CW01214137

# Researching the Global Education Industry

Marcelo Parreira do Amaral
Gita Steiner-Khamsi
Christiane Thompson
Editors

# Researching the Global Education Industry

Commodification, the Market and Business Involvement

palgrave
macmillan

*Editors*
Marcelo Parreira do Amaral
Institute of Education
University of Münster
Münster, Germany

Gita Steiner-Khamsi
Teachers College
Columbia University
New York, NY, USA

Christiane Thompson
Theory and History of Education
Goethe-University Frankfurt am Main
Frankfurt am Main, Germany

ISBN 978-3-030-04235-6     ISBN 978-3-030-04236-3  (eBook)
https://doi.org/10.1007/978-3-030-04236-3

Library of Congress Control Number: 2018966800

© The Editor(s) (if applicable) and The Author(s) 2019
This work is subject to copyright. All rights are solely and exclusively licensed by the Publisher, whether the whole or part of the material is concerned, specifically the rights of translation, reprinting, reuse of illustrations, recitation, broadcasting, reproduction on microfilms or in any other physical way, and transmission or information storage and retrieval, electronic adaptation, computer software, or by similar or dissimilar methodology now known or hereafter developed.
The use of general descriptive names, registered names, trademarks, service marks, etc. in this publication does not imply, even in the absence of a specific statement, that such names are exempt from the relevant protective laws and regulations and therefore free for general use.
The publisher, the authors and the editors are safe to assume that the advice and information in this book are believed to be true and accurate at the date of publication. Neither the publisher nor the authors or the editors give a warranty, express or implied, with respect to the material contained herein or for any errors or omissions that may have been made. The publisher remains neutral with regard to jurisdictional claims in published maps and institutional affiliations.

Cover designed by Tom Howey

This Palgrave Macmillan imprint is published by the registered company Springer Nature Switzerland AG
The registered company address is: Gewerbestrasse 11, 6330 Cham, Switzerland

# Contents

1  Introduction: Researching the Global Education Industry      1
   *Christiane Thompson and Marcelo Parreira do Amaral*

2  Serial Entrepreneurs, Angel Investors, and Capex Light
   Edu-Business Start-Ups in India: Philanthropy, Impact
   Investing, and Systemic Educational Change                  23
   *Stephen J. Ball*

3  The Political Turn of Corporate Influence in Education: A
   Synthesis of Main Policy Reform Strategies                  47
   *Clara Fontdevila and Antoni Verger*

4  Advocacy Networks and Market Models for Education           69
   *Christopher Lubienski*

5  UNESCO, Education, and the Private Sector: A
   Relationship on Whose Terms?                                87
   *Natasha Ridge and Susan Kippels*

6  Embedding Education Research in the European
   Economic Imaginary?                                            115
   *Marcelo Parreira do Amaral*

7  The Global Education Industry, Data Infrastructures, and
   the Restructuring of Government School Systems                 135
   *Bob Lingard*

8  The Transformation of State Monitoring Systems in
   Germany and the US: Relating the Datafication and
   Digitalization of Education to the Global Education
   Industry                                                       157
   *Sigrid Hartong*

9  International Education Hubs as Competitive Advantage:
   Investigating the Role of the State as Power Connector in
   the Global Education Industry                                  181
   *Marvin Erfurth*

10 The Globalized Expert: On the Dissemination and
   Authorization of Evidence-Based Education                      203
   *Christiane Thompson*

11 Digitization, Disruption, and the "Society of
   Singularities": The Transformative Power of the Global
   Education Industry                                             225
   *S. Karin Amos*

12 Writing Global Education Policy Research                       251
   *Stephen Carney*

13  Conclusion: Changing Education in the GEI—Rationales,
    Logics, and Modes of Operation                                273
    *Marcelo Parreira do Amaral and Christiane Thompson*

**Index**                                                        291

# Notes on Contributors

**S. Karin Amos** is Professor of Education at University of Tübingen, Germany, with a special focus on International and Comparative Education as well as Intercultural Pedagogy. Her research interests include international governance in education, the relation between the concepts governance and governmentality as well as the question of the relation between political and pedagogical formations.

**Stephen J. Ball** is Distinguished Service Professor of Sociology of Education at the University College London, Institute of Education, UK. His main areas of interest are in sociologically informed education policy analysis and the relationships between education, education policy, and social class.

**Stephen Carney** is Associate Professor in Comparative Education Policy at Roskilde University in Denmark. His research focuses on global educational reform and comparative method. He has studied university governance in Denmark, teacher preparation in England and China, and school development in Nepal and India. He has been President of the Comparative Education Society in Europe (CESE) since 2016.

**Marvin Erfurth** is Research Associate and PhD candidate in International and Comparative Education at the University of Muenster, Germany. His main research interests include Global Education Policy, Higher Education Research, and International and Comparative Education. His dissertation focuses on the implications of International Education Hubs on Higher Education Policy and

Governance, a qualitative empirical study of the United Arab Emirates and Singapore.

**Clara Fontdevila** holds a degree in Sociology from the Universitat Autònoma de Barcelona and is a PhD candidate at the Department of Sociology of the same university, with a thesis research project on the settlement of the post-2015 global education agenda. She has previously collaborated with Education International on different investigations, as well as on the 2012 evaluation report of the Civil Society Education Fund. Her areas of interest are private-sector engagement in education policy, education and international development, and the global governance of education.

**Sigrid Hartong** is post-doctoral research fellow at the Helmut-Schmidt-University Hamburg, Germany, with a special focus on International and Comparative Education and also Educational Governance. Her research interests include the growing datafication/digitalization of education, standardization policies, policy network analysis, as well as (problems of) inclusive education.

**Susan Kippels** is a research fellow at the Sheikh Saud bin Saqr Al Qasimi Foundation for Policy Research, Ras Al Khaimah, United Arab Emirates. She holds a dual bachelor's degree (Economics and Arabic) from the University of Notre Dame as well as a master's degree (International Education Policy) from the Harvard Graduate School of Education. Her research interests include philanthropy and education, private education in the Gulf, and Arab migrant teachers.

**Bob Lingard** is Professorial Fellow in the Institute for Learning Sciences and Teacher Education at the Australian Catholic University, Brisbane, Australia. His work is situated within the sociology of education and focuses on education policy, with a particular focus on the impacts of globalization and on the work of the OECD.

**Christopher Lubienski** is Professor of Education Policy at Indiana University. He is also a fellow with the National Education Policy Center at the University of Colorado, a visiting professor at East China Normal University in Shanghai, and an adjunct professor at Murdoch University in Western Australia. He is co-leader and convener of the Scholar Strategy Network's K-12 Working Group. His research focuses on education policy, reform, and the political economy of education, with a particular concern for issues of equity and access.

**Marcelo Parreira do Amaral** is Professor of International and Comparative Education at the University of Münster, Germany. He is member of NESET II (Network of Experts on the Social Aspects of Education) funded by the European Commission. His main research interests include international and comparative education, in particular the role and activities of international organizations on education policy and governance and its implications for education research, practice, and policy.

**Natasha Ridge** is Executive Director of the Sheikh Saud bin Saqr Al Qasimi Foundation for Policy Research, Ras Al Khaimah, United Arab Emirates, after having served as the Acting Director of Research at the Dubai School of Government. She has a number of publications including *Education and the Reverse Gender Divide in the Gulf States: Embracing the Global, Ignoring the Local*. She holds a Doctorate of Education in International Education Policy from Columbia University and her latest research focuses on the role and impact of Arab father involvement, philanthropy and education, and access and equity in the Gulf education sector.

**Gita Steiner-Khamsi** is Professor of Comparative and International Education at Teachers College, Columbia University in New York, USA, as well as the Graduate Institute for International and Development Studies, Geneva, Switzerland. Her work focuses on globalization, transnational policy borrowing and lending as well as school reform and teacher policy in developing countries, mostly in post-Soviet Central Asia and Mongolia. She is a past president of the Comparative and International Education Society (CIES) and co-editor of the series World Yearbook of Education (Routledge).

**Christiane Thompson** is Professor of Theory and History of Education at the Goethe-University Frankfurt am Main, Germany. She has been Research Professor of Education funded by the German Research Foundation on the cultural theory and research of Bildung and education. Her main research areas are the philosophy of education, the analysis of educational processes at the crossing point of language and power as well as critical theory of education. Most recently, her research focuses on the forms and practices of authorization within the field of education/educational policy and on the consequences for educational theory and practice.

**Antoni Verger** is Associate Professor at the Department of Sociology of the Universitat Autònoma de Barcelona, and general deputy of the European Master program *Education Policies for Global Development*. A former post-doctoral fellow at the Amsterdam Institute for Social Science Research, Verger's research analyzes the relationship between global governance institutions and education policy. He has specialized in the study of public-private partnerships, quasi-markets, and accountability policies in education. He coordinates the ERC-funded project REFORMED—*Reforming Schools Globally: A Multiscalar Analysis of Autonomy and Accountability Policies in the Education Sector*.

# List of Figures

Fig. 2.1    A simplified network of investments in edu-business in India    25
Fig. 5.1    Sources of UNESCO's funding, January–June 2016 (Source: UNESCO, 2016)    98
Fig. 8.1    Framing the ongoing transformation of state-level monitoring systems    171
Fig. 10.1   Result depiction in one of the reports. (Revel, 2015, p. 7)    216

# List of Tables

| | | |
|---|---|---|
| Table 2.1 | Components of the impact investing network | 27 |
| Timeline 5.1 | UNESCO's funding crises and private sector initiatives | 95 |
| Table 5.1 | UNESCO's private sector education projects broken down by foundations and corporations, as of January 1, 2016 | 98 |
| Table 5.2 | Expand existing market share: Select private sector funded UNESCO projects (January 1, 2016) | 100 |
| Table 5.3 | Penetrate new markets: Select private sector funded UNESCO projects (January 1, 2016) | 101 |
| Table 5.4 | Improve the organizational image: Select private sector funded UNESCO projects (January 1, 2016) | 103 |
| Table 8.1 | Policies around the transformation of state-level education monitoring systems in the US and Germany between 2001 and 2017 | 170 |

# Introduction: Researching the Global Education Industry

## Christiane Thompson and Marcelo Parreira do Amaral

In September 2017, the third Global Education Industry (GEI) Summit[1] took place in Luxembourg to discuss opportunities for better networking between industry and schools. The latter were seen as "learning ecosystems" that are "at the crossroads of innovation," which although often still seen as "bulwarks of outdated practices" may become innovative if well supported. It was organized jointly by the Luxembourg Ministry of Education, Children and Youth, the European Commission (EC), and the Organization for Economic Development and Cooperation (OECD). Its aim was to give a selected number of ministers, senior policy makers, and industry leaders opportunities to accelerate change, making industry

---

C. Thompson (✉)
Theory and History of Education, Goethe-University Frankfurt am Main, Frankfurt am Main, Germany

M. Parreira do Amaral
Institute of Education, University of Münster, Münster, Germany
e-mail: parreira@uni-muenster.de

© The Author(s) 2019
M. Parreira do Amaral et al. (eds.), *Researching the Global Education Industry*,
https://doi.org/10.1007/978-3-030-04236-3_1

actors consolidated partners in education. In his opening speech, Andreas Schleicher, head of the DG Education at OECD, presented the future aims and tasks as follows:

> To turn digital exhaust into digital fuel, to change education practice; that requires us to get out of the 'read-only' mode of our education systems, in which information is presented in a way that cannot be altered. [...] What if we could get our teachers working on curated crowdsourcing of educational practice? Wouldn't that be so much more powerful than things like performance-related pay as an approach to professional growth and development? Technology could create a giant open source community of educators and unlock the creative skills and initiative of its teachers. Simply by tapping into the desire of people to contribute, to collaborate and to be recognized for that. (2017, 5:24)

Schleicher's introductory speech already depicts a central motif of the GEI Summit: an extensive rhetoric of innovation and modernization that calls for a radical break with the educational system as it has been run so far. The past of education is presented as a divided, isolated, hierarchical practice that has been essentially a technology- and innovation-hostile island—an island largely severed from the real world and incapable of being innovative. The future of education is painted in bright colors, modeled as an ecosystem of collaborative consumption; creative, entrepreneurial, and innovative, education is portrayed as a future that can only be achieved through transparent collaboration, powered by powerful digital reputational metrics.

The reader may note how the rhetoric of innovation is embellished as a practice of empowerment and liberation. Schleicher mobilizes the image of a "giant open source community of educators" that is completely freed from the bureaucratic regulations that have dominated the past of education: in his view, the cartel-like business model of governments, academia, textbook publishers, and software providers have limited and fragmented education into a "read-only" system. The digital technologies are interpreted as the source for a complete reorganization of the education sector—a "creative destruction" to put it in terms of the famous political economist Joseph Schumpeter (1993). Therefore, it comes as no surprise that educational innovation, for Schleicher, is thrust forward by extensive entrepreneurialism.

To be sure, this is one of the central ideas behind the GEI Summit: the gathering of policy actors in education and representatives from the industry: "The time is ripe to establish a dialogue between ministers of education and the global education industry," as it was pointed out in the introductory announcement to the first OECD Summit 2015 in Finland.[2] The Summit's aim was and is to establish a platform that allows businesses and generally actors from the economic sector to further their economic interests and penetrate the educational sector accordingly. Thus, the GEI Summits may be taken as a paradigmatic illustration for the current developments of the GEI: the capitalization of the educational sector on a global scale.

This book examines the emergence of new providers and policy actors in education and, more specifically, reflects on how the fast advance of the GEI is likely to transform conceptualizations of ("good") education. Drawing systematic attention to the rationales, processes, and impacts of current developments of the GEI, the book discerns particular expressions and manifestations of the GEI phenomenon. The contributions to this book investigate not only the influence of private and philanthropic actors on education as well as educational policy-making but also the changing role of the state within the GEI. Further, the book explores the role that digital technology and data infrastructures play in the rise and expansion of the GEI, for example, by aligning the allocation of research funding to economic imperatives. Last but not least, the book examines the rationales as well as the rhetoric of the GEI, that is, how the reorganization of education is strategically legitimized.

Following the threads of the GEI requires educational policy research to transgress the usual country-based design. The chapters of this volume build on a global perspective in order to grasp and theorize these complex developments. The reconstruction and conceptualization of agency in complex networks is of utmost importance to understand the roles of philanthropists, international organizations, and other mediating figures in the GEI. As Stephen Ball explains in his chapter, researching the GEI means to follow and analyze the flow of relations, ideas, and money. It is central to understand how local edu-preneurs draw on global references and are able to use them to their own advantage. Generally, we are faced with complex and heterogeneous relations in the expansion of the GEI. This has immense consequences for disclosing the operation of transnational organizations, philanthropic foundations with a global reach, states, and so on. However, being entrenched with new edu-economic imaginaries, educational policy studies will have to re-evaluate whether its own central concepts still enable it to grasp the current developments in appropriate ways.

In the remainder of this introduction, we address some of the concepts that are used to apprehend phenomena related to the GEI in order to show how they need to be resituated in terms of the GEI. Starting from the state of the art concerning the GEI, we will turn toward central categories such as commodification and financialization, placing them in the ongoing discourse of the GEI. The conceptual framework provided here will also demonstrate how the studies presented in the chapters are of utmost importance for educational researchers, policy makers, and graduate students in a range of academic disciplines who are trying to gain a better understanding of these developments. In the final section of the introduction, we present a short overview over the chapters included in the book.

## The Global Education Industry

In the first section, we have already touched upon the central imaginary of the GEI, that is, the establishment of an "ecosystem" or policy infrastructure that is oriented toward business opportunities concerning educational goods and services on a global scale. In fact, the recurring Summits illustrate a number of aspects that are central to our researching the GEI. First, the Summits draw our attention to the *size* and *global influence* of the institutions and actors that arrange the Summit and take part in them. Researching the GEI precisely focuses on the increasing impact that comes from these platforms, coalitions, and connections of very different actors toward a global market sphere of education. Second, they also indicate that the emergence of the GEI is strongly related to the

## Introduction: Researching the Global Education Industry 5

*delegitimization* of how (public) education has been organized so far, which raises key questions as to the social aspects of education as a public good. We mentioned Schleicher's criticism of the educational system remaining in a "read-only" mode. The GEI is about constructing and fostering educational imaginaries of innovation and modernization that call for the substitution or disruption of education systems as we know them. Third, the Summits allow us to discern how *policy-making* lies at the heart of establishing the GEI. In other words, they structure, facilitate, and optimize business opportunities, for example, for the IT industry to promote and market information and communications technology (ICT) in schools. As defined by Antoni Verger and colleagues:

> The GEI is an increasingly globalized economic sector in which a broad range of educational services and goods are produced, exchanged and consumed, often on a for-profit basis. The GEI is constituted by its own sets of processes, systems of rules, and social forces, which interact in the production, offer and demand of educational services and goods. (Verger, Lubienski, & Steiner-Khamsi, 2016, p. 4)

Researching the GEI thus entails analyzing these sets of processes, systems of rules, and social forces and structures, as mentioned by Verger et al. However, reconstructing these processes, rules, forces, and structures poses education (policy) research some important analytical challenges. Examining the GEI has to avoid presupposing the global coherence or unity, as we need to discern clearly between the lenses and concepts we use to apprehend these phenomena and the research object. In this context an important issue is the fact that the term "Global Education Industry" has been appropriated by its proponents in order to brand its imaginaries of a worldwide innovation (cf. OECD, 2017; Schleicher, 2017; Tooley, 2001). Related to this, the analytical categories used to grasp the dynamics and impact of the GEI in the education field need to be sharpened, a topic we return to in the next section. In addition, the manifold actors involved in the GEI operate in diverse contexts and networks, and have various relations among themselves and with state agencies. Thus, discerning these differences in type, capacity, and scope as well as in logics of action and practice becomes crucial. Finally, extant research has rightfully stressed the importance of going beyond economic theory that focuses primarily on rationality and interests to include sociological description and analyses of non-economic and non-material factors as well as of the institutional and social contexts that make, maintain, and transform industry sectors. Against this background, researchers in the field turned to Pierre Bourdieu's concept of field to understand the GEI as a contested and socially structured space (Lingard, Rawolle, & Taylor, 2005; Verger et al., 2016, p. 11).

In summary, in researching the GEI, education policy research has to emphasize its analytic perspective and present studies that can unveil and theorize adequately the complexity, the different manifestations, and the functioning of the GEI. In this sense, research needs to examine the rationales and logics of action of myriad players as well as their modes of operation. Assessing the impact of these developments, as we argue in this volume, will greatly profit from recent social theory literature assessing the current social, cultural, technological, and political transformations in which the ascendance of the GEI is embedded.

In the following paragraphs, we concisely recapitulate the manifold actors in the GEI by referring to the recent literature. The next section discusses central categories of analysis of the GEI.

When contemplating the globalized market of education, *large companies and corporations* come to mind. They have become key actors in the field of education. A very good example of this is Pearson, the world's largest edu-business that is becoming a public policy actor globally (Hogan, Sellar, & Lingard, 2016; Porter, 2014). Alongside these bigger companies, one can find a growing number of *philanthropic foundations*, like The Michael & Susan Dell Foundation (see Ball, in this volume). Even though these foundations are independent from the companies, their programs and ideas are geared toward opening market opportunities for the respective companies (Au & Lubienski, 2016). A third important group within the GEI are *international organizations* like the OECD, the World Bank, and the United Nations Educational, Scientific and Cultural Organization (UNESCO) (Ridge & Kippels, in this volume; see also Rizvi & Lingard, 2010). The example of the Programme for International Student Assessment (PISA) studies shows plainly the enormous power and influence the OECD has gained since 2000 in setting educational agendas and market opportunities (Spring, 2015). The *state* is another actor of the GEI that should not be overlooked. In the context of the GEI, the state takes over important functions, especially as facilitator or moderator of marketization (Au & Lubienski, 2016) as well as provider of funding. However, the state can also be a competitor that partakes in constructing the imaginary of "educational excellence" (see Erfurth, in this volume).

In addition to these actors with global reach, there are numerous actors that (also) take up the function of mediation and facilitation in the GEI. These might be *renowned individuals*, like the already-mentioned Andreas Schleicher or James Tooley, a professor at the University of Newcastle. As Ball has shown in his research, Tooley is an important figure providing ideas regarding how to assemble and coordinate policy networks (Ball, 2012, p. 38). Furthermore, the scaling of policy infrastructures is dependent on *advocacy networks*, that is, more or less organized circles or groups that agree in furthering particular educational ideas and projects (see Lubienski, in this volume). A third group of actors exert their mediating and facilitating role in the GEI by *consultancy and advice*. In the German context, for example, consultancy corporations are increasingly approached for remodeling universities as science businesses (Mautner, 2005; see also Gunter & Mills, 2017).

The reference to the university can be taken as an indication that this list of important actors in the GEI is not yet complete: educational institutions also become actors within the GEI, for they undergo entrepreneurial transformations. Thus, it is not only the growing number of private schools that operate for profit that play a role in the GEI. Rather the emergence of the GEI turns pre-schools, schools, universities, continuing education—not to mention students, parents, teachers, and so on—into entrepreneurial actors. Universities, for example, compete for the best students and best graduation rates to secure their (global) market position, or they open a branch campus abroad. This process of globalization is fueled by the growing sector of digital technology. An illustrative example is the fast-growing business *Udacity*, a company that offers online classes as a means for companies to train their employees (see Amos, in this volume).

Given the multiplicity of actors, the various levels of their engagement, and their global reach, it is crucial to understand the common reference points and aims that enable concerted action within the GEI. In other words, what are the rationales, semantics, and imaginaries that produce the symbolic order of the GEI? How can we understand the emergence and expansion of the GEI given the diversity of actors and relationships? It is one of the aims of this collection to delineate the corresponding processes, rationales, logics, and modes of operation of the GEI. From there, it will be possible to give a theoretical account of the current developments and clarify what this means for education.

In the following paragraphs, we reflect on the central categories of the GEI. They may arguably be viewed as both its products and its producers. In other words, they help throw into sharper relief the different rationales and logics that underpin the various manifestations of the GEI. We address them in order to bring into view the dynamics and differentiation that the GEI brings to the educational sector.

## Central Categories of the GEI

There are numerous concepts that are used to grasp the penetration of economic rationales into the educational sector. *Economization, marketization, privatization, commodification,* and *financialization*—all these concepts highlight different aspects of the neoliberal process: they have to be seen in relation to the complexity of the neoliberal process in its multifaceted and multiscalar quality. In the context of the GEI, they can be helpful to grasp the quantitative and qualitative changes that the educational sector has undergone in the recent past (Mundy, Green, Lingard, & Verger, 2016; Normand, 2016).

In the field of education, the category of *economization* is used to refer to the process of rephrasing or reformulating educational processes in the language of economic transaction. This reformulation of education was an important step to situate education in a market environment. The emergence of new public management in times of the crises of public funding of education was and is an important entry point to anchor economic thinking, norms, and procedures in the provision, management, and evaluation of education (see Hartong, Hermstein, & Höhne, 2018). With the rise of the GEI, we notice the unlimited global reach and power of economic actors to place and sell their products. We also observe that the *development and enactment of educational policies* can be described as a field of *strategic interaction and trade* (Verger, 2012).

To be sure, the construction of tradable commodities is of utmost importance for the economic penetration of the education sector. *Commodification* precisely means the construction of education as a tradable good to be advertised and exchanged like other products of consumption or use. Education becomes implemented in the exchange of values. It is important here to recognize how this value exchange is permeated by political rationalities (Appadurai, 2012). These rationalities imply—to put it in Foucauldian terms (Foucault, 2000)—governmentalities, that is, forms and ways to constitute subjectivities by provoking specific modes of governing oneself and others. This is how entrepreneurialism is implemented in learning and schooling. Focusing on the GEI, the emphasis has to be directed toward the ways that entrepreneurialism is transformed into a global agenda and reform project (Verger, Fontdevila, & Zancajo, 2016). Furthermore, the establishment of policy infrastructures that increasingly enable the construction of commodities, for example, by data mediation services, cannot be overestimated (Hartong, 2016). Privatization (see below) and commodification have to be seen in close connection, but the later *emphasizes the cultural dimension of transforming the meaning and understanding of education into a tradable or consumable good that can be marketed globally.*

Ever since the beginning of modern political liberalism, the notion of the "(free) market" was linked to the idea (or ideology) of an impersonal and neutral institution that mediates social interests. In classical economic thinking, the market is the sphere where individual efforts can be transformed into individual wealth and social advancement. There is an operative and symbolic coalition within the imagery of the "market" that has become the core of neoliberal market rationality: the "market" is the sphere where social prosperity and individual well-being are realized. To be sure, the role of education in this cannot be overestimated. On the level of the GEI, *marketization* refers to the production of *market readiness* for those educational goods, services, and policies but also people that are deemed indispensable for economic growth, public health, social, and individual well-being on a global scale. At the same time, the established market relations weaken former structures and infrastructures of education (Lawn, 2013).

*Privatization* understood as the shift of public money into the private sector and provision of education by private agents that were formerly provided by public agents (Fitz & Beers, 2002, p. 139) has long been a topic that had to be treated in the context of nation states and their respective traditions as well as institutional frameworks (Adamson, Astrand, & Darling-Hammond, 2016; Burch, 2009; Robertson & Verger, 2012; Verger, 2016). Verger, Fontdevila, et al., (2016) have delineated six paths toward education privatization that discern the contextual dispositions, agents, and mechanisms of privatization, for example, "education privatization as a state reform" (as in Chile and UK) or "scaling up privatization" (as with the school reform in the US; see Verger, Fontdevila, et al., 2016, p. 11). In the context of the GEI, one may notice the increase of complexity that comes with the globalization of policy infrastructures as well as the global diffusion of privatization (ibid.) while at the same time recognizing the concentration of power and agenda-setting capacities (e.g. in the World Bank or the OECD).

Increasingly, education has become an object of investment and means of profit making by the interests of education businesses, technology companies, and philanthropic organizations on a global scale (Verger, Fontdevila, et al., 2016). Related to the processes discussed above, the term *financialization* refers to contemporary changes in social formation due to an increasing role financial capital plays in everyday life (van der Zwan, 2014). As Peters and Besley note, "Credit and investment are metaphors that now help determine an individual's (and family's) place in society […] [instigating] a new finance culture that includes fundamental shifts in attitudes to money, investment, credit, [and] risk" (Peters & Besley, 2015, p. 22). This apparent shift in the relationship between society and finance, however, instigates veiled effects expressed in "a deepening culture of risk-taking and strategic deployment of assets" (ibid.). More and more realms of social life depend on the hidden workings of financial services—and education is no exception, although to a lesser extent in some countries "where education remains largely publicly funded and so always politicized" (ibid., p. 35). When viewing education services globally—including not only its provision and management but also research, publishing, testing, and so forth—the last few decades brought about the emergence of global players in the field. Education has developed into a substantial global business with low market capitalization, resulting in global players' efforts to tap into this business with expectations of high profit margins (cf. Ball, 2012, pp. 116–136; Spring, Frankson, McCallum, & Banks, 2017). The term *financialization* in education, therefore, describes the growing dependence of education provision, management, research, and so on, on finance capital (loans, borrowing, student debt, impact investment, etc.) as well as the financial operations in the stock market with education products and services (brokering, investing, speculating, etc.).

Related to the concepts discussed above, we also refer to the *digitalization* of education to call attention to a key driver of the global market in education. Over the last two decades, we have experienced the establishment of powerful imaginaries and objectives concerning "digital technology and education." To mention just a few: digital learning environments stand for the optimization and individualization of learning. The establishment and accessibility of the Internet have been praised as a space to make knowledge accessible and enable social participation. Furthermore, the use of digital technology is said to provide knowledge management "without frictional loss": along with the growing computing capacities, the storage, analysis, and prognostic evaluation of data promises to be a powerful instrument of educational governance (Sellar & Lingard, 2014). Briefly, the innovation, optimization, and the increasing accessibility of learning and learning processes fuel the digital transformation of the educational sector.

For the expansion of the GEI, the significance of digitalization cannot be overestimated. In the coming years, the e-learning market is expected to reach a market share worth hundreds of billions of US dollars. Furthermore, technological innovations in education, for example, the use of digital devices in classrooms, open up new markets and new customers. In his contribution to this volume, Ball mentions the enormous opportunities that digital technologies can unfold for educational innovation in the Global South. Along with the digital forms of educational provision comes an understanding of learning and of the learning subject that is oriented toward competitiveness and effectiveness. This brings about far-reaching changes of social interaction and communication within educational institutions (for universities cf. Selwyn, 2014).

Another dimension of digitalization that is highly relevant for the GEI is that the collection and management of large data infrastructures offer new modes of educational governance (Fenwick, Mangez, & Ozga, 2014; Lawn, 2013). Data infrastructures have to be seen as an essential complement for managing and monitoring educational institutions (see Hartong, in this volume). Policy researchers have remarked that digitalization has brought about a de-territorialization of governance (Lewis & Lingard, 2015). They also represent a necessary ingredient of new public management because they translate and mediate the measurability of educational processes. Moreover, the analysis and manipulation of data can be used to develop ever more and better educational products and services. As Karin Amos argues in her contribution, there is a disruptive quality in the development of the digital domain. To be sure, the GEI Summits discussed at the beginning of this introduction are precisely geared toward the uprooting of traditional education through digital innovation. The complexity and intransparency of how data is collected, algorithmically evaluated, shared, and used (in ever-growing data networks), therefore, represent an important task for the educational policy and practice research (Williamson, 2016, 2017).

## Researching the GEI: An Overview of the Book

Most of the authors in this collection presented their research at a Symposium on the *Emergence of a Global Education Industry* held in February 2017 at the Goethe University Frankfurt in Germany.[3] The contributions to the symposium focused on the various manifestations of the GEI, types, features, and networks, and on the consequences these manifestations have for educational research, policy, and practice. One approach to grasping the manifestations of the GEI is to discuss different actors and networks that influence not only the provision, management, and evaluation of education but also both policy-making and research activities in the education sector. The chapters included in this volume examine how education has become an object of investment and profit through the involvement of philanthropic organizations (e.g. the Michael and Susan Dell Foundation, the Gates Foundation), international organizations (for instance, UNESCO or the European Commission), local policy networks, and education businesses and technology companies operating on a global scale.

The analyses of the GEI provided in this book also include the rationales and activities of the abovementioned agents of the GEI as well as the close collaboration of governmental and non-governmental agents. The chapters further systematically discuss these actors' strategies for exerting influence and producing "evidence" to promote preferred policy ideas, suggesting conceptual tools that can illuminate policy advocacy networks. In this context, the role of global infrastructures such as large digital data systems used in school monitoring are examined with respect to their impact on education governance.

Regarding educational theory, the contributions to this volume examine the impact and consequences of the advance of the GEI for conceptualizing and reflecting about education—for instance, in terms of changes in education provision by large international firms and their impact on the organization of educational institutions and practices. What does the strong intertwinement of policy and research imply for the distribution of funding? How does the popularization of "expert knowledge" constitute and regulate an "evidence-based educational laboratory"? Finally, how do digital innovations exert a disruptive quality on educational institutions? The chapters address these developments and dynamics and offer important conceptual explorations of the challenges related to education policy research, of the narratives and modes of communication in this field, including recognizing their significance for social theory and for our aim of revealing power struggles and self-imposed dependencies.

In his chapter, Stephen J. Ball investigates the topology of education in India with a particular emphasis on small and medium-sized edubusinesses. More precisely, the study focuses on the role of serial entrepreneurs and of angel investors as well as the proliferation of education start-up businesses. Ball reconstructs how reform and profit are interrelated and how a business ecosystem emerges in which educational and social problems are transformed into business opportunities. What is remarkable about this development in the Indian education sector is how it supplements and displaces the state's provision of education.

Clara Fontdevila and Antoni Verger examine the emerging strategies of legitimization that the corporate sector employs for the purpose of shaping educational policy. Based on a comprehensive literature review, the authors present five different strategies that reinforce the privatization of education: lobbying, networking and brokerage, knowledge mobilization, supporting and instrumenting community-based advocacy, and the sponsorship of pilot experiences. The analysis demonstrates the wide range of strategies that corporate actors utilize, even though they are not necessarily concerned with direct education provision. As Fontdevila and Verger show, the corporate actors draw not only on economic capital but also political as well as symbolic capital to influence educational policy.

Christopher Lubienski is concerned with advocacy networks in the context of market-based educational policies. The chapter presents the findings of an empirical study on the networks of intermediaries that process, present, and promote evidence for policy makers in and across several major American metropolitan areas. Overall, the study indicates that intermediary organizations operate at quite a distance to traditional expertise and to measures of evaluating knowledge claims. His chapter points to the shortcomings of a popular approach to studying advocacy coalitions, namely the Advocacy Coalition Network developed by Sabatier and colleagues. Lubienski characterizes education policy networks as "marketplace of ideas" diverging from the usual meaning: ideas do not compete for supremacy, but rather, they are bought and sold among the policy networks.

Natasha Ridge and Susan Kippels' chapter turns toward UNESCO and its relationship with various private sector organizations. Referring to UNESCO's budget crises, the authors recapitulate the organization's opening toward the private sector. The analysis exposes the educational as well as ethical conflicts that arise from UNESCO's partnerships with private actors. Particularly, it captures the change from a multilateral donor organization that is committed to "education for all" to a brand for sale. The private sector involvement may, in some cases, even lead to a participation in activities that go against UNESCO's education mission, thereby putting its reputation at risk.

The role and position of educational research in the current policy agenda of the European Union is the topic of Marcelo Parreira do Amaral's chapter, which links policy developments at European and national levels as well as in science to the GEI. With a particular focus on the Horizon 2020 research framework program, he investigates the impact of knowledge generation activities in the social sciences and the humanities: it is the so-called European Knowledge-Based Economy that dominates our understanding of as well as the orientation of educational research. Referring to a call for proposals on lifelong learning, Parreira do Amaral illustrates the tensions and limitations within this approach to educational research. Using Germany as an exemplary case, it is shown how the changing knowledge regime has an impact on educational research as well as on the social epistemology of the educational field. He raises concerns about the implications and risks of a completely "embedded" educational research, that is, one where there is no difference or distance to the dominant economic imaginaries.

In his chapter, Bob Lingard addresses aspects of privatization and commercialization of public schooling systems that are seldom noticed or recognized: the role of edu-businesses with respect to the establishment of data infrastructures for the governing of school systems. Here, the establishment of network governance comprising edu-businesses and philanthropic as well as state actors is particularly relevant. The chapter draws on two case studies that investigate the relation of ed-techs to data infrastructures: the Australian National Schools Interoperability Program (NSIP) and the InBloom data infrastructure initiative in the US. The first case discloses the networked governance mode through collaboration between governments and ed-tech companies. The second case follows the attempts to provide a single platform for sharing data about schooling. Finally, Lingard discusses the issues of data privacy raised by the public.

Sigrid Hartong deals with the expanding datafication and digitalization in the sphere of education. More specifically, her chapter reconstructs the complex, cross-sectoral, and cross-scalar relations of the digital expansion in school administration and school monitoring at state level in the US as well as in Germany. As Hartong shows, for both countries, there is a coincidence of transforming the state-level monitoring system and the rise of supra-state (federal) standardization. Since the 2000s, this serves as the basis for actor networks between ed-tech vendors, state actors, philanthropic figures, and intermediary figures, such as the *National Center for Education Statistics* in the US. In comparison, the German reforms in the past two decades appear less commodity oriented than those in the US. On this point, the changes of education through digital transformation as well as the power of ed-tech are hardly called into question.

The chapter by Marvin Erfurth examines the role of International Education Hubs (IEH) in terms of the establishment of an interconnected global education policy space. The IEH, created in order to attain a competitive advantage in the global economy, brings together global players in the provision of education, training, research, as well as education policy. As the author shows, the IEHs are of particular interest for understanding the roles of the state as power connector. Drawing on the theoretical approaches of Cultural Political Economy, Erfurth analyzes the educational and social imaginaries in the United Arab Emirates' Vision 2021 and how this creates a semiotic-discursive space of a uniting effort to prevail in the global knowledge-based economy.

In her chapter on the globalized expert, Christiane Thompson examines the popularization and proliferation of evidence-based education as a global project of innovation. As the discursive analysis of a TED talk by Andreas Schleicher shows, everyone is addressed to take up the position of global expertise. The chapter demonstrates the significance of the globalized expert in Pearson's data platform "The Learning Curve" as well as in its online learning platform "Revel." Particular focus is placed on authorization, that is, practices and strategies that are used to present evidence-based knowledge as legitimate or reasonable. By inviting everyone to participate as a globalized expert, Pearson can present itself as a quasi-public actor that works for educational innovation while at the same time strengthening its market position.

The topic of the chapter by Karin Amos is the role of digitization and algorithmization in the rise of the GEI. Amos provides a succinct analysis of how successful start-ups in higher education transform education from a modern to a late-modern institution in a disruptive fashion. Using the case of an e-advising system at the University of Arizona, Amos shows how the implementation of digital instruments follows the idea of personalized medicine: to bring out the best in every individual. The development of personalization and singularization (Reckwitz) is characterized by the paradoxical surrendering of autonomy to gain autonomy and by the elimination of the public aspect of education.

The chapter by Stephen Carney unfolds around a critique of education policy research that strongly favors the superordinate view of method and research. According to Carney, what is often missed in education policy studies is the global complexity of the GEI and the incommensurability of perspectives for the subaltern. Referring to the story of Ganesh, an exploited Nepali migrant worker who returned injured from the United Arab Emirates, Carney portrays the "imaginative scape" that is constituted by education reform, development ideology, hard labor, and consumerism in Nepal. In view of this imaginative scape that is "always intoxicating and necessarily fraught with risk," Carney sketches the rather chaotic ensemble of reason, desire, fear, and seduction that captures public education.

The concluding chapter by Marcelo Parreira do Amaral and Christiane Thompson goes beyond the description and analysis of the different expressions and manifestations of the GEI phenomenon by discerning different but overlapping rationales, logics, and modes of operation identified from a more synthetic reading of the chapters included in this volume. The chapter closes by raising questions as to the social dislocations gaped open by the GEI phenomena and interrogations of theoretical lenses that guide our analyses.

**Acknowledgments** The research presented in this volume has profited from engaging discussions during the Symposium "*Economization, Commodification, Digitalization: The Emergence of a Global Education Industry*" held in Frankfurt/Main, Germany, in February 2017. We would like to thank the Goethe University Frankfurt, Germany; the Westfälische Wilhelms-University Münster, Germany; the Teachers College, Columbia University, New York, USA; NORRAG, Geneva, Switzerland; as well as the Freunde und Foerderer of the Goethe University Frankfurt, Germany, for their logistic and financial support. But principally, we want to thank the participants who provided pertinent insights and invaluable comments on the first drafts of the chapters. We thank in particular Frank-Olaf Radtke, Isabell Diehm, Johannes Bellmann, Thomas Höhne, Florian Waldow, Wivian Weller, and Sieglinde Jornitz. Thanks also go out to those who provided administrative support for the preparation of the symposium and for the preparation of the manuscripts, in particular Nicole Stelter, Tomoko Kojima, and Marvin Erfurth.

## Notes

1. Third Global Education Industry Summit, Luxembourg, 25–26 September 2017. Retrieved online: http://globaleducation.onetec.eu/index.html [last 21 July 2018].
2. In 2015, Helsinki hosted the Summit; in 2016, the summit took place in Jerusalem, Israel. See the Annexes provided in OECD (2017) for brief reports of the meetings. In 2018, the Summit will take place in Estonia in September in Tallinn. Retrieved online: https://www.eu2017.ee/news/press-releases/preparations-were-made-paris-next-years-global-oecd-summit-educational [last 21 July 2018].
3. See: "*Economization, Commodification, Digitalization: The Emergence of a Global Education Industry.*" Symposium at Goethe-University, Frankfurt am Main, Germany, 16–17 February 2017. Retrieved online: http://www.symposium-gei.eu/Symposium/ [last 21 July 2018].

## References

Adamson, F., Astrand, B., & Darling-Hammond, L. (Eds.). (2016). *Global Education Reform: How Privatization and Public Investment Influence Education Outcomes*. New York: Routledge.

Appadurai, A. (2012). *The Social Life of Things: Commodities in Cultural Perspective*. Cambridge: University Press.

Au, W., & Lubienski, C. (2016). The Role of the Gates Foundation and the Philanthropic Sector in Shaping the Emerging Education Market. Lessons from the US on Privatization of Schools and Education Governance. In A. Verger, C. Lubienski, & G. Steiner-Khamsi (Eds.), *World Yearbook of Education 2016: The Global Education Industry* (pp. 28–43). New York: Routledge.

Ball, S. J. (2012). *Global Education Inc. New Policy Networks and the Neoliberal Imaginary*. London/New York: Routledge.

Burch, P. (2009). *Hidden Markets: The New Education Privatization*. New York: Routledge.

Fenwick, T., Mangez, E., & Ozga, J. (Eds.). (2014). *World Yearbook of Education 2014: Governing Knowledge: Comparison, Knowledge-Based Technologies and Expertise in the Regulation of Education.* New York: Routledge.

Fitz, J., & Beers, B. (2002). Education Management Organisations and the Privatisation of Public Education: A Cross-national Comparison of the USA and Britain. *Comparative Education, 38*(2), 137–154.

Foucault, M. (2000). Gouvernementalität. In U. Bröckling, T. Lemke, & S. Krasmann (Eds.), *Gouvernementalität der Gegenwart. Studien zur Ökonomisierung des Sozialen* (pp. 41–67). Frankfurt/M, Germany: Suhrkamp.

Gunter, H. M., & Mills, C. (2017). *Consultants and Consultancy: The Case of Education.* Cham, Switzerland: Springer.

Hartong, S. (2016). Between Assessments, Digital Technologies, and Big Data: The Growing Influence of 'Hidden' Data Mediators in Education. *European Educational Research Journal, 15*(5), 523–536.

Hartong, S., Hermstein, B., & Höhne, T. (Eds.). (2018). *Ökonomisierung von Schule?* Weinheim, Germany/Basel, Switzerland: Juventa.

Hogan, A., Sellar, S., & Lingard, B. (2016). Corporate Social Responsibility and Neo-Social Accountability in Education. The Case of Pearson plc. In A. Verger, C. Lubienski, & G. Steiner-Khamsi (Eds.), *World Yearbook of Education 2016: The Global Education Industry* (pp. 107–124). London: Routledge.

Lawn, M. (2013). A Systemless System: Designing the Disarticulation of English State Education. *European Educational Research Journal, 12*(2), 231–241.

Lewis, S., & Lingard, B. (2015). The Multiple Effects of International Large-Scale Assessment on Education Policy and Research. *Discourse: Studies in the Cultural Politics of Education, 36*(5), 621–637.

Lingard, B., Rawolle, S., & Taylor, S. (2005). Globalizing Policy Sociology in Education: Working with Bourdieu. *Journal of Educational Policy, 20*(6), 759–777.

Mautner, G. (2005). The Entrepreneurial University. A Discursive Profile of a Higher Education Buzzword. *Critical Discourse Studies, 2*(2), 95–120.

Mundy, K., Green, A., Lingard, B., & Verger, A. (Eds.). (2016). *Handbook of Global Education Policy.* Chichester, UK: Wiley.

Normand, R. (2016). *The Changing Epistemic Governance of European Education. The Fabrication of the Homo Academicus Europeanus?* Cham, Switzerland: Springer.

OECD. (2017). *Schools at the Crossroads of Innovation in Cities and Regions.* Paris: OECD Publishing. https://doi.org/10.1787/9789264282766-en

Peters, M. A., & Besley, T. (2015). Finance Capitalism, Financialization, and the Prospects for Public Education. In M. A. Peters, J. M. Paraskeva, & T. Besley (Eds.), *The Global Financial Crisis and Educational Restructuring* (pp. 21–49). New York: Peter Lang.

Porter, M. E. (2014). Foreword. Education Presents and Immense Opportunity for Companies to Create Shared Value. In FSG Consulting (Ed.), *Shared Value Initiative. The New Role of Business in Global Education*. Retrieved online at: https://www.sharedvalue.org/new-role-business-global-education. Last 19 July 2018.

Rizvi, F., & Lingard, B. (2010). *Globalizing Education Policy*. New York: Routledge.

Robertson, S. L., & Verger, A. (2012). Governing Education through Public Private Partnerships. In S. L. Robertson, K. Mundy, A. Verger, & F. Menashi (Eds.), *Public Private Partnerships in Education. New Actors and Modes of Governance in a Globalizing World* (pp. 21–42). Cheltenham, UK: Edward Edgar.

Schleicher, A. (2017). *Schools at the Crossroads of Innovation in Cities and Regions*. Video Presentation at the 3rd Global Education Industry Summit, Luxembourg, 25–26 September 2017. Retrieved online: http://globaleducation.onetec.eu/. Last 21 July 2018.

Schumpeter, J. A. (1993). *Theorie der wirtschaftlichen Entwicklung*. Berlin, Germany: Duncker & Humblot.

Sellar, S., & Lingard, B. (2014). The OECD and the Expansion of PISA: New Global Modes of Governance in Education. *British Educational Research Journal, 40*(6), 917–936.

Selwyn, N. (2014). *Digital Technology and the Contemporary University: Degrees of Digitalisation*. London: Routledge.

Spring, J. (2015). *Economization of Education: Human Capital, Global Corporations, Skills-Based Schooling*. London: Routledge.

Spring, J., Frankson, J. E., McCallum, C. A., & Banks, D. P. (Eds.). (2017). *The Business of Education: Networks of Power and Wealth in America*. New York: Routledge.

Tooley, J. (2001). The Global Education Industry: Lessons from Private Education in Developing Countries. In *The International Finance Corp*. Washington, DC.

van der Zwan, N. (2014). Making Sense of Financialization. *Socio-Economic Review, 12*, 99–129.

Verger, A. (2012). Framing and Selling Global Education Policy: The Promotion of Public-Private Partnerships for Education in Low-Income Contexts. *Journal of Education Policy, 27*(1), 109–130.

Verger, A. (2016). The Global Diffusion of Education Privatization: Unpacking and Theorizing Policy Adoption. In K. Mundy, A. Green, B. Lingard, & A. Verger (Eds.), *The Handbook of Global Education Policy* (pp. 64–80). Chichester, UK: Wiley.

Verger, A., Fontdevila, C., & Zancajo, A. (2016). *The Privatization of Education: A Political Economy of Global Education Reform.* New York: Teachers College Press.

Verger, A., Lubienski, C., & Steiner-Khamsi, G. (Eds.). (2016). *World Yearbook of Education 2016: The Global Education Industry.* New York: Routledge.

Williamson, B. (2016). Digital Education Governance: Data Visualization, Predictive Analytics, and 'Real-time' Policy Instruments. *Journal of Education Policy, 31*(3), 123–141.

Williamson, B. (2017). *Big Data in Education: The Digital Future of Learning, Policy and Practice.* London: SAGE.

# 2

# Serial Entrepreneurs, Angel Investors, and Capex Light Edu-Business Start-Ups in India: Philanthropy, Impact Investing, and Systemic Educational Change

Stephen J. Ball

This chapter addresses a gap in the existing literature on the Global Education Industry (GEI) and explores some possibilities for new forms of research that might fill this gap. Most work on the GIE has focused on the role and growth of the 'big players'—the multi-national corporations (e.g. Pearson, McKinsey, Microsoft, and News Corporation) or major global philanthropic foundations (Gates, Broad, Walton, Omidyar, etc.)—and has sought to map their national and global reach, their programs and investments, and ambitions for growth. Far less attention has been directed to the other end of the education market and the role of micro-, small-, and medium-sized edu-businesses. Furthermore, existing work tends to focus on the substantive programs and initiatives of and relationships among these big players, and their participation in and influence on 'policy conversations' of various sorts (Hogan, Sellar, & Lingard, 2014), and their interaction with multilateral agencies (OECD, the

---

S. J. Ball (✉)
Institute of Education, University College London, London, UK
e-mail: stephen.ball@ucl.ac.uk

© The Author(s) 2019
M. Parreira do Amaral et al. (eds.), *Researching the Global Education Industry*,
https://doi.org/10.1007/978-3-030-04236-3_2

World Bank, the EU) (Mundy, 2010). This focus, with some exceptions, neglects the growing importance of impact investing and the financial aspects of business practices and market dynamics in education.

This chapter then has a primary focus on investment and the role of *serial entrepreneurs* and *angel investors* (see below) and the proliferation of education start-up businesses in India, but in doing so it also demonstrates the role of multi-national philanthropic foundations and local and international investment houses in the facilitation of the development of a global/local business eco-system 'at the bottom of the pyramid' (Prahalad, 2008) (or what is sometimes called 'bottom[1] billion capitalism' or 'social capitalism') (Ball & Junemann, 2015).[2] Social capitalism and impact investing are not the same thing, but distinctions between them are blurred. In the former, competitive advantage remains the primary basis on which companies are held to account. In the case of the latter, attempts are made to establish a clear and measureable development or beneficiary impact. However, there are examples of impact investing where returns are given priority over impact (see UNITUS and SKS Microfinance). Furthermore, the meaning of 'impact' in the rhetoric of business philanthropy is often unclear and impact reports are frequently unpublished or difficult to access.

I suggest that impact investments and 'bottom billion' investments in for-profit providers, of a variety of kinds, operating in 'the education space', are bringing about significant changes to the topology of Indian education and contributing to the construction of a shadow education state (Wolch, 1990). Special attention is paid to the role of nodal actors or boundary spanners in policy and business development. The chapter also signals issues related to changes in education policy processes and governance and the concomitant changes to the form and modalities of the state that I have explored elsewhere (Ball, 2016, 2017) and gestures toward the key role of technology—Ed-Tech—in the growth of the GEI and education reform.

This discussion begins with a particular point of entry into an international network of impact investing organizations (see Fig. 2.1), that is, the Michael and Susan Dell Foundation (MSDF). It then moves via one of MSDF's third-party investment vehicles, the UNITUS Seed Fund, to focus on one of UNITUS' Indian partners, Sylvant Advisers, with whom

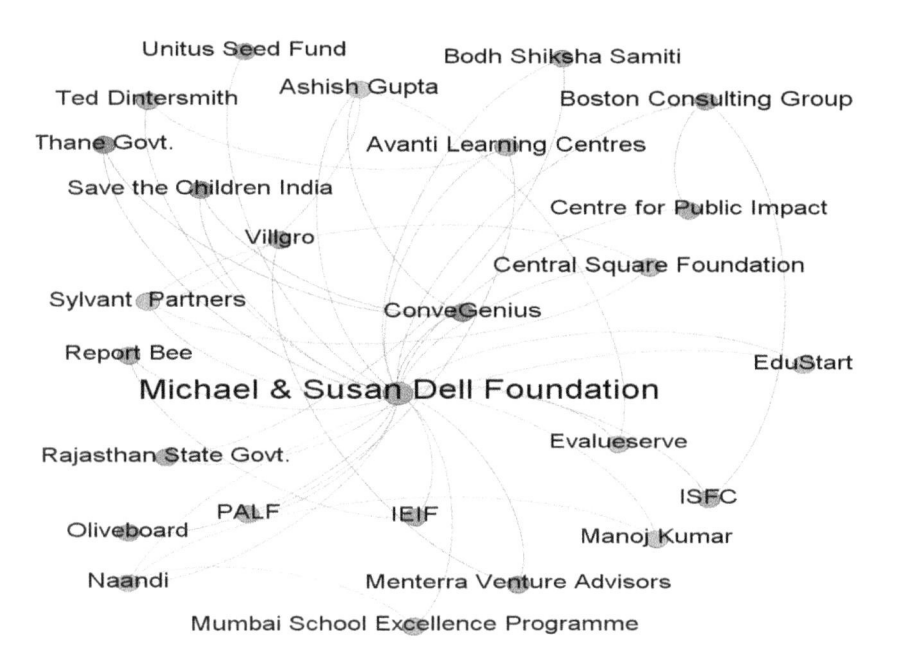

Unitus Seed Fund   Bodh Shiksha Samiti
Ted Dintersmith   Ashish Gupta
                                    Boston Consulting Group
Thane Govt.
                  Avanti Learning Centres
Save the Children India
                                    Centre for Public Impact
            Villgro
                                    Central Square Foundation
Sylvant Partners
                  ConveGenius
Report Bee
                                            EduStart
         Michael & Susan Dell Foundation

Rajasthan State Govt.              Evalueserve

                                            ISFC
            PALF       IEIF
Oliveboard                         Manoj Kumar

    Naandi         Menterra Venture Advisors
         Mumbai School Excellence Programme

**Fig. 2.1** A simplified network of investments in edu-business in India

they collaborate to run the StartEdu Competition (see below) and thence to a closer look at the activities, roles, and relationships of one member of Sylvant's team, Madan Padaki.[3] This takes serious McCann and Ward's (2012, p. 42) argument for research to 'follow' and 'study through' policies (or in this case investments) and the need to attend to not only the 'whos' and 'whats' but also the 'wheres' of edu-business—as places and events in which the 'past, present and potential futures of education coexist' (McCann & Ward, 2012, p. 48). The universals that circulate here are investment and its concomitant subject the entrepreneur.

This approach to researching and the analysis of the field of edu-business is based on what Ong (2007) calls an *analytics of assemblage* and the techniques of a global 'network ethnography' (Junemann & Ball, 2018)—that is, an analysis that relates together a set of global practices, language, people and places, sites and events, and organizational forms that are joined-up in a network of social, commercial, and discursive relations. Roy (2012) claims that a 'thick description' of networks requires a thick description of connections and connectivity. However, as Roy (p. 34) makes clear network ethnography is 'less a practice of specific methods and more an orientation, a way of undertaking problematizations of the world'. Gupta and Ferguson (1997) state: 'what would once have appeared as a logical impossibility—ethnography without the ethnos—has come to appear, to many, perfectly sensible, even necessary' (p. 2). This involves 'studying up' (Roy, 2012), and the generation of an intimate ethnography of elite actors, and mapping and following the flows of relations, ideas, and money that connect and animate the spaces of (education) policy and business in which such actors operate and interact. Thus, Roy (2012, p. 755) describes the challenge of a global ethnography as 'ethnography of circulations' rather than ethnography of locations. It is money that circulates in the forms of investment and loans, buying and selling, and as the discourse, sensibilities, and values of financialization that produces conduits of opportunity for investment. In relation to all of this, Ong (2006) urges us to produce more ethnographic case studies to examine experiments in and developments of neoliberalization, arguing that an ethnographic perspective reveals specific alignments of market rationality, sovereignty, and citizenship that mutually constitute 'distinctive milieus of labor and life at the edge of emergence'. That is to say, 'The interplay of optimizing rationality, political institutions and actors defines a particular configuration, i.e. a milieu of transformation that is also for the analyst, a space of problematization' (Ong, 2007, p. 5). The problematization and the apparatus in this case is investment practices and their relation to edu-business and its growth. The chapter draws primarily on internet documents including press releases, company websites, online newspaper articles, interviews, and online ephemera.

A partial, simplified, schematic, and indicative representation of the network in question here is presented in Fig. 2.1 and a more extensive table of participants is provided in Table 2.1 (see below). This network is full of overlaps (investment, philanthropy, business, government); it is multi-faceted, multi-directional, and multi-layered. It is not easy to see 'through' the welter of activity and actors to comprehend the effects being wrought. It is based, as Jessop (1998, p. 33) explains, 'on negotiation and

Table 2.1 Components of the impact investing network

| Technology | Finance | Edu-businesses | Philanthropy and third sector | Government | Entrepreneurs |
|---|---|---|---|---|---|
| | Sylvant Advisers PALF | LabinApp GetSetSorted Integra Vedantu | MSDF EDGE Forum Makeroom Samarthanam Trust SVP India | DOEACC | Madan Padaki |
| Entlogics Concur Technologies Apple Amazon Aslan Computing | NovakBiddle UNITUS Seed Fund Goldman Sachs Boston Common Asset Management Bain Capital | Lodestar GuruG Manipal Education and Medical Group Pearson | USAid TiE Deshpande Foundation Wadhwani Foundation Sorenson Impact Foundation 500 StartUps | Ministry of IT Planning Commission of India | PV Boccasum Bill Gates Vinod Khosla Diego Piacentini Hari Kumar Steve Singh Geeta Aiyer Bob Gay T.V. Mohandas Pai Dr. Ranjan Pai Hemendra Kothari Mike Murray Dave McClure |
| NComputing | UNITUS Incubator Accelerator Program | MeritTrac | | | |

(continued)

**Table 2.1** (continued)

| Technology | Finance | Edu-businesses | Philanthropy and third sector | Government | Entrepreneurs |
|---|---|---|---|---|---|
| Microland | StartEdu | Manipal Education Group | MillionJobsMission | | Anand Sudarshan |
| | RubanBridge | | Tata Trusts | | Kartik Kilachand |
| Adea Solutions | | Littlemore Innovation Labs iStar | Indo-America Chamber of Commerce | | Srikanth Iyer |
| Microsoft | StartEdu TVS Capital | Communikids Head High Services | | | |
| | Lets Venture Edcubator | Education Initiatives Curiositi Cue Math | | | |
| Sun Systems Wipro | | | | | |
| Infosys | UpGrad | Hippocampus | | | Will Poole |
| Aditi Technologies | | VidyaNext | | | Pradeep Singh |

positive coordination in task oriented "strategic alliances" based on a (perceived or constructed) coincidence of interests and dispersed control of the interdependent resources needed to produce a joint outcome which is deemed mutually beneficial'. It connects up reform efforts, and reform assumptions around the globe, through the investment activities of 'high net worth' individuals and foundations, with local business initiatives and 'disruptions' in 'the education space' of India. The methods of impact investing draw on those of business investment to address the needs of the 'poor' and to bring about changes in the landscape of educational provision (through new private provision and services) and the reform of education (through partnerships and policy initiatives with the state and the negotiation of legal frameworks for for-profit activity in education services).

It is easy to get lost in the labyrinth of the network, the jargon of the field, and the claims of the participants. The research challenge is to make some sense of the 'interconnectedness, multiplexity and hybridisation' (Amin, 1997, p. 129) that animates the social and commercial relations displayed. The researcher must plot a journey through the network, choosing a starting point, taking turnings, finding dead ends, and confronting ambushes and surprises. There is a need to balance some sort of order of representation against the messiness, instability, and change of the field depicted. Within this labyrinth and given the limits of the chapter, some of the connections indicated here must be left as loose ends to be followed up and explored later, and some organizations and people will have to 'stand' as examples for others and as indicators of more general trends and processes.

The focus here is on India. India is by no means 'typical' but it is interesting and important in relation to education reform and education business and impact investing. It is one of the world's fastest-growing economies and one of the youngest countries in the world in terms of the age structure of its population—India has over 550 million people below the age of 25 years. Over 32 percent of the 1.2 billion population is in the age group 0–14, which means that the number of people in India who need primary and secondary education alone exceeds the entire US population—which poses enormous challenges to the government in terms of educational provision and skill development but also creates a window of opportunity and receptivity for business (Kingdon, 1995). 'India is at a unique point in human history with an extraordinary size and proportion of youth ... We are seeking the best of entrepreneurial energy and commitment to participate in this opportunity'[4] (Anand Sudarshan, Founder & Director at Sylvant Advisors). India is regarded as 'The Global Epicentre of Impact Investing' (Thillai Rajan, Koserwal, & Keerthana, 2014). The term *impact or social investing* refers to investing with the implicit intention of generating positive social impact, along with a return on capital. Social impact investments in India attracted $500 million in 2015 and are expected to increase to US$1 billion (about INR6700 crore) by 2020, according to the Impact Investors Council (IIC):

> India is globally regarded as a major hub for impact investing, with a highly evolved ecosystem comprising diverse stakeholders, well regarded successes in Bottom of the Pyramid entrepreneurship, pioneering investors, and a wide array of enterprise enablers. An analysis of impact investment trends from the year 2000 shows that USD $1.6b has been invested in 220+ enterprises across India. It also reveals that around 60% of total impact investments have been made in just 15 enterprises, and that Healthcare, agri-business and clean energy are the leading sectors outside financial inclusion, attracting investments of $341m. (Intellecap, 2014)

In various ways, the national government in India and the government of some states have welcomed and sought to facilitate the participation of new actors—commercial, not-for-profit, and philanthropic—in education service delivery (see Verger, Fontdevila, & Zancajo, 2016, pp. 144–150).

## MSDF

India is one of the three countries in which the MSDF is active. MSDF was created as a charitable foundation in 1999 by Michael Dell (Founder and CEO of Dell Computers) and his wife Susan. It is a distinct entity, formally separate from the Dell Corporation and its CSR wing the Dell Foundation. Its origins are in central Texas, USA, but now it has offices in New Delhi and Cape Town. MSDF partners with governments, a wide range of international and non-governmental organisations, entrepreneurs, UN bodies, investment houses, global management consultancy firms, and edu-businesses, and, in doing so, 'systematically seeks to transform the education system in the cities and countries of operation' (website). It seeks 'to improve the lives of under privileged children living in urban poverty primarily, though not exclusively, through education' (website). The foundation's work focuses on issues of student and teacher performance. MSDF is an active player in a global education policy network involving multiple and multifaceted relationships with other policy actors, like ARK, BMGF, Omidyar Network, Central Square Foundation, McKinsey, Pearson, Centre for Public Impact (Boston Consulting Group), and so on. Since its inception, MSDF has committed $1.23 billion to non-profits, edu-businesses, charities, and social enterprises in the US, India, and South Africa through donations, equity stakes, and social impact bonds, and it provides incubation and support for business development, and, since 2006, has invested over INR745 crore ($120 million) in India.[5] While it describes itself as a catalytic investor, MSDF operates across the whole spectrum of philanthropic modalities but is committed to *'a hands-on approach, close relationships with partner organizations, and data-driven mindset'* and is *'driven by pragmatism, which means that every investment decision is based on sound, business-minded factors, hard data and realities on the ground'*[6] (MSDF website).

> Besides mapping investment opportunities against programmatic goals (for instance, ensuring an investment helps to expand access to high-quality after-school learning for poor children in Indian cities), we also evaluate potential investments to make sure they meet a second criteria: "additionality." In other words, we look at the broader landscape to determine whether our dollars fill a specific market gap that more traditional investors, with their purer focus on profits, are unlikely to prioritize.
> We then evaluate each potential investment with an eye toward a nuanced view of risk and reward that goes well beyond conventional "impact first" or "finance first" considerations. We know for instance, that dependent on the context in which we invest – whether we're providing seed stage funding, funding to extend access to a far greater number of people, or funding to help lower-price points – the relative balance of financial and social returns will (and should) shift.
> The bottom line is that, if impact investors want to shape market forces so that they address at least some of the huge gaps faced by the poor, we need to remain agile. We have to move beyond the current either/or debate, and embrace a certain amount of necessary complexity. (Goel, 2014, n.p.)

## UNITUS Seed Fund and 'Technology Veterans'

UNITUS (managed from Seattle and Bangalore) is funded by a group of partners, mainly 'technology veterans' as they are called, including institutional investors like *MSDF, the Deshpande Foundation,*[7] *Wadhwani Foundation,*[8] *and Sorenson Impact Foundation,*[9] and individual investors like Bill Gates (Microsoft), Vinod Khosla (Sun Microsystems), Mike Murray (Microsoft and Apple), Dave McClure (Aslan Computing, Microsoft, Intel, 500 StartUps), Diego Piacentini (Amazon), Hari Kumar (Formerly Goldman Sachs), Steve Singh (Concur Technologies), Geeta Aiyer (Boston Common Asset Management), and Bob Gay (Co-Founder of Bain Capital). UNITUS also includes Indian investors such as T.V. Mohandas Pai (formerly Infosys CFO), Dr. Ranjan Pai (CEO of Manipal Education and Medical Group), and Hemendra Kothari (Chairman, DSP Blackrock). UNITUS began with an initial $8 million (rising to $25 million) and a second tranche of £50 million—it is a spin-off from UNITUS Labs (founded by Dave Richards [Real Networks]). These are, as they are called, 'high net worth individuals', and they are part of what Diane Ravitch calls *The Billionaires Boys Club* (Ravitch, 2016). UNITUS funds 'early stage start ups focused on low-income customers' in areas of activity that do not attract 'grand slam investments', it various offers risk capital, growth funds, bootstrapping, and mezzanine financing. 'The new fund (UNITUS) will serve to help fill the pipeline for later-stage funds' like the Khosla Impact Fund (which invests from 500k to several million) and the UNITUS Impact Fund.[10] Technology is a key point of interest to the fund in part because of its low per-unit costs and marginal costs and potential access to low-income and remote consumers. Technology start-ups are 'capex light' (i.e. low in capital expenditure). 'Approximately 17 per cent of business plans that UNITUS Seed Fund (USF) has received are from the education sector' (Madan Padaki).

> Lots of private schools have adopted technology and the government is also ready to spend on technology. So we believe the time is right for disruption to happen and we want to help start-ups do that. (Srikanth Iyer, venture partner, UNITUS Seed Fund)[11]

UNITUS is one example of and one form of social capitalism—its aim is to 'do well by doing good' by focusing investment on initiatives at 'the bottom of the pyramid'. That is, the application of what Bill Gates calls 'creative capitalism' to the solution of social problems, problems it is argued that governments cannot solve, or as Vinod Khosla put it 'Investors, entrepreneurs and businesses can create wealth for themselves by providing value to the masses' (Vinod Khosla). In effect, philanthropists and impact investors are assuming the 'socio-moral duties that were heretofore assigned to civil society organizations, governmental entities and state agencies' (Shamir, 2008).

> We're incredibly excited about the growth and profitability we're seeing in for-profit education startups that are serving the masses in India today. However, despite the phenomenal consumer demand, not enough new entrepreneurs are capitalizing on this Rs. 6 lakh crore (USD $100 billion) market opportunity. To trigger momentum, we are partnering with some of India's best incubators to identify, support and develop new companies in this rapidly growing market. (Will Poole, managing partner at UNITUS Seed Fund)

Several of the US-based UNITUS investors, both individuals and foundations, are part of the Indian diaspora who are keen to 'give something back' to their country of origin.

## Sylvant Advisers: StartEdu

Among many other local partnerships, UNITUS collaborates with an Indian management consultancy firm Sylvant Advisors to run StartEdu—StartEdu is a nationwide program to identify, incubate, and invest in early-stage education and Ed-Tech start-ups that are serving India's masses—that is, the 20 crore families living on under INR20,000 per month. Launched in December 2014, the initiative has had three editions with participation from over 250 Indian companies. Sylvant itself 'works with entrepreneurs and early stage companies to accelerate their growth. Beginning with critical investment or fund raising effort, drafting business strategies, providing operational support and being a part of an entire growth lifecycle are the key levers to accelerate the growth of these entrepreneurial ventures, providing operational support and being a part of an entire growth journey' (website). Sylvant is based in Bangalore and was co-founded by Anand Sudarshan (former CEO of Manipal Global Education—India's largest edu-business), Madan Padaki (former co-founder and CEO of MeritTrac Services, a skill assessment and testing company and co-founder Head Held High Services, a social enterprise for rural youth), and PV Boccasam (serial entrepreneur and General Partner at NovakBiddle Venture Partners, US—the world's largest private equity investor in education). Sylvant currently has a portfolio of 14 education start-ups including GuruG (which is also invested in by MSDF through the Indian Educational Investment Fund), Lodestar, Entlogics, and LabInApp (EduStart winner and UNITUS investment recipient), a science learning app that uses 3D virtual laboratories and real-time computer graphics technology. The winner of the second StartEdu competition was GetSetSorted, an integrated career guidance portal business:

> The fourth edition of StartEdu includes two-day bootcamps in five cities across India, from which 20 companies will be handpicked. They will get access to mentorship on growth strategies from industry players such as S. Chand Publishers, Pearson Affordable Learning Fund and Integra. The final winners can also pitch for seed-round investments from UNITUS of up to Rs 3 crore.[12]

The winner of each competition is provided with three mentoring sessions with UNITUS Seed Fund partners Srikanth Iyer (formerly CEO of Pearson India, founder HomeLane) or Will Poole (chairman of NComputing, co-founder VidyaNext), or Sylvant partners Madan Padaki or Anand Sudarshan. Sylvant Advisors, in partnership with LetsVenture, also runs The Edcubator 'India's first Education-focused virtual incubator!' A large proportion of the StartEdu applicants are Ed-Tech companies aiming to supplement or displace government schooling, as Madan Padaki explains[13]:

With greater internet and smartphone penetration, ed-tech entrepreneurs can more efficiently cater to cities with lower public education standards. Models and processes like gamification, simulation, and so on are also pushing innovation in this segment. For instance, Vedantu is trying to build a marketplace targeting tutors as well as students and bring their interaction online. Flinnt is an app to improve student-teacher interaction that sells to schools and other institutions.[14] Not surprisingly, the most populated category focuses on the students and digitising both in-classroom and outside classroom educational needs ... tablet and mobile-based startups like Edutor[15] transform the tablet PC into an educational device, which then enhances the learning experience. Cloud-based ERP Fedena[16] provides user-friendly dashboards with login access for teachers, non-teaching staff, students, parents and management personnel of the target institution. Curiositi offers a customised programme involving learning kits that integrates with a school's science curriculum and transforms science into activity-based learning.

Flow of capital in the ed-tech sector has shown a clear upward trend, with consistent growth since 2010. While evaluating these startups, most of the investors look out for the potential of efficient scaling. Strong tech innovation has proven to be a key enabler for scaling businesses into successful enterprises across sectors. Hence a lot of edupreneurs are now experimenting with the tech aspect alone, a notch up here or a new twist there!

Besides tech-innovation and scalability, the aspect of customer acquisition also remains a huge challenge. The big question still posed: Are the schools motivated by these transformations? Will these tech propositions actually appeal to them, or will they still stick to their brick-and-mortar methods to attain the ultimate goal of educating students?

The education sector is indeed witnessing swift growth with greater adaptation of the digital platform. However, in the chase for introducing the best or the most exciting technology as a potential tool, it is critical that the founders stay focused on the underlying problem and not just on the technology itself!

Ed-Tech solutions are a key component of the re-envisioning of 'the education space' as a space of profit, and a re-envisioning of profit as a means to address social inequality and social exclusion. Digitalization also reworks and reorients the student (Selwyn, 2014), the means and meaning of learning, and the social relations of learning—but at the same time offers possibilities of educational advantage. New markets and new customers for IT are also being created here and the colorful and euphoric blogposts and interviews which promote and advertise these services conjure up 'dream images' of entrepreneurial redemption. This is a vibrant alternative to the saturated high-end IT market in the global north. There is also a complex relation between the interests of small profits (start-ups), big profits (investors), and even bigger profits (large hardware and software providers working toward 'a technology enabled future').

> India is considered among the most digitally mature economies today and credit to the Indian government and India Inc. on driving our country's digital transformation agenda. Dell Technologies, will collaborate with customers, partners and consumers to drive human progress and create a technology enabled future. With a proactive government, digitally inspired business leaders and an advanced partner ecosystem, India has the required potential to lead the world's digital transformation journey. (Alok Ohrie, President & Managing Director, India Commercial, Dell EMC)

## Madan Padaki

> We wanted to lend our shoulder to the wheel for good entrepreneurial ideas in education to contribute in building and scaling them as well. Second, this is a good opportunity for us to look at the education ecosystem in India, assess gaps and find ways to plug them. (Madan Padaki, partner at Sylvant and Sylvant and CEO of Head Held High speaking about EduStart)[17]

Padaki holds a degree in engineering from the National Institute of Engineering, University of Mysore, and an MBA from S.P. Jain Institute of Management and Research. In 2011, he was conferred The Young Education Leader Award by EDGE Forum—a forum of leading educationists and educational institutions in India. (See Madan Padaki speaking on the TEDx Gateway). Madan Padaki is a relatively new kind of globally networked, locally based, boundary-spanning, edu-business investor and policy actor. He is a businessman, angel investor, government adviser, serial entrepreneur, philanthropist, and social capitalist. He has worked as a senior executive for TNCs (Wipro Corporation, Infosys Technologies, and BFL Software [now EDS Mphasis]), founded his own businesses, invests in and incubates business start-ups, and serves on government and business organizations.[18] He is a senior advisor to Tata Trusts, serves on the Governing Council of TiE[19] Bangalore, the Indo-American Chamber of Commerce, and also serves on the Governing Council of DOEACC, an organization of the Ministry of IT, Government of India that has the role to evaluate IT education in India. He speaks about and acts in a space that presents business solutions to educational problems. He has received awards and recognition both for his business activities and for his contribution to rural development. He is regarded as a 'thought leader' and 'social change leader'. He leads the Makeroom—Action Agenda for Change 2020—Core team, Global Action on Poverty, and is a fundraiser for Samarthanam Trust[20] and lead partner of SVP India, which is a 'community' of 200+ corporate leaders, entrepreneurs, active citizens, and philanthropists committed to solving complex social issues through personal philanthropy, advocacy, and capacity building. He represents and espouses a potent blend of business acumen and moral responsibility and is complexly positioned in the reframing 'of socio-moral concerns from within the rationality of capitalist markets' (Shamir, 2008, p. 3) where, as noted above, doing good becomes good for business. Tensions between social good and private interests are miraculously resolved. 'Moral considerations thus "lose", so to speak, their transcendental attributes or at least their character as liabilities and re-emerge as business opportunities' (Shamir, 2008, p. 14). He is a nodal actor in a global financial and business network that is investing in and building capacity and opportunity for edu-businesses. In various capacities, he is a participant in investments in India and the US, and he partners (in various enterprises) edu-businesses large and small. He embodies what Amin (1997, p. 129) calls the 'intermingling of global, distant and local logics'.

## Discussion

What is outlined here is a set of neoliberal doubles that rest on a mutually beneficial relation between reform and profit. Reform creates a future of profit opportunities, both at the general level in a shift from state to private provision and the concomitant commodification of education, and at the substantive level. The reform process and reform initiatives themselves create a raft of profit opportunities (particularly in relation to digitalization—pedagogy, teacher education, assessment, data analytics, big data, etc.). This is a marketplace of social solutions. Solutions are proffered and sold, and both profit and social returns are sought (Eggers & Macmillan, 2013). In relation to this, Blowfield and Dolan (2014) suggest that 'the very notions of the poor, poverty, beneficiary and development worthiness are being constructed around what is material, instrumental and comprehensible to business' (p. 35). This might be seen as part of a bigger narrative that entails 'the financialisation of development'[21] and the escalation of levels of debt both for businesses and for consumers.[22] There is also another general process here that 'grows' new markets and encourages new consumers especially via the digitalization of education, which serves the interests of multi-national hardware and software companies. There is a second double embedded here, which involves working (endogenously) with and (exogenously) against the state. Partnerships and contracts with the state are part of the process of reworking education as a commodity or more precisely a monetized 'service'; at the same time, a set of alternative forms of private provision (and a 'shadow state') are created to supplement and/or displace state provision. Other doubles are the rhetorical assertion of moral and financial complementarity—'doing well by doing good' (these are 'angel investors'!!!), for example. Alongside this there are possibilities of 'worldmaking' for super-rich philanthropists, that is the enactment of personal beliefs and commitments through investment, advocacy, and processes of dissemination, whereby the personal becomes political in the form of technical solutions to social problems. My argument here is that 'development agents' like MSDF are contributing to both the re-imagination of the 'educational space' as a market and the production of an infrastructure of organizations, processes, and subjects in whose relations and market exchanges become a sensible and necessary form for the production and consumption of education, marking out a new topology for Indian education. One concomitant effect of this, although there is no space to explore it here, is a reworking of the educational experience and what it means to teach and to learn. Another is that within this *dispositif* of reform and its molar and molecular processes, the educational subject is re-formed in relation to a de-statization of *government*. MSDF operates to 'fill in' the space created by educational reform arrangements with pedagogical/technological innovations like *blended learning* and thence produces new opportunities, in terms of demand, for the IT business. However, the interplay and inter-reliance here between venture philanthropy, impact investing, support and advice from foundations, and longer-term business interests is often unclear. The investments described and the processes of reform both grow the retail consumer base for hardware, software, and online services and nudge education policy toward Ed-Tech 'solutions' which generate wholesale sales opportunities. As Bhanji (2012, p. 315) has argued, referring to the case of Microsoft in Jordan and South Africa, these *localization* processes—donation, investment, contracting, partnerships, and so on—enables (in this case) MSDF, 'to shape policy goals, directives, and decisions in favor of the use of commercial software and services in schools' and as a consequence 'public policymaking is being enmeshed in private sector activities in education'. The hardware and software are themselves actors in the network and means and ends of reform (Dussel, 2018).

What we see here may be one particular form and instance of what Porter (1990) calls strategic clusters. That is 'geographic concentrations of interconnected companies, specialized suppliers, service providers, firms in related industries, and associated institutions in particular fields that compete but also cooperate'. We might call this an investment cluster. Porter's argument is that proximity and flexibility enable change and dynamism— edu-business in India is a case in point. New markets and opportunities for profit are being sought everywhere in the cluster outlined here. There are multiple and murky blurrings between the state, the third sector, and the economy, between public and private, between philanthropy and profit. Philanthropy is a sliding signifier in all of this and the state is enrolled in these processes as an active, facilitative 'audience' and interlocutor. Business works with and against the state, at the same time. Generally, there is in India a receptive policy and political environment for reform and for the participation of business and other actors in service delivery and in policy itself, a wide and welcoming 'policy window'.[23] This new environment creates a role for new knowledges and those actors with expertise based on those knowledges to become significant in the development and enactment of neoliberal governmentality. As Ong (2006) argues, there is a new relationship between government and knowledge through which governing activities are recast as non-political and non-ideological problems that need technical solutions.

Also evident is that various segments, adjuncts, and aspects of education in India, and the work of philanthropy, are fully integrated into a global financial infrastructure animated by a global financial super class of investors and technology entrepreneurs, and the executives and senior staff of both the investment vehicles and the service providers involved are typically business school educated and/or have backgrounds in IT, the latter in banking or investment, often with leading global brands (HSBC, Morgan Stanley, Goldman Sachs, etc.). This infrastructure is layered and complex, is constantly evolving, and is made up of multi-faceted partnerships, collaborations, and exchanges. There are financial, discursive, and arguably social 'returns' achieved here, a commodifying and marketing effect, making education ever more business and market 'ready'. This is enabled by and enables the movement of global education 'forms' (like accountability and assessment, blended learning, and leadership) and policies (like Charter schools) through the networks of this infrastructure, mainly but not exclusively from North to South (Ball, Junemann, & Santori, 2017). As Larner and Laurie (2010, p. 225) suggest, 'there are multiple actors, multiple geographies and multiple translations involved in the process of policy transfer'.

This is a good example of what Ong (2006) names a *milieu of transformation* at 'the edge of emergence'. Several things are happening here. The overall effect is an on-going commercialization and commodification of education. Furthermore, these actors and their investments (with investment as 'an optimising rationality') '*sustain a transformative <u>direction</u> in reform*' efforts (Peck, 2013, p. 145, emphasis in original) and respond to aspiration and advantage seeking and stimulate demand, form consumers and soak up surplus demand. Arguably, as MSDF is aspiring to achieve, the India education system (in part and in some places) is being 'transformed' by the myriad of initiatives, programs, products, services, partnerships, and interventions in 'the education space'. This transformation is multi-faceted—it acts upon the meaning and 'value' of education, upon the practice of philanthropy and the practices of the state, and establishes an infrastructure of business practices and commercial services within education, all of which contribute to changing 'how education is represented and understood' (Ball et al., 2017, p. 143). Impact investing does not simply impact on issues of access, participation, and performance of low-income communities—if indeed it does do that—it has impact on the form of educational provision, the educational space, governance, and the form and modalities of the state. Contemporary philanthropy in the form of impact investing is a space of mediation between the state, economy, and ethics as a heterogeneous space of government it produces 'blurred' subjects (investors, entrepreneurs, aid workers) coalescing the subject of right with the economic subject. 'Through the market and society the art of government is deployed with an increasing capacity of intervention, intelligibility and organization of the whole of juridical, economic and social relations from the standpoint of entrepreneurial logic' (Lazzarato, 2006).

**Acknowledgments** I am very grateful to Shelina Thawer for her support for and comments on this paper, and to Carolina Junemann and Antonio Olmedo for their comments.

# Notes

1. In 2013, according to McKinsey GI and the Omidyar Network, there were 835 million people in India with incomes of under $4.26 a day—representing a spending power of $360 billion.
2. This is the idea that businesses can solve problems that governments cannot and make a profit (generating 'shared value') and making business into a 'development agent' and government into a 'commodifying agent' (Ball, 2012). His proposal is that companies that engage in serving the poor should be given public recognition as their reward for these investments. He encourages companies to compete with each other to do the most good (in addition to making profits) and governments should create market incentives for this behavior. But there is a more general business context to all of this: 'Meeting the needs of low income customers' is also about seeking out profit opportunities at 'the bottom of the pyramid' (BoP) or 'markets for the poor' (M4P) (Blowfield & Dolan, 2014).

This is especially important in the highly saturated technology market. Sorry can't add a comment on a footnote: I think this is important and could be moved to the main text. Also, when you say this, isn't it important to problematize 'impact' anyway? It is usually difficult to understand how these businesses see and measure impact, in part as you say below, because impact evaluations go unreported. 'Meeting the needs of low income customers' as such, as customers and consumers, can be portrayed as impact from a business perspective, but is paying for a service that in many cases should have been provided for free, really 'social benefit'? The rhetoric of impact seems a convenient promotion and branding strategy of these businesses that I think we should be careful to take on uncritically.

3. This is a technique of analysis I have tried before (Laboring…), using one nodal actor within a network as a paradigm case both to provide examples of the network discourse in play and the diversity of relationships and activities that constitute the effectivity of the network.
4. http://gosylvant.com/Ourteam.html
5. https://www.msdf.org/press-releases/michael-susan-dell-foundation-funds-landmark-state-wide-school-quality-improvement-program/, accessed 13/05/16.
6. https://www.msdf.org/about/foundation-team/, accessed 13/05/16.
7. Deshpande Foundation is a non-governmental organization founded in 1996 in the US by Dr. Gururaj and Jaishree Deshpande to accelerate the creation of sustainable and scalable enterprises that have significant social and economic impact. Gururaj Deshpande is an Indian American venture capitalist and entrepreneur, who is best known for co-founding the Chelmsford, MA-based internet equipment manufacturer Sycamore Networks. His net worth, at its peak, exceeded $4 billion.
8. The Wadhwani Foundation is a philanthropic organization founded by Dr. Romesh Wadhwani. The Foundation's mission is 'to accelerate economic development in India and other emerging economies'. The Wadhwani Foundation principally works through partnerships with like-minded individuals, organizations, corporations, and governments. Founded in 2000, the Foundation launched its first initiatives in entrepreneurship development. The National Entrepreneurship Network (NEN), opened in 2003, is now the largest entrepreneurship community in India. Wadhwani is Executive Chairman of Symphony Teleca Corporation, MSC Software Inc., Symphony Health Solutions Inc., and

Shopzilla Inc. Wadhwani is also the largest limited partner in each of Symphony's private equity funds, the third of which closed recently at $870 million.
9. SIF describes itself as helping 'governments, nonprofits, social enterprise, and philanthropy get better results through a clear focus on mission-aligned, long-term outcomes. Center strategies include: Designing programs that incorporate research-based best practices; Tracking performance to understand what's "working"; Using data to improve program performance over time; Re-allocating resources toward more evidence-based models; and Developing innovative funding strategies to scale proven models'. James Lee Sorenson founded Sorenson Media in 1995, where he built a team that developed the world's leading digital compression software.
10. https://techcrunch.com/2013/01/03/unitus-seed-fund/
11. http://economictimes.indiatimes.com/articleshow/45546117.cms?utm_source=contentofinterest&utm_medium=text&utm_campaign=cppst
12. https://yourstory.com/2016/06/edtech-startup-tips-startedu-2016/
13. Extracts from https://yourstory.com/2015/07/ed-techs-classroom-experience/
14. Flinnt is India's most exciting learning app for K-10 students. On Flinnt, students can learn from free and paid courses mapped to CBSE, NCERT, NSO, IMO, IEO, ASSET, and other Olympiads.
15. Edutor helps emerging technologies engage learners while driving effectiveness in educational institutions' teaching-learning processes.
16. An online school management system.
17. Read more at: http://economictimes.indiatimes.com/articleshow/45546117.cms?utm_source=contentofinterest&utm_medium=text&utm_campaign=cppst
18. Padaki's first entrepreneurial venture was in 2000, when he co-founded MeritTrac, a skill assessment and training company. Manipal Education Group (MEG) bought a 70 percent stake in MeritTrac in which he, along with his founding team, continues to lead MeritTrac as an independent entity. In 2011, he transitioned to Manipal Education from MeritTrac to head up Strategy, Innovation and International Partnerships before moving out in 2013. MeritTrac is today India's largest skills assessment company and is recognized as a thought leader in the sector, having won several awards like the NASSCOM Innovation Award and Deloitte's

Fast 50 India Award. MeritTrac has also been featured extensively in several books on entrepreneurship and is also a case study at INSEAD. He was also the CEO of Erudient, a global education management company. Erudient is now active in North America, Europe, Australia, and Asia Pacific with clients across these geographies and operates out of offices in New York and Singapore.
19. TiE is a non-profit, global community of entrepreneurs. 'We believe in the power of ideas to change the face of entrepreneurship and growing business through our five pillars; mentoring, networking, education, incubating and funding' (website).
20. 'Samarthanam Trust for the Disabled is a non-profit engaged in empowering persons with disabilities and distress in socio-economic-cultural fronts through its various initiatives on Education, Livelihood, Environment, Health & Nutrition, Sports, Culture and Rehabilitation' (website).
21. See Young (2010).
22. MSDF invests directly or indirectly in several loan companies and UNITUS has been a major funder of the SKS microfinance bank.
23. The state is not 'of a piece' in all of this. Different parts of the state, and levels of the state (regional, national, federal, or local), engage with solution providers differently. There are different degrees of enthusiasm and appetite for change.

# References

Amin, A. (1997). Placing Globalisation. *Theory, Culture and Society, 14*(2), 123–137.
Ball, S. J. (2012). *Global Education Inc.: New Policy Networks and the Neoliberal Imaginary*. London: Routledge.
Ball, S. J. (2016). Following Policy: Networks, Network Ethnography and Education Policy Mobilities. *Journal of Education Policy, 31*(5), 549–566.
Ball, S. J. (2017). Laboring to Relate: Neoliberalism, Embodied Policy, and Network Dynamics. *Peabody Journal of Education, 92*(1), 29–41.
Ball, S. J., & Junemann, C. (2015). *Pearson and PALF: The Mutating Giant*. Brussels: Education International. Retrieved from https://download.ei-ie.org/Docs/WebDepot/ei_palf_publication_web_pages_01072015.pdf. Accessed 3 Jan 2018.

Ball, S. J., Junemann, C., & Santori, D. (2017). *Edu.Net: Globalisation and Education Policy Mobility*. London: Routledge.

Bhanji, Z. (2012). Transnational Private Authority in Education Policy in Jordan and South Africa: A Case Microsoft Corporation. *Comparative Education Review, 56*(2), 300–319.

Blowfield, M., & Dolan, C. S. (2014). Business as a Development Agent: Evidence of Possibility and Improbability. *Third World Quarterly, 1*(1), 22–42.

Dussel, I. (2018). Digital Technologies in the classroom: A Global Education Reform? In E. Hultqvist, S. Lindblad, & T. Popkewitz (Eds.), *Critical Analyses of Educational Reforms in an Era of Transnational Governance*. Cham, Switzerland: Springer.

Eggers, W., & Macmillan, P. (2013). *Solution Revolution: How Business, Government, and Social Enterprises Are Teaming Up to Solve Society's Toughest Problems*. Deloitte Global Services.

Goel, G. (2014). *Impact Investing: Are Conventional Impact Measures Too Limiting? (Part 1 of 2)*. Online at: https://www.msdf.org/blog/2014/07/impact-investing-conventional-impact-measures-limiting-part-1-2/. Accessed 3 Jan 2018.

Gupta, A., & Ferguson, J. (1997). Discipline and Practice: 'The Field' as Site, Method and Location in Anthropology. In A. Gupta & J. Ferguson (Eds.), *Anthropological Locations: Boundaries and Grounds of a Field Science*. Berkeley, CA: University of California Press.

Hogan, A., Sellar, S., & Lingard, B. (2014). Pearson, Edu-business and New Policy Spaces in Education. *EERA Annual conference*.

Intellecap. (2014). *Invest. Catalyze. Mainstream: The Indian Impact Investing Story*. Retrieved from https://www.microfinancegateway.org/sites/default/files/mfg-en-paper-invest-catalyze-mainstream-the-indian-impact-investing-story-apr-2014.pdf. Accessed 3 Jan 2018.

Jessop, B. (1998). The Rise of Governance and the Risks of Failure. *International Social Science Journal, 155*(1), 29–45.

Junemann, C., & Ball, S. J. (2018). On Network(ed) Ethnography in the Global Education Policyscape. In D. Beech (Ed.), *Handbook of Ethnography*. Hoboken, NJ: Wiley.

Kingdon, J. W. (1995). *Agendas, Alternatives, and Public Policies*. New York: HarperCollins.

Larner, W., & Laurie, N. (2010). Travelling Technocrats, Embodied Knowledges: Globalising Privatisation in Telecoms and Water. *Geoforum, 41*(2), 218–226.

Lazzarato, M. (2006). Biopolitics and Bioeconomics. *Multitudes*. Retrieved from http://www.multitudes.net/category/archives-revues-futur-anterieur-et/bibliotheque-diffuse/post-operaisme/lazzarato/. Accessed 3 Jan 2018.

McCann, E., & Ward, K. (2012). Assembling Urbanism: Following Policies and 'Studying Through' the sites and Situations of Policy Making. *Environment and Planning, A44*(1), 42–51.

Mundy, K. (2010). "Education for All" and the Global Governors. In M. Finnemore, D. Avant, & S. Sell (Eds.), *Who Governs the Globe*. New York: Cambridge University Press.

Ong, A. (2006). Mutations in Citizenship. *Theory, Culture and Society, 23*(2–3), 499–531.

Ong, A. (2007). Neoliberalism as a Mobile Technology. *Transactions of the Institute of British Geographers, 32*(1), 3–8.

Peck, J. (2013). Explaining (with) Neoliberalism. *Territory, Politics, Governance, 1*(2), 132–157.

Porter, M. (1990). *The Competitive Advantage of Nations*. New York: Free Press.

Prahalad, C. K. (2008). *The Fortune at the Bottom of the Pyramid*. Upper Saddle River, NJ: Wharton School Publishing.

Ravitch, D. (2016, December 13). Big Foundations Paved the Way for Trump's Assault on Public Schools. *Chronicle of Philanthropy*. Retrieved from https://dianeravitch.net/?s=billionaire+boys+club. Accessed 3 Jan 2018.

Roy, A. (2012). Ethnographic Circulations: Space-time Relations in the Worlds of Poverty Management. *Environment and Planning A, 44*(1), 31–41.

Selwyn, N. (2014). *Digital Technology and the Contemporary University: Degrees of Digitalisation*. London: Routledge.

Shamir, R. (2008). The Age of Responsibilitization: On Market-Embedded Morality. *Economy and Society, 37*(1), 1–19.

Thillai Rajan, A., Koserwal, P., & Keerthana, S. (2014). The Global Epicenter of Impact Investing: An Analysis of Social Venture Investments in India. *The Journal of Private Equity, 17*(2), 37–50.

Verger, A., Fontdevila, C., & Zancajo, A. (2016). *The Privatization of Education: A Political Economy of Global Education Reform*. New York: Teachers College Press.

Wolch, J. (1990). *The Shadow State: Government and Voluntary Sector in Transition*. New York: The Foundation Center.

Young, S. (2010). Gender, Mobility and the Financialisation of Development. *Geopolitics, 15*(3), 606–627.

# 3

# The Political Turn of Corporate Influence in Education: A Synthesis of Main Policy Reform Strategies

Clara Fontdevila and Antoni Verger

## Introduction and Purpose of the Study

A growing body of research points to the increased presence of private actors in education policy-making processes, frequently in connection with the advancement of a pro-market agenda. The emerging role of corporate actors as policy-shapers leads Ball and Youdell (2008) to identify the "privatization of education policy" as an emerging form of education privatization. According to these two authors, privatization occurs when private sector actors participate in policy formation processes through a broad range of activities, including consulting, research, and evaluation. Lubienski (2016) also highlights the growing presence of private interests and actors in education policy-making processes to argue that, in some countries, it is more prevalent than the privatization of schooling.

Processes of education policy privatization echo broader dynamics of social change and redistribution of power affecting a wide variety of

C. Fontdevila (✉) • A. Verger
Department of Sociology, Universitat Autònoma de Barcelona, Barcelona, Spain
e-mail: clara.fontdevila@uab.cat; antoni.verger@uab.cat

fields. Garsten and Sörbom (2017) refer to the *political turn of corporations* in order to capture the growing influence exerted by the corporate sector over the political sphere as both agenda-setters and policy-shapers. While corporate engagement in policy matters is not entirely new, the current scale and intensity are unprecedented. Nevertheless what remains unclear are the specific channels, mechanisms, and resources that endow corporate actors with increased authority and legitimacy in the policy domain (Hillman, Keim, & Schuler, 2004). Research on *policy influence strategies* remains scarce, and tends to address this theme in a piecemeal approach focused on specific organizations and individuals or areas of activity. As a result, we know little about the operating principles, procedures, and strategies the corporate sector deploys when actively contributing to education policy-making and policy-shaping processes.

Another limitation of research on corporate actor influence on policy-making is the lack of a global perspective. Research tends to focus on Western countries, Anglo-Saxon in particular. Meanwhile the so-called Global South (Srivastava & Baur, 2016) has received only limited attention. This is largely the consequence of less developed regions being on the periphery of research production and dissemination. Focusing on Southern and non-Western countries means reconsidering the most well-established categories of policy influence. The conceptual and theoretical tools developed for the study of policy influence in liberal democracies are ill suited to capturing the emerging policy influence dynamics of the Global South.

Based on these considerations, we will describe the broad variety of repertoires of action mobilized by the corporate sector to exert policy influence in different educational settings. We systematize different strategies deployed by the corporate sector to promote education privatization reforms, illustrating each with case studies of corporate influence in various countries. Market reforms are an entry point to explain a broader political trend, namely the increasing number of sources use by private actors to influence education policy-making. Market reforms constitute one of the approaches embraced most consistently by the corporate sector in education. This preference is the result of a mix of material interests, as well as the belief among businesses in the effectiveness of the market as a provider and distributor of incentives in every societal sphere, including education.

# Methodology and Scope of the Research

## Methods of Data Collection and Analysis

Methodologically, our study draws on the results of a systematic literature review (SLR) on the political economy of education privatization. SLR is an approach oriented toward the systematization and synthesis of available evidence on a specific theme, characterized by the use of explicit and transparent methods (Gough, Thomas, & Oliver, 2012). Systematization allows us to identify six different approaches to education privatization, revealing the emergent role of non-state actors as a cross-cutting trend that impacts most of them (see Verger, Fontdevila, & Zancajo, 2017). We reviewed 227 documents, approximately one-third of which explicitly discussed the role of corporate actors in promoting privatization reforms. The primary studies included peer-reviewed articles in academic journals (retrieved through electronic databases), as well as technical reports and other articles suggested by key informants with a regional expertise, or identified through hand-searching. The integration of these sources allowed us to compensate for the literature gaps typical of SLRs, whose search tools tend to privilege research produced by, and focused on, Anglo-Saxon contexts. We relied on common theories of policy change, as well as literature describing the role of interest groups, think tanks, philanthropic organizations, and policy entrepreneurs, to make the data in each study comparable. The combination of empirical material and theoretical sources enabled us to induce five different strategies frequently deployed by the corporate sector to gain influence in privatization policies and reforms.

## Conceptual Framework

Our conceptual framework is based on the *strategies of influence* that Binderkrantz defines as "the overall approaches taken by groups when they pursue political goals" (2005, p. 696). This is not to say that the policy influence exerted by the private sector is solely the product of a *deliberate* strategy. We focus on the toolkit, or repertoires of action, private actors use to influence policy.

We also build on a broad understanding of the corporate sector, encompassing a wide range of individual and collective non-state actors both for-profit, or closely connected to profit-making organizations. Our notion of corporate sector comprises both corporations and corporate-funded private organizations—including philanthropies, think tanks, lobbying firms, and policy institutes (for a similar approach, see Bull & McNeill, 2007, or Garsten & Sörbom, 2017). We combine these categories to capture the spectrum of strategies, networks, and resources mobilized by the corporate sector. This diversity could not be appreciated if we focused on firms because, as has been well documented, corporations have engaged in the establishment of new organizations that directly or indirectly work on their behalf (Barley, 2010, Garsten & Sörbom, 2017). These organizations capitalize on their undefined role to enjoy greater flexibility and access to policy spaces. A broad, inclusive approach is necessary to make sense of the different ways corporations influence education in different settings.

This generic understanding of the corporate sector in education is similar to the notion of the Global Education Industry as advanced by Verger, Lubienski, and Steiner-Khamsi (2016). Our category integrates an array of corporate organizations, including *edu-businesses* operating at different levels, such as private schools, testing companies, teacher training, school improvement services, business conglomerates offering non-core education services, and philanthropic foundations. We also include individual actors—particularly policy entrepreneurs—who are usually connected to corporate players.

## Policy Influence Strategies: A Synthesis

In this section, we present five strategies the private sector uses to influence policies promoting privatization. These are lobbying, networking and brokerage, knowledge mobilization, grassroots mobilization, and sponsorship of pilot experiences.

## Lobbying

Lobbying is often seen as the best way for corporations to influence policy-making. Much study has been devoted to corporate lobbying processes and analyzing the determinants of its forms and success (see Fulton & Stansbury, 1985; De Bruycker, 2014). Milbrath defines lobbying as "the stimulation and transmission of a communication, by someone other than a citizen acting on his own behalf, directed to a governmental decision-makers with the hope of influencing his decision" (1963, p. 8). Lobbying encompasses a wide range of activities, including administrative strategies (like contacting key decision-makers or participating in advisory committees), and parliamentary strategies (such as the participation in parliamentary committees and, more generally, contact with different individuals in the legislative branch).[1]

Lobbying practices pay a role in the enactment of education privatization reforms in the UK and the US. In the UK, for instance, there is the Private Sector Education Group (PSEG) made up of 14 top private education sector companies with access to key education policy-makers such as ministers and top civil servants (Fitz & Hafid, 2007). In the US, private education providers have the Education Industry Association, which is strongly engaged in American education politics at multiple levels (Bulkley & Burch, 2011). Other similar private organizations also have a long history of lobbying for market-driven education policies as a way to improve education performance, empower parents, and, ultimately, stimulate economic development (Holyoke, Henig, Brown, & Lacireno-Paquet, 2009; see also Bulkley & Burch, 2011; Fitz & Beers, 2002; Fusarelli & Johnson, 2004).

Beyond the US and the UK, however, examples of corporate influence via lobbying practices are rather sparse. This is probably because, as Béland (2005) notes, the *parapolitical* sphere differs significantly from one country to another—with Anglo-Saxon political systems being known for their openness to interest groups, and the existence of transparency rules that make lobbying visible to the public. Nonetheless, even in these cases, lobbying appears to be only the tip of the iceberg of a much broader range of strategies to influence the private sector. In Britain, for instance, Fitz and Hafid (2007) note how—because of the lack of a formal structure and the informal spaces and relations through which they operate—the means by which non-state actors influence policy are invisible to most citizens. This is why it is essential to explore more subtle channels of influence, such as those presented below.

## Networking and Brokerage

Networks are key to processes of policy change. Policy networks tend to be integrated by actors who share certain beliefs and ideologies in relation to particular policy issues, and are usually articulated hierarchically (cf. Bull, Bøås, & McNeill, 2004). The theoretical and methodological insights provided by social network analysis—both in its quantitative and ethnographic approaches—are especially useful for capturing relational power dynamics and hierarchies within policy networks.

The policy network research agenda has been especially evident in the study of education market reform. Ball and colleagues have used ethnographic network analysis to explore the impact of philanthropies in the expansion of education markets in both developed and developing countries (Ball, 2012; Santori, Ball, & Junemann, 2015; Junemann, Ball, & Santori, 2016). Their work consistently highlights the amount of influence deployed by a dense network of loosely affiliated, like-minded individuals and organizations, and particularly the policy-shaping capacity associated with their brokerage positions—that is, the adoption of bridging and/or bonding roles as an instance of policy agency likely to have an impact on policy change (cf. Christopoulos & Ingold, 2011). As advanced by Medvetz's (2012, 2014) work on organizations as boundary spanners, the policy influence of the corporate sector greatly relies on being embedded in policy networks within larger policy systems connected to different social spheres.

In fact, networks are not always or necessarily structured purposefully. Connectivity is also routinely "nourished" through routine casual encounters such as business meetings and social events. For instance, informal communication networks have played an important role in the promotion of low-fee private schools (LFPSs) in the Global South (Ball,

2012; Santori et al., 2015; Junemann et al., 2016). An emerging body of research highlights the pluri-scalar dynamics in which pro-LFPSs networks operate. This research shows that the network of international promoters of LFPSs include international organizations, aid agencies, individual consultants, and private foundations. These actors meet on a regular basis with private-school owners and other types of *edupreneurs* at numerous events, conferences, and seminars—including the IFC Private Education Conference, the International and Private Schools Education Forum, the Qatar Foundation's World Innovation Summit for Education (WISE), and the Global Education and Skills Conference. According to Junneman et al. (2016), these meetings provide opportunities for "talk and touch," that is, personal contact, which produces and consolidates trust among the different members of the network. Participants in these events share ideas, learn about "best practices" and local edupreneurs, visit private schools, or participate in other pilot experiences (Santori et al., 2015). These events expand and strengthen networks, intensify the exchange of information and ideas, and facilitate business. These spaces also entrench a discourse in the international education arena on the desirability of including both private sector and for-profit motives in educational development strategies.

However, policy networks do not always operate behind the scenes. In fact, one of the emerging strategies of networking is the establishment of (relatively) formalized alliances between key actors in the field to provoke policy change. In contrast to informal networks, formal coalitions have a public profile and larger capacity to convene "strange bedfellows" (Heaney, 2006). Brazil offers an illustrative example of the role of the corporate sector in establishing formal coalitions in education policy. In recent years, a national business coalition, *Todos Pela Educaçao* (TPE), has developed a high public profile in Brazilian educational politics. According to Martins (2013), this coalition has contributed to constructing new hegemonic educational projects with a focus on pro-market policies. To advance its proposals, TPE has relied on a powerful communication strategy, solid technical support, and good connections with all three branches of government. In fact, TPE has become a model for other education business coalitions in Latin America where there is even a supranational network, Latin American Network of Civil Society Organizations for Education (known as REDUCA in its Spanish acronym), which was created with the support of the Inter-American Development Bank, and is composed of 14 national coalitions (Martins & Krawczyk, 2016).

## Knowledge Mobilization

In many countries, research on education is no longer either exclusively academic or only informed by traditional peer-reviewed sources. Evidence informing education policy debates is increasingly based on the knowledge produced, funded, gathered, and interpreted by corporate-based intermediary organizations and related advocacy groups. These groups are not neutral knowledge brokers, but rather possess a particular political and economic agenda. Philanthropic foundations, think tanks, as well as policy institutes backed by the corporate sector, are increasingly involved in the management and production of knowledge oriented toward policy-making (DeBray, Scott, Lubienski, & Jabbar, 2014; Lubienski, Scott, & DeBray, 2014; Scott & Jabbar, 2014). Lubienski, Brewer, and La Londe (2015) describe this as *idea orchestration,* which they define as "the arrangement of financial, empirical, political and institutional support through networks to advance policy ideas" in which philanthropies and major funders play a central role (p. 2).

The popularization of pro-market reforms among policy-makers and the general public is a result of the production and dissemination of evidence on education reforms conducted by philanthropic organizations. This trend is particularly prominent in the US, where the dissemination of ideas on the advantages of markets and choice in education is funded by philanthropic foundations such as the Eli and Edythe Broad, Michael and Susan Dell, Bill and Melinda Gates, Heritage, Hewlett, and the Walton family. These groups occasionally produce their own research, although more frequently they contribute to knowledge mobilization by supporting like-minded organizations that specialize in it. These *intermediary organizations* (DeBray et al., 2014) are part of an increasingly complex, multi-directional, knowledge-producer-to-consumer relationship where private foundations use funding policies to influence the agendas of academics and research centers. Foundations can also strategically use the results in an intense array of dissemination activities (Henig, 2008). As documented by Lubienski et al. (2015), philanthropy plays a key role in funding intermediary organizations and networks whose function is to "collect, package and promote, but not necessarily produce, research evidence aligned with the agendas of their funders" (p. 7). As these authors note:

> The main point is that, whether knowledge production services are performed in-house or outsourced to an IO [intermediary organization] which relies on funding, venture philanthropies have created integrated policy networks in which funding provides the financial, empirical and political resources to accomplish the multiple tasks necessary to see their agendas implemented. (Lubienski et al., 2015, p. 8)

The engagement of the corporate sector in the production and funding of research has impacted the policy research field in many ways (DeBray et al., 2014). Philanthropies use research to advance their agendas and are not afraid to blur the boundaries between research and advocacy for this purpose (DeBray-Pelot, Lubienski, & Scott, 2007). This has resulted in a tactical, political use of research by policy-makers, who are increasingly willing to instrumentalize evidence in order to provide empirical evidence for their positions.

To some extent, the success of the philanthropic sector in knowledge production and dissemination depends not so much on the consistency and empirical reliability of the information produced, but on framing strategies and the generation of so-called *echo-chamber effects*. The echo-chamber effect is the repeated reference to a limited group of usually low-quality, like-minded studies, which creates the illusion of a general consensus around a policy solution. Such dynamics are particularly frequent in relation to issues that generate uncertainty and/or where evidence is still inconclusive, as is the case with most forms of education privatization policy. As Lubienski, Weitzel and Lubienski note:

> In these types of policy sectors where there are both real demands for empirical evidence of effectiveness and widespread consumption of non-empirical 'evidence', the use of research evidence may be more susceptible to politicization. (2009, p. 135)

The case for vouchers and school-reform policies in the US is a good example of these tensions around knowledge production and use. Here, evidence is often employed by political groups to provide academic legitimacy to their ideological preferences (Belfield & Levin, 2005; see also Goldie, Linick, Jabbar, & Lubienski, 2014). Due to the politicized nature of debates around vouchers and charter schools, relatively neutral research sources are unusual in the public discussion of these themes (Belfield & Levin, 2005; Boyd, 2007; Kirst, 2007; Vergari, 2007). Research justifying the policy agenda on privatization generally lacks the necessary rigor, while university-based, referenced, peer-reviewed research is sidelined or misused.

Similar dynamics exist in relation to the promotion of LFPSs in low- and middle-income countries. During the last decade, a growing body of research has analyzed the effects of LFPSs on quality education and equity, with contradictory results. Nonetheless, LFPSs advocates use existing sources of evidence in a selective way to focus on research claiming they are higher quality and more efficient (Srivastava, 2016). One of the most active players in this promotional work is the policy entrepreneur James Tooley. On the basis of research conducted in poor areas of India, Kenya, Ghana and Nigeria, Tooley emphatically advocates for the advancement of the LFPSs model in a variety of international forums (Ball, 2012). And while he and his research team are generally more nuanced when discussing the advantage of the LFPSs sector in academic circles (Srivastava, 2014), it is his more journalistic material that has been widely diffused across high-level policy circles.

The changing uses of knowledge are also reflected in the centrality of the media in the education policy debate. Market advocates increasingly turn to innovative channels in order to reach the general public and make the case for particular policy solutions (Goldie et al., 2014; Lubienski et al., 2015). Conservative media outlets in the US have played a crucial role in the strategy of school choice advocates (Boyd, 2007). In several Latin American countries, the "knowledge outputs" produced or directly supported by philanthropic foundations are often published in the press. New philanthropists devote substantial resources to consolidating their presence as columnists of widely-distributed newspapers and magazines, or ensuring that they are invited to comment on central policy issues in a variety of media so that they gain the status of educational "specialists" in public debates about education (see for instance Santa Cruz & Olmedo, 2012).

Likewise, school choice campaigners in the US use film documentaries such as *The Cartel, The Lottery, Waiting for Superman,* and *Won't Back Down* to popularize their message and "trigger an emotional reaction in people" (Cave & Rowell, 2014, p. 237). According to Lubienski et al., the production and promotion of these advocacy documentaries "represents a new approach to informing and moving the opinions of a broader audience to help inform policymaking" (2014, p. 139). It is worth noting that these films were funded by the Gates and Broad foundations, and other related intermediary organizations (Lubienski et al., 2015).

## Supporting and Instrumenting Grassroots Advocacy

The sponsorship or encouragement of different forms of grassroots advocacy constitutes a distinct corporate strategy of policy influence. Corporate actors might resort to outside pressure as a means to influence policy with "public appeals through the media and mobilization of group members and citizens" (Binderkrantz, 2005, p. 695). *Outside lobbying* is similarly used as a way of "bringing pressure to bear on Congress by making appeals publicly and encouraging grassroots supporters to contact Congress directly" (Heaney, 2006, p. 898).

In the education field, particularly in the US, the philanthropic sector has actively supported interest groups and civil society organizations whose agenda is aligned to their own pro-market agenda. As Lubienski et al. recall:

> Policy networks in the US have been associated with a number of organisations that describe themselves as grassroots—that is, community-based organisations and movements representing broad-based support. However, whether those organisations emerge organically from community concern or are cultivated by seed money from venture philanthropists and their IOs is not always clear, causing some to label these as 'grass-top' efforts. (2015, p. 11)

Foundations such as the Broad, Dell, Gates, Heritage, Hewlett, and the Walton family have actively supported pro-school choice interest groups and the emerging civil rights movements supporting it. This has been documented in the cases of the National Alliance for Public Charter Schools, the Center for Education Reform, the Hispanic Council for Reform and Educational Options, and the Black Alliance for Educational Options (BAEO) (Scott, 2009, *inter alia*). BAEO, for instance, advocates for the radical alteration of urban schools educating African-American students. According to Apple and Pedroni (2005), BAEO represents the most explicit African-American support for vouchers, school choice, and other conservative ideas. While BAEO enjoys support within black communities throughout the country, particularly in poor inner city areas, most of its leaders have a middle-class background, and, more importantly, this organization's popularity and presence in poor communities are connected to the financial support provided by government agencies and private philanthropies (Apple & Pedroni, 2005; DeBray-Pelot et al., 2007; Lubienski et al., 2015).

Likewise, wealthy individuals and their philanthropic organizations also sponsor pro-charter school and voucher campaigns. The Gates Foundation and other donors connected with Gates provided $8.32 million to influence the *Yes On 1240* campaign, organized by the Washington Coalition for Public Charter Schools, to convince the citizens of Washington State to vote in favor of the Charter Schools Initiative (I-1240). This amount, representing around 80% of the campaign's total budget, is essential to understanding why, after losing three previous popular referenda, the Charter Schools Initiative became state law in December 2012 (Au & Ferrare, 2015; Au & Lubienski, 2016).

## Sponsorship of Pilot Experiences: Leading by Example

Decision-making in complex policy sectors such as education generates much uncertainty. For this reason, the development of new educational models and demonstration projects has become an attractive promotional reform strategy in the eyes of the philanthropic sector. This strategy of "leading by example" is less likely to trigger immediate opposition, given the relatively lower levels of public, journalistic, or research scrutiny that small-scale interventions tend to generate. To a great extent, this approach allows the corporate sector to act with relative autonomy vis-à-vis traditional educational stakeholders—including education authorities, teachers' unions, or community groups. Given the bureaucratized and highly professionalized nature of the education field in most countries, the direct allocation of funds to alternative education providers, in the eyes of the private sector, is one of the most promising venues of political engagement in the promotion of policy change (Reckhow & Snyder, 2014).

Especially in the US, an important part of philanthropic funding supports private education initiatives, such as particular charter school chains or blended education programs that involve more intense uses of ICT in classrooms, as a way to demonstrate that they are a desirable policy option. These dynamics convert philanthropic organizations into *jurisdictional challengers* in that they replicate and replace functions typically performed by traditional public sector institutions (Reckhow & Snyder, 2014). Reckhow and Snyder (2014) distinguish between two different types of jurisdictional challengers in education: first, organizations providing "alternative modes of running schools" (such as charter schools) and, second, organizations providing alternative "sources of human capital in education," particularly in relation to teacher training and certification. By analyzing the giving patterns of the 15 largest education foundations in the US, Reckhow and Snyder (2014) document how, in the last decade, major philanthropies have invested heavily in both types of jurisdictional challengers, charter schools in particular.

Such a trend must be understood in connection with significant changes in philanthropy during the last few decades in the US. One of the main differences between traditional and venture philanthropy is that the latter operates through entrepreneurial and donor-driven funding programs, and treats donations as investments from which significant returns are expected (Scott, 2009; Scott & Jabbar, 2014). Whereas traditional philanthropies make donations to support specific programs and interventions, the aim of venture philanthropies is more ambitiously oriented toward promoting macro educational transformations. A number of recently created philanthropies, including the Gates, Broad, Lumina, and Joyce foundations, have embraced this new paradigm and are investing heavily in transforming education systems through the promotion of school choice and the expansion of private provision (Scott, 2009; Scott & Jabbar, 2014).

For these philanthropic organizations, sponsoring pilot experiences or providing private providers with financial support are central means of policy influence. Their goal is that the experience, if successful, becomes a model for public policy. Venture philanthropists in the US finance specific charter schools and charter management organizations such as Green Dot Public Schools, the KIPP network, and Uncommon Schools. By converting these schools into models of excellence and best practice, philanthropies can demonstrate that their reforms work, and encourage governments to adopt their approach (Bulkley & Burch, 2011; DeBray-Pelot et al., 2007; Scott, 2009). These initiatives are increasingly welcomed by public authorities to the extent that Lubienski et al. have coined the term "disintermediation" to refer to the process through which "state and local authorities are often willing to serve as 'pilot' sites for philanthropists' reforms in exchange for resources" (Au & Lubienski, 2016; Lubienski, 2016)" (2015, p. 4). Disintermediation processes reflect the increasingly important role of these private donors in producing different forms of evidence around educational reform—by mobilizing their economic capital and investing it in policy programs of their choice.

Pilot experiences and scaling up strategies can also be found in countries of the Global South, where philanthropic organizations promote market-oriented interventions by developing and consolidating the private sector through a variety of funding initiatives. Frequently, these foundations aspire to be key players in the education-for-development field through corporate social responsibility programs. In countries like India, for example, most philanthropic foundations are set up by private corporations. Because for-profit education in India is illegal, some of these foundations are contracted by the government to run "underperforming" schools. One example is the Bharti Foundation, funded by the telecommunications company Airtel, that is in charge of 50 government schools in Rajasthan. Another example is the NGO established by the wife of the CEO of Infosys, which runs various schools for the poor in Bangalore (Nambissan & Ball, 2010). The fact that corporate social responsibility has become a new global norm legitimates the increasing presence of the business sector in education networks, particularly in the South (Bhanji, 2016; Nambissan & Ball, 2010).

The evolution of the LFPSs sector also illustrates these education reform dynamics. While originally controlled by local stand-alone providers, this schooling sector is increasingly populated by a number of large-scale corporate-backed school chains—including the APEC schools, Bridge International Academies (BIA), and the Omega Schools. All of these chains have received crucial support from philanthropic organizations, private companies, and finance corporations, such as Pearson and Bill Gates Investments, meaning this shift in scale is largely due to the support of foreign investors (Srivastava, 2016). The investment power of these companies and foundations ultimately endows them with the capacity to reshape the education landscape through transformation on the supply-side. In addition to supporting particular school chains, corporate funding contributes to the establishment of formal public-private partnership arrangements between governments and LFPSs in a growing number of countries such as Uganda, India, or Pakistan (Barber, 2013; Srivastava, 2014, 2016).

The most recent example of this can be found in Liberia. In 2016, the Liberian government announced the Partnership Schools for Liberia—an ambitious reform that originally put the BIA chain in charge of managing every public school in the country. Due to the disapproval of the international aid community, BIA is ultimately not the only private school provider; however, the reform follows their model (Verger, Steiner-Khamsi, & Lubienski, 2017). In Liberia, we see how getting ones foot in the door as the first provider can create the assumption that an organization's strategy for reform is the best.

## Concluding Remarks

Though the corporate or private sector in education has frequently been perceived as a provider of education services, it increasingly plays a diverse range of roles in the policy field. The power of private education providers in reform processes is ultimately a function of their level of presence in the education system. In this chapter, we have focused on corporate actors who do not necessarily have an interest in direct education provision, yet still greatly influence education policy. These actors exert a growing power in the politics of education as agenda-setters by following five different strategies to influence the policy domain. Our list is not exhaustive, but simply provides a preliminary outline of corporate influence in educational reform. There could be other strategies—we just focus on those most frequently discussed by existing literature because of their effectiveness and impact in terms of policy change.

Corporate actors are diversifying their repertoire of ways to influence education policy processes. They do not solely rely on economic capital but also on political—through access to decision-makers and privileged positions vis-à-vis bureaucrats and policy-makers—as well as symbolic capital—through markers of scholar proficiency, and recognition as "authorized" producers of knowledge—as well. This diversification of resources echoes Garsten and Sörbom's (2017) observations on corporate actors as policy *bricoleurs* who alternate between the market and politics, depending on the circumstances.

The role of the private sector in education policy-making is still an emerging field. Our review has identified a number of gaps in existing research, as well as future possible directions. Among them is analyzing the intersection between context (institutional frameworks, levels of economic development, political climate) and strategy. In other words, what are the factors that structurally determine the selection and effectiveness of specific policy influence-seeking strategies? Study on the impact of organizational features and resources allocation on corporate strategy preferences could also advance our understanding of the changing role of the corporate sector in education policy. More empirical research is also necessary to understand the ideological, economic, and political motives behind corporate sector engagement in reform, and how these might be more conducive to some strategies than to others. At a more conceptual level, it would be necessary to better delimit and analyze the internal diversity of corporate involvement in education. Given the changing structure of the education policy field, and the emergence of hybridized organizational forms in which both public and private actors are involved, the construction of neat categories might be neither possible nor desirable (cf. Ball, 2017). In a nutshell, further research on this topic is necessary for a richer understanding of the transformative potential of the corporate sector and the challenges it generates in the education policy landscape.

## Note

1. The term has frequently been used in opposition to outsider or insider strategies relying on public appeals, grassroots, and media mobilization or other forms of pressure, and roughly equates to the notion of insider lobbying (Heaney, 2006) or direct strategies (Binderkrantz, 2005).

## References

Apple, M. W., & Pedroni, T. C. (2005). Conservative Alliance Building and African American Support of Vouchers: The End of Brown's Promise or a New Beginning? *Teachers College Record, 107*(9), 2068–2105.
Au, W., & Ferrare, J. J. (2015). Other People's Policy: Wealthy Elites and Charter School Reform in Washington State. In W. Au & J. J. Ferrare (Eds.), *Mapping Corporate Education: Power and Policy Networks in the Neoliberal State* (pp. 147–164). New York/Abingdon: Routledge.
Au, W., & Lubienski, C. (2016). The Role of the Gates Foundation and the Philanthropic Sector in Shaping the Emerging Education Market: Lessons from the US on Privatization of Schools and Education Governance. In A. Verger, C. Lubienski, & G. Steiner-Khamsi (Eds.), *World Yearbook of Education 2016: The Global Education Industry* (pp. 27–43). New York/Abingdon: Routledge.
Ball, S. J. (2012). *Global Education Inc.: New Policy Networks and the Neoliberal Imaginary*. New York/Abingdon: Routledge.
Ball, S. J. (2017, November). *Philanthropy and the Changing Topology of Global Education: The Economization of the Moral*. Keynote Address at the Philanthropy in Education-Global Trends, Regional Differences and Diverse Perspectives Symposium, Geneva, Switzerland.
Ball, S. J., & Youdell, D. (2008). *Hidden Privatisation in Public Education*. Brussels: Education International Retrieved from http://download.ei-ie.org/docs/IRISDocuments/Research%20Website%20Documents/2009-00034-01-E.pdf
Barber, M. (2013). *The Good News from Pakistan: How a Revolutionary New Approach to Education Reform in Punjab Shows the Way Forward for Pakistan and Development Aid Everywhere*. London: Reform Retrieved from www.reform.uk/wp-content/uploads/2014/10/The_good_news_from_Pakistan_final.pdf

Barley, S. (2010). Building an Institutional Field to Corral a Government: A Case to Set an Agenda for Organization Studies. *Organization Studies, 31*(6), 777–805. https://doi.org/10.1177/0170840610372572

Béland, D. (2005). Ideas and Social Policy: An Institutionalist Perspective. *Social Policy & Administration, 39*(1), 1–18. https://doi.org/10.1111/j.1467-9515.2005.00421.x

Belfield, C., & Levin, H. M. (2005). Vouchers and Public Policy: When Ideology Trumps Evidence. *American Journal of Education, 111*(4), 548–567. https://doi.org/10.1086/431183

Bhanji, Z. (2016). The Business Case for Philanthropy, Profits, and Policy Making in Education. In K. Mundy, A. Green, R. Lingard, & A. Verger (Eds.), *Handbook of Global Policy and Policy-making in Education* (pp. 419–432). West Sussex: Wiley-Blackwell.

Binderkrantz, A. (2005). Interest Group Strategies: Navigating Between Privileged Access and Strategies of Pressure. *Political Studies, 53*(4), 694–715. https://doi.org/10.1111/j.1467-9248.2005.00552.x

Boyd, W. L. (2007). The Politics of Privatization in American Education. *Educational Policy, 21*(1), 7–14. https://doi.org/10.1177/0895904806297728

Bulkley, K. E., & Burch, P. (2011). The Changing Nature of Private Engagement in Public Education: For-profit and Nonprofit Organizations and Educational Reform. *Peabody Journal of Education, 86*(3), 236–251. https://doi.org/10.1080/0161956X.2011.578963

Bull, B., Bøås, M., & McNeill, D. (2004). Private Sector Influence in the Multilateral System: A Changing Structure of World Governance? *Global Governance, 10*(4), 481–498. https://doi.org/10.2307/27800543

Bull, B., & McNeill, D. (2007). *Development Issues in Global Governance. Public-private Partnerships and Market Multilateralism*. New York/Abingdon: Routledge.

Cave, T., & Rowell, A. (2014). *A Quiet Word: Lobbying, Crony Capitalism and Broken Politics in Britain*. London: The Bodley Head-Vintage.

Christopoulos, D., & Ingold, K. (2011). Distinguishing Between Political Brokerage & Political Entrepreneurship. *Procedia Social and Behavioral Sciences, 10*, 36–42. https://doi.org/10.1016/j.sbspro.2011.01.006

De Bruycker, I. (2014). *How Interest Groups Develop their Lobbying Strategies. The Logic of Endogeneity*. Paper Prepared for the European Consortium for Political Research (ECPR) General Conference, Glasgow.

DeBray, E., Scott, J., Lubienski, C., & Jabbar, H. (2014). Intermediary Organizations in Charter School Policy Coalitions: Evidence from New Orleans. *Educational Policy, 28*(2), 175–206. https://doi.org/10.1177/0895904813514132

DeBray-Pelot, E. H., Lubienski, C. A., & Scott, J. T. (2007). The Institutional Landscape of Interest Group Politics and School Choice. *Peabody Journal of Education, 82*(2/3), 204–230. https://doi.org/10.1080/01619560701312947

Fitz, J., & Beers, B. (2002). Education Management Organisations and the Privatisation of Public Education: A Cross-national Comparison of the USA and Britain. *Comparative Education, 38*(2), 137–154. https://doi.org/10.1080/03050060220140j18

Fitz, J., & Hafid, T. (2007). Perspectives on the Privatization of Public Schooling in England and Wales. *Educational Policy, 21*(1), 273–296. https://doi.org/10.1177/0895904806297193

Fulton, J. M., & Stanbury, W. T. (1985). Comparative Lobbying Strategies in Influencing Health Care Policy. *Canadian Public Administration, 28*(2), 269–300. https://doi.org/10.1111/j.1754-7121.1985.tb00514.x

Fusarelli, L. D., & Johnson, B. (2004). Educational Governance and the New Public Management. *Public Administration and Management, 9*(2), 118–127 Stable URL www.spaef.com/file.php?id=192

Garsten, C., & Sörbom, A. (2017). Introduction: Political Affairs in the Global Domain. In C. Garsten & A. Sörbom (Eds.), *Power, Policy and Profit Corporate Engagement in Politics and Governance* (pp. 1–24). Cheltenham, UK/Northampton, MA: Edwar Elgar Publishing.

Goldie, D., Linick, M., Jabbar, H., & Lubienski, C. (2014). Using Bibliometric and Social Media Analyses to Explore the "Echo chamber" Hypothesis. *Educational Policy,28*(2),281–305.https://doi.org/10.1177/0895904813515330

Gough, D., Thomas, J., & Oliver, S. (2012). Clarifying Differences Between Review Designs and Methods. *Systematic Reviews*, (28), 1 Retrieved from http://link.springer.com/content/pdf/10.1186%2F2046-4053-1-28.pdf

Heaney, M. T. (2006). Brokering Health Policy: Coalitions, Parties, and Interest Group Influence. *Journal of Health Politics, Policy and Law, 31*(5), 887–944. https://doi.org/10.1215/03616878-2006-012

Henig, J. R. (2008). *Spin Cycle: How Research Gets Used in Policy Debates: The Case of Charter Schools.* New York: Russell Sage Foundation.

Hillman, A. J., Keim, G. D., & Schuler, D. (2004). Corporate Political Activity: A Review and Research Agenda. *Journal of Management, 30*(6), 837–857. https://doi.org/10.1016/j.jm.2004.06.003

Holyoke, T. T., Henig, J. R., Brown, H., & Lacireno-Paquet, N. (2009). Policy Dynamics and the Evolution of State Charter School Laws. *Policy Sciences, 42*(1), 33–55. https://doi.org/10.1007/s11077-009-9077-3

Junemann, C., Ball, S., & Santori, D. (2016). Joined-up Policy: Network Connectivity and Global Education Governance. In K. Mundy, A. Green, R. Lingard, & A. Verger (Eds.), *Handbook of Global Policy and Policy-making in Education* (pp. 535–553). West Sussex: Wiley-Blackwell.

Kirst, M. C. (2007). Politics of Charter Schools: Competing National Advocacy Coalitions Meet Local Politics. *Peabody Journal of Education, 83*(2/3), 184–203. https://doi.org/10.1080/01619560701312939

Lubienski, C. (2016). Sector Distinctions and the Privatization of Public Education Policymaking. *Theory and Research in Education, 14*(2), 193–212. https://doi.org/10.1177/1477878516635332

Lubienski, C., Brewer, T. J., & La Londe, P. G. (2015). Orchestrating Policy Ideas: Philanthropies and Think Tanks in US Education Policy Advocacy Networks. *The Australian Education Researcher, 43*(1), 55–73. https://doi.org/10.1007/s13384-015-0187-y

Lubienski, C., Scott, J., & DeBray, E. (2014). The Politics of Research Production, Promotion, and Utilization in Educational Policy. *Educational Policy, 28*(2), 131–144. https://doi.org/10.1177/0895904813515329

Lubienski, C., Weitzel, P., & Lubienski, S. T. (2009). Is There a "Consensus" on School Choice and Achievement? Advocacy Research and the Emerging Political Economy of Knowledge Production. *Educational Policy, 23*(1), 161–193. https://doi.org/10.1177/0895904808328532

Martins, E. M. (2013). *Movimento Todos Pela Educação: Um projeto de nação para a educação brasileira* (Master dissertation). Retrieved from Biblioteca Digital da UNICAMP. (Accession Order No 000915751).

Martins, E. M., & Krawczyk, N. R. (2016). Entrepreneurial Influence in Brazilian Education Policies: The Case of Todos Pela Educação. In A. Verger, C. Lubienski, & G. Steiner-Khamsi (Eds.), *World Yearbook of Education 2016: The Global Education Industry* (pp. 78–89). New York/Abingdon: Routledge.

Medvetz, T. (2012). Murky Power: "Think Thanks" as Boundary Organizations. In D. Courpasson, D. Golsorkhi, & J. J. Sallaz (Eds.), *Rethinking Power in Organizations, Institutions, and Markets* (pp. 113–133). Bingley: Emerald Group Publishing Limited.

Medvetz, T. (2014). Field Theory and Organizational Power. Four Modes of Influence among Public Policy "Think Tanks". In M. Hilgers & E. Mangez (Eds.), *Bourdieu's Theory of Social Fields. Concepts and Applications* (pp. 221–237). New York/Abingdon: Routledge.

Milbrath, L. W. (1963). *The Washington Lobbyists*. Chicago: Rand McNally.

Nambissan, G. B., & Ball, S. (2010). Advocacy Networks, Choice and Private Schooling of the Poor in India. *Global Networks, 10*(3), 324–343. https://doi.org/10.1111/j.1471-0374.2010.00291.x

Reckhow, S., & Snyder, J. W. (2014). The Expanding Role of Philanthropy in Education Politics. *Educational Researcher, 43*(4), 186–195. https://doi.org/10.3102/0013189X14536607

Santa Cruz, E., & Olmedo, A. (2012). Neoliberalismo y creación de "sentido común": Crisis educativa y medios de comunicación en Chile. *PRO, 16*(3), 145–168.

Santori, D., Ball, S. J., & Junemann, C. (2015). mEducation as a Site of Network Governance. In W. Au & J. J. Ferrare (Eds.), *Mapping Corporate Education: Power and Policy Networks in the Neoliberal State* (pp. 23–42). New York/Abingdon: Routledge.

Scott, J. (2009). The Politics of Venture Philanthropy in Charter School Policy and Advocacy. *Educational Policy, 23*(1), 106–136. https://doi.org/10.1177/0895904808328531

Scott, J., & Jabbar, H. (2014). The Hub and the Spokes: Foundations, Intermediary Organizations, Incentivist Reforms, and the Politics of Research Evidence. *Educational Policy, 28*(2), 233–257. https://doi.org/10.1177/0895904813515327

Srivastava, P. (2014, March). *Contradictions and the Persistence of the Mobilizing Frames of Privatization: Interrogating the Global Evidence on Low-fee Private Schooling.* Paper Presented at the Annual Conference of the Comparative & International Education Society (CIES), Toronto, Ontario, Canada.

Srivastava, P. (2016). Questioning the Global Scaling Up of Low-fee private Schooling: The Nexus Between Business, Philanthropy, and PPPs. In A. Verger, C. Lubienski, & G. Steiner-Khamsi (Eds.), *World Yearbook of Education 2016: The Global Education Industry* (pp. 248–263). New York: Routledge.

Srivastava, P., & Baur, L. (2016). New Global Philanthropy and Philanthropic Governance in Education in a Post-2015 World. In K. Mundy, A. Green, R. Lingard, & A. Verger (Eds.), *Handbook of Global Policy and Policy-making in Education* (pp. 433–448). West Sussex: Wiley-Blackwell.

Vergari, S. (2007). The Politics of Charter Schools. *Educational Policy, 21*(1), 15–29. https://doi.org/10.1177/0895904806296508

Verger, A., Fontdevila, C., & Zancajo, A. (2017). Multiple Paths Towards Educational Privatization in a Globalizing World: A Cultural Political Economy Approach. *Journal of Education Policy, 32*(6), 757–787. https://doi.org/10.1080/02680939.2017.1318453

Verger, A., Lubienski, C., & Steiner-Khamsi, G. (2016). The Emergence and Structuring of the Global Education Industry: Towards an Analytical Framework. In A. Verger, C. Lubienski, & G. Steiner-Khamsi (Eds.), *World Yearbook of Education 2016: The Global Education Industry* (pp. 3–24). New York/Abingdon: Routledge.

Verger, A., Steiner-Khamsi, G., & Lubienski, C. (2017). The Emerging Global Education Industry: Analysing Market-making in Education Through Market Sociology. *Globalisation, Societies and Education, 15*(3), 325–340. https://doi.org/10.1080/14767724.2017.1330141

# 4

# Advocacy Networks and Market Models for Education

Christopher Lubienski

In much of the world, policymakers, philanthropists, and experts are demanding evidence on the effectiveness of proposed approaches for addressing issues, often as an indicator of the suitability of different interventions for receiving funding and support. For instance, in the US, the federal No Child Left Behind Act of 2001 famously uses the term "scientifically based" over 100 times, referring to research and practices that have an empirical basis and would be favored under the legislation. Similarly, the "effective philanthropy" movement promotes business-style performativity measures of impact and cost-effectiveness to evaluate and endorse humanitarian efforts across the globe. But in education policy in particular, there are serious questions not only about the degree to which policies are actually evidence-based but also how evidence is produced, whether it is useful, how policymakers access or use evidence on policy proposals, and how new forms of advocacy networks convey ideas across time and space, and perhaps—in doing so—re-shape those ideas.

---

C. Lubienski (✉)
School of Education, Indiana University, Bloomington, IN, USA
e-mail: clubiens@iu.edu

© The Author(s) 2019
M. Parreira do Amaral et al. (eds.), *Researching the Global Education Industry*,
https://doi.org/10.1007/978-3-030-04236-3_4

As a case in point, education policies emerging from neoliberal economic models have proliferated rather rapidly around the world in recent decades. Interestingly enough, this expansion has occurred despite a paucity of evidence on their effectiveness in addressing their education goals. Instead, proponents often refer to the effectiveness of such approaches outside of education, and then—reflecting the general global trend of market penetration into traditionally non-market sectors—have argued that such market logic should be extended into state systems of mass education. Supporting this logic, an infrastructure of rapid production and dissemination of data has emerged through advocacy organizations and networks, research outfits, policy entrepreneurs, bloggers, and other internet-based thought-shapers. These factors are both responsible for, and benefit from, removing traditional barriers to the rapid dissemination of information, but at the same time create a new information landscape that can both democratize and undercut access to quality information (Lubienski, Scott, & DeBray, 2014). But it is not at all clear that the information advanced through this vast infrastructure is even utilized in policymaking (DeBray, Scott, Lubienski, & Jabbar, 2014; Jabbar, LaLonde, DeBray-Pelot, Scott, & Lubienski, 2015; Lubienski, Scott, & DeBray-Pelot, 2015; Scott, Jabbar, Goel, DeBray, & Lubienski, 2015).

Thus, even as policymakers pay lip service—if not actual attention—to the need for evidence-based decision-making, the sources for information have become more diverse, and the information itself more diffuse and disputed. And governments' capacity to collect and weigh evidence that could illuminate policy proposals is often being diminished and contracted out to non-state actors. This is happening at the same time that advanced methods of knowledge production have become more nuanced, sophisticated, and precise, albeit also arcane and thus necessarily opaque. Into the chasm between research production and policymaking, we are seeing the entrance of networks of new actors—intermediaries—that seek to collect, interpret, package, and promote evidence for policymakers to use in forming their decisions (Lubienski, Scott, & DeBray, 2011).

Traditionally, researchers have considered the movement of policy ideas in a number of ways that help explain the patterns of knowledge production, transfer, and use. But some are less helpful for understanding the emerging landscape of new policy networks, and few truly explain the drivers for information across those networks. In particular, the advocacy networks around market-oriented models of education policy represent a newer phenomenon with attributes that require new methodological approaches, and new perspectives for conceptualizing the relationships, pathways, motivations, and behaviors of participants in those networks (DeBray et al., 2014; Gulson, Lingard, Sellar, Takayama, & Lubienski, 2017).

In this chapter, I briefly review a number of approaches to considering policy transfer, focusing on education issues in general, and market-based policies in particular. In the next section, I outline the concept of advocacy networks, and highlight the emerging role of intermediaries within those networks. Then after considering some of the current approaches to understanding how policy ideas transfer across nodes, actors, and contexts, I describe an ongoing, multi-site study that examines this issue through a mixed-methods investigation of actors working in policy networks. In reporting some of the Phase 1 findings from the study, I note a few of the limitations of one of the most popular theoretical perspectives for understanding such networks. The concluding discussion introduces some theoretical considerations for analyzing policy transfer through a lens of economic transaction.

## The Question of Policy Proliferation

The era of public policymaking that followed the decline of the Soviet Union marked a notable period of standardization of social policy in many places around the globe, as formerly centralized economies and social systems moved rapidly toward Western liberal ideals and neoliberal public policy models. The 1990s saw a global movement toward liberalization, privatization of state-dominated sectors, and encouragement of private ownership and enterprise not only in the former Soviet Bloc, but in South Asia, Africa, and Latin America, not to mention moves even further in this direction in established market systems such as the US. Even before the fall of the Berlin Wall in 1989, liberal Western nations with lengthy traditions of state welfare policies, such as in New

Zealand, England, and Sweden, had begun to move toward more decentralized, market-style arrangements for social services such as education. As a more recent continuation of this trend, we are seeing the spread of state-funded autonomous schools in many nations: for instance, Free Schools and Academies in England, Partnership Schools in New Zealand, and charter schools in Columbia, the US, and Canada.

The question is why do some such ideas, models, and practices multiply when they do, while others do not? Is it that evidence of their effectiveness recommends them across contexts? Is it that governing bodies (often supra-national ones) or institutional cultures promote or encourage the adoption of particular practices? Do policy entrepreneurs spread the gospel of a particular approach across contexts? Moreover, *how* do such ideas spread, in terms of routes, mechanisms, and drivers?

Scholars have long noted the tendency of some policies—some more than others—to be reproduced, emulated, adapted, or co-opted, in substance or symbolically. Sometimes, of course, this happens through coercive measures, such as imperialism or the imposition of structural adjustment policies. But scholars have been more recently drawn to how policy ideas spread by more nuanced means.

For instance, many observers (and some policymakers) see idea diffusion as simply the natural proliferation of innovations or effective approaches that have generated a track record of proven effectiveness (Steiner-Khamsi, 2012). While there is a compelling internal logic to this view, analyses drawing on this perspective tend to slight the role of power, influence, and concerted efforts to promote ideas and agendas (Cresswell & Merriam, 2011). Some of the education policy literature highlights the "viral" spread of ideas, as a standardizing force, but also one whose effects can be localized (Anderson-Levitt, 2003).

World Culture Theory, drawing from neoinstitutionalist sociology, is more explanatory, positing that different systems are isomorphic to increasingly standardized models (Meyer & Rowan, 1992; Ramirez, 2012). Partly due to a liberal notion of progress, but also due to a yearning for legitimacy, as countries emulate practices, policies, and approaches from what are leading models. But such more unitary perspectives have tended to take a satellite view of the issue and fail to consider contextual issues driving changes within specific systems (Verger, 2014). Other approaches in the mobility literature have looked largely at the created spaces and networked pathways through which policy ideas move, and are sometimes refashioned.

Overall, much of this literature is useful for descriptive analyses of the patterns of proliferation of policy ideas. But with some notable exceptions, these perspectives do not always account for the complexity and agency involved in the actual transmission of those ideas. For the research described below, we drew on the Advocacy Coalition Framework (ACF) first outlined by political scientist Paul Sabatier and colleagues (Sabatier & Jenkins-Smith, 1999). The framework has particular usefulness when—as is the case with incentivist policies—there is apparent uncertainty around factual issues and policy objectives are heavily contested by myriad actors in policy arenas. Such actors will find allies and build network relationships with other actors with whom they share core values, although they may differ on secondary policy and strategy issues; for instance, incentivist networks may form around school choice, but actors may disagree over emphasizing choice within or beyond the state sector.

The ACF has an advantage in that it goes beyond the traditional "iron-triangle" conception of actors (interest groups, legislators, and the bureaucracy) and incorporates not only multiple levels of government but also non-state actors such as think tanks, university-based researchers, the media, and advocacy groups into the policy equation. Thus, it conceptualizes networks as incorporating a range of actors working in a more or less concerted fashion, covering multiple functions, such as idea creation, political lobbying, and shaping public perceptions of an issue. Focusing on policy subsystems, or issue-based networks, ACF draws attention to the use of different strategies and instruments, which could include public opinion, litigation, or legislation, for instance, or demonization of opposing coalitions, over time (Sabatier, Hunter, & McLaughlin, 1987). ACF is particularly useful for considering how advocacy of (and opposition to) policy ideas shapes the issue, question, and policy solution, and presents many advantages when considering an issue such as different strategies in the advocacy around incentivism.

## Studying Advocacy Networks

The question of how policy ideas move and change is becoming more relevant in an age, and in places, where the increasingly sophisticated nature of much research evidence makes it less accessible to broader audiences, where the policy process is less transparent and more open to interest groups, and where traditional forms of accountability between policymakers and their broader constituencies are diminished. Such conditions have become more prevalent in a number of places, particularly where economic inequality and the susceptibility of political systems to private resources have privileged the influence of private actors in public policymaking. In the wealthier nations, the US has become one of the leading sites in this trend, due in a large part to policies that allow for the accumulation of massive wealth by a few people and philanthropies, and a political system that encourages private funding of individuals and ideas (Gilens & Page, 2014).

The political-institutional context in the US makes it a useful site for re-evaluating not only the emerging landscape around policymaking but also for examining how evidence shapes and is shaped by that landscape. In particular, one of the inherent features of these landscapes is the increasing presence of policy advocacy networks, populated largely by intermediary organizations that seek to assemble, interpret, and advance information for policymakers to utilize in the policymaking process. Importantly, this is happening in a context where research evidence on education policy (especially relative to other sectors) is frequently discounted for a number of reasons, including that education research is often extremely sophisticated or theoretical; that the field of education is inherently ideological (Aristotle, 1946), and less susceptible to empirical evidence; and that many people went to school and feel that experience gives them the necessary expertise and common sense to promote policy preferences. Consequently, to meet the demand—whether it be substantive or symbolic—for research to be "used" (however that may be defined) in policymaking, intermediaries have rapidly populated the education policy landscape in the US.

Since 2011, the Research on Intermediary Organizations (RIO) in Education Policy project has been examining these issues by investigating policy advocacy networks in and across several major American metropolitan areas (Lubienski et al., 2011). Drawing on an ACF, investigators have focused on the role of intermediary organizations (IOs) as they network with policymakers, researchers, and with each other in packaging and promoting research evidence in and between New York City (in Phases 1 & 2), New Orleans (Phase 1), Denver (Phase 1), Los Angeles (Phase 2), as well as from Washington, DC (Phase 2). These cities were chosen because they have been leading sites for different versions of "incentivist" policies—that is, generally market-oriented reforms such as charter schools or merit pay for teachers that seek to align policy goals and institutional environments in order to encourage individuals and organizations toward particular desired behaviors. Researchers have so far conducted over 200 interviews with policymakers, researchers, and especially with actors in networks of IOs on their use and sources of—or audience for—evidence on incentivist policies, and their relationships with other actors and organizations in or outside the networks.

While this is an ongoing study now a year into its second phase, the longevity of the project at this point offers some useful insights into how advocacy networks are constituted and intersect, how they operate and, in doing so, shape research evidence and its use, and how they impact the political economy of evidence production and use.

Some of the findings pertinent to present discussion include[1]:

- policymakers either report little evidence of using research, or display diluted conceptions of research "evidence," at least in this area of education policy;
- the pace of a policy's movement or expansion is not linked to evidence of its efficacy;
- sources cited tend to be based on relationships, reputation, and access;
- our approach of conceptualizing IOs as discrete actors was misguided. We conceived of IOs as actors operating in the space between researchers and policymakers. While this is true, the diversity of organizational forms in this space, acting in this regard, is not limited to discrete

actors. Many organizations play multiple roles that also include the intermediary function;
- the most effective IOs operate in networks where they often play a convening role, are resourced to do research and/or advocacy, and often serve as agenda-setters on behalf of national organizations or policymakers;
- funders play a central role as connectors and facilitators, primarily through IOs;
- in some cases, we are seeing what could be called privatized public policymaking, as private, non-state actors are ultimately making policy decisions (Layton, 2014; Lubienski, Brewer, & La Londe, 2016);
- local and meso-level networks typically do not include a capacity to produce or assess more than basic evidence on proposed or implemented policies, so that function is often left to outside actors;
- the research that is valued tends to marginalize that produced by most university-based researchers;
- there is a notable lack on non-partisan research brokers;
- IO networks (or IONs) reflect and promote echo chambers. (Goldie, Linick, Jabbar, & Lubienski, 2014)

These findings together indicate that IOs operate in a space largely removed from more traditional forms of expertise, with increasingly obsolete forms of quality control to evaluate information claims. This is a crucial concern, since it suggests that funders are employing a strategy of using IOs in policy networks to establish new channels linking knowledge production, from a wider and less reliable range of producers, with (what are presumably) knowledge users in policymaking circles.

However, in addition to insights on IOs and their networks, a further finding from our study involves the recognition of the limits of the ACF for understanding these patterns. While the ACF is one of several theoretical frames for analyzing policy networks and policy implementation, it exhibits some significant shortcomings in several key areas when applied to the issues we study, including:

- accounting for, or helping to examine, the over-production of "evidence," and the variation in that over-production across contexts;

- the strong presence of policy brokers, which ACF conceptualizes as relatively scarce because of the need to establish trust;
- predicting behaviors in and of policy networks;
- addressing not just potential pathways by which information travels through policy networks, but also the drivers of movement through those pathways.

In fact, some of these concerns apply to many of the other theoretical approaches to understanding the movement of policy ideas across contexts. Drawing from the study described here, the next section outlines some theoretical considerations for conceptualizing policy movements in a way that may ultimately address some of these issues.

## Policy Networks as Marketplace

In 1990, political economists John Chubb and Terry Moe (1990) championed the idea of markets as a metaphor for how education systems could be more effectively organized. They argued, based on their analysis of a national US dataset, that schools set in more market-like institutional environments are driven by "decentralization, competition, and choice" (p. 67). Thus, lumping all three of these "basic features of markets" together under the banner of "choice," they concluded: "Without being too literal about it, we think reformers would do well to entertain the notion that choice *is* a panacea" (p. 217, emphasis in original).

Of course, inasmuch as this was a metaphor (Henig, 1994), it was a thinly disguised one, and was commonly taken (as intended) as a prescriptive model for organizing school systems, under the logic that schools had been unnaturally shielded from market forces, despite the fact that they—like most individuals and organizations—are responsive to competitive incentives of the marketplace, according to this line of thinking.

Following that logic, and—as has been a global trend—extending it to previous non-market area (Kuttner, 1997; Sandel, 2012), we might consider a "marketplace of ideas" in policy advocacy networks. As with some other markets, they can exhibit serious information problems, suggesting the possibility of market-oriented analytical frameworks for understanding these issues. That is, without taking the metaphor too far or too literally, we might conceive of the transmission of ideas across policy networks in transactional terms in order to better understand these dynamics and obstacles, including the "push-pull," supply and demand forces that drive the movement of ideas.

In this sense, such a market has "producers" and "consumers" of information—although that "consumption" may be largely symbolic (which, as noted below, is still significant). Connecting the knowledge creators and knowledge users are the intermediaries or "brokers" who seek to gather, process, package, and promote their goods and services to both producers and consumers. Such "selling" does not necessarily entail the exchange of money or goods/services with monetary value—although it may. It can instead utilize a currency of prestige, legitimacy, affiliation, or position within a network.

For instance, on the demand side, many of our informants in the RIO study spoke of which "research evidence" they choose to use not in terms of its rigor or applicability to a policy problem. Instead, they were much more likely to refer to a well-known individual or institution—typically with which they were seeking to suggest to the interviewer some sort of affiliation—as proof of their connection to prestige and credibility. Informants would mention, for instance, that they had hosted a speaker from a well-known think tank to lecture and advise them, had learned of some findings from a popular blogger, or would cite a study out of a notable institution like Brookings, Harvard, or Stanford without really being able to discuss the quality or applicability of the report in question. Likewise, on the supply side, researchers, and representatives of organizations that produce research, are eager to show where their work has been used or cited by policymakers.

More importantly, IOs, as brokers in these markets, see it as their role to connect research information with users, be those in policy circles, public forums, or social media. And, from our data, it appears likely that brokers may operate in hierarchies just as do the buyers and sellers they seek to serve. Of course, they typically (but not always) select evidence that aligns with the agendas they represent, even as those transactions span local, national, or international networks. But those selections also seem to be shaped by the prestige of their (potential) clients on both the supply and demand sides, and their ability to connect with those clients is influenced by the IO's position in the network. A local IO in Denver, for instance, is likely to promote information from a local researcher to city- and state-level policymakers—not only because of the particular relevance of that research on that context (indeed, that is not always the case), but because neither information users nor (too often) information producers have the capacity to deal in more sophisticated data and analyses, which is often left to better resourced organizations that are more prominent in the policy networks (see, for instance, A+ Denver, 2012). And IOs' positions within the network hierarchies might be demonstrated by measures such as their citation counts, press penetration, or the prestige of the members on their boards—which are often populated by CEOs, hedge-fund managers, reformers, politicians, and sometimes professors. Thus, low-end brokers may specialize (although not always exclusively) in serving lower-end buyers and sellers, while mid- and high-end brokers may have their own market segments to serve.

In this regard, information that travels through these networks might be regarded as a positional good to some degree. Policymakers "using" or otherwise associating themselves with evidence from more prestigious sources enjoy added credibility. On the supply side, even though researchers may like to see their work embraced by broad audiences and cited widely, researchers whose work is "used" in elite policy circles enjoy particular prestige, even if that "use" is not broadly known—for example, in a high court case, or in the formation of legislation. However, it is important to note that "use" is an intentionally vague concept. Information may be "used" substantively: for example, by helping a policymaker arrive at a particular position. Yet in the RIO project, there was virtually no evidence that information consumers "use" research evidence that way. For instance, informants are asked to offer examples of when evidence changed their position on an issue, and almost all were unable to provide examples. Instead, it is helpful to think of "use" in ways that are similar to how we can envision currency in these policy networks "markets"—in more symbolic ways. Indeed, scholars have pointed to multiple ways that research can be used in contexts such as are described here. For instance, research evidence can be used conceptually or in a confirmatory manner (Weiss, 1979); it might be used (or misused) tactically (Davies & Nutley,

2008); it can be utilized in "hortatory applications" where it serves a symbolic role to exhort supporters (i.e., McDonnell, 2004); or in "decision accretion," where evidence is used gradually to limit the range of future possible policy options (Weiss, 1980).

The problem of information asymmetries inherent in these networks offers an interesting issue from which to explore the usefulness of a transactional conception of policy networks. As has been suggested above, the sophisticated and arcane nature of the production of much research evidence moving through these networks can give undue advantages to those "selling" or promoting the information. At the same time, buyers or users without the ability to observe or evaluate production processes are at a disadvantage. Inasmuch as this information is a positional good, users might not prioritize the ability to monitor quality but instead be satisfied with their association with a brand-name producer, such as a prestigious think tank, a funder, or university center. However, the possibility of an embarrassing fiasco where research turns out to be unreliable or simply wrong (e.g., Williams, 2014) suggests that buyers and sellers with different capacities for evaluating research need to form some level of trust.

To some extent, the institutional environment in which education policy networks operate appears to reflect monopolistic competition, where multiple sellers are generally similar but also all somewhat unique in consumers' eyes, and there are few barriers for new providers to enter the field. Thus, for example, the Center for Education Reform promotes all forms of school choice, while the Friedman Foundation promotes research on school choice, but specializes in voucher advocacy. Each has control over a smaller segment of the market. The actual distinctions—if any exist—between products might not be clear to consumers, so promotion again often happens in terms of branding or affinity grouping.

But in instances of over-supply—as in this case where multiple producers and brokers are trying to "sell" seemingly endless supplies of information to policymakers—where there is a particular need to promote one's product, different aspects of the good may suggest different arrangements and implications for developing and maintaining trust. If the trustworthiness of a good is readily apparent to a prospective buyer, promotion is often done based simply on direct evidence of a good's merits relative to alternatives, as when shopping for fresh food one could sample, or clothes one could try on. In such a case in policymaking, a user would be able to evaluate the relative merits of two contradictory studies based on their methods and data, if those are apparent and understandable. But sometimes the trustworthiness of a good is something that can be assessed only after buying it—for instance, whether or not the food in the can is spoiled, or if scaling-up a program based on evaluation actually leads to better results. In other cases, a good's relative quality can never be truly assessed. Then promotion is often based more on branding or affinity grouping. This is often the case with marketing of gasoline or supplements, for instance, or using branding and loyalty programs to encourage users to feel inclusion in a group. For the topic at hand, this might mean that one counts oneself as a supporter of a reform organization, a follower of a given think tank's blog, or a formal member of an organized advocacy group like the American Legislative Exchange Council.[2]

What this all indicates, then, is that we can conceive of education policy networks as a "marketplace of ideas," but not in the usual sense of that phrase, where a range of ideas themselves compete for supremacy. Instead, it is a site where ideas can be seen as being bought and sold. If we can accept this market metaphor in observing the behaviors of actors within policy networks, then it may also be useful to leverage market-oriented analytical approaches in investigating these networks.

# Conclusion

Many education policymakers in recent years have promoted the idea of creating more information for use by "consumers" to foster an education marketplace—for instance, through uniform metrics such as standardized test results, school ratings or league tables, or through parent information centers. Yet the degree to which such market-oriented policies themselves are based on hard evidence of their effectiveness is highly questionable, and highly contested. In an age of overabundance of both official and unofficial information being directed to sway policymakers (even, or especially, when they apparently may not use it), researchers need to understand how information moves, and what drives such movement, particularly across a changing institutional landscape in education policy.

Advancing from previous work on the "push-pull" factors that drive information mobility, uptake, and use, this conceptual analysis considers ways that we think about the socio-political coalitions that have been promoting evidence, using the case of market models for education through policy networks in the US. It draws on a large empirical study in order to consider ways of better understanding these issues in education policymaking. As noted, the study has been illuminating ways in which policymakers express a rhetorical allegiance to the idea of evidence-based policy, but quite often "use" research evidence in a cursory, nominal, or "symbolic" manner. Nonetheless, networks of advocacy organizations work diligently to promote their preferred "research" to policymakers, even if only for symbolic use. Yet existing theoretical perspectives have fallen short in helping us understand the role of these networks in facilitating the movement of ideas from research producers to policymakers.

As an alternative to the many theoretical perspectives that do not sufficiently explain the movement of policy ideas through advocacy networks, this chapter suggests using an economic-transactional lens to conceive of the relationships between different actors in these networks. Such an approach may help us to theorize and analyze the movement of information across networks, the drivers of such movement, and the roles of different actors in the networks.

However, this chapter is simply an initial foray into this complex question, and is thus inherently faced with challenges for validating, expanding, or altering the proposed approach. The thinking is based on only a defined set of policies in the US, and draw on a small set of (major) cities to derive and examine the ideas at the core of this analysis. As such, they are better suited for building theory than testing hypotheses, much less generalizing to other localities and countries. Nonetheless, the idea of transactional policy analysis outlined in this chapter suggests some potential areas for further investigation. For instance, future research may consider why policymakers cleave to the symbolic use of research even when—on the face of it—they do not use empirical evidence in weighing policy alternatives. Or research may weigh the factors and conditions that lead actors to engage in symbolic forms of currency transactions. Research may also address how the marketplace of ideas might incentivize policymakers to adopt more substantive utilization of research. Furthermore,

more attention will need to be paid not only to questions of currency or capital in such transactions, but how those become commonly used in a given network. Moreover, there are questions as to how not just currency, but other factors in these networks, such as roles, density, and distribution may differ across contexts. For instance, how is research evidence from a local program treated in national-level networks? Do brokers from one context bring additional (or diminished) credibility to networks in another context?

Still, while cognizant of such questions, this chapter suggests the usefulness of considering alternative frameworks and perspectives to consider complex policy issues. Ultimately, it may contribute to a discussion about improving the quality and use of information in policymaking processes.

**Acknowledgments** The author would like to thank his colleagues on the RIO project, especially Professors Elizabeth DeBray and Janelle Scott, whose thinking has influenced the argument in this chapter. Of course, the author alone is responsible for the interpretations and analyses in this chapter. An earlier version of this chapter was published in Policy Futures in Education, Vol. 16(2): 156–168.

# Notes

1. Further information on the study and its findings is available; see (DeBray et al., 2014; Jabbar et al., 2015; Lubienski et al., 2015; Scott et al., 2016; Scott et al., 2015; Scott, Lubienski, DeBray, & Jabbar, 2014).
2. ALEC is an organization that draws together corporate sponsors with state-level legislators in the US, promoting a conservative agenda around issues such as school choice and privatization.

# References

A+ Denver. (2012). *School Achievement in Denver: The Impact of Charter Schools*. Retrieved from Denver, CO: A+ Denver.

Anderson-Levitt, K. (Ed.). (2003). *Local Meanings, Global Schooling: Anthropology and World Culture Theory*. Basingstoke, UK: Palgrave Macmillan.
Aristotle. (1946). *The Politics of Aristotle* (E. Barker, Trans.). Oxford, UK: The Clarendon Press.
Chubb, J. E., & Moe, T. M. (1990). *Politics, Markets, and America's Schools*. Washington, DC: Brookings Institution.
Cresswell, T., & Merriam, P. (2011). Geographies of Mobility: Practices, Spaces, Subjects. In T. Cresswell & P. Merriam (Eds.), *Geographies of Mobility: Practices, Spaces, Subjects* (pp. 1–17). Farnham: Ashgate.
Davies, H. T. O., & Nultey, S. M. (2008). *Learning More about How Research-based Knowledge Gets Used: Guidance in the Development of New Empirical Research*. New York, NY: William T. Grant Foundation.
DeBray, E., Scott, J., Lubienski, C., & Jabbar, H. (2014). Intermediary Organizations in Charter School Policy Coalitions: Evidence from New Orleans. *Educational Policy, 28*(2), 175–206. https://doi.org/10.1177/0895904813514132
Gilens, M., & Page, B. I. (2014). Testing Theories of American Politics: Elites, Interest Groups, and Average Citizens. *Perspectives on Politics, 12*(3), 564–581. https://doi.org/10.1017/S1537592714001595
Goldie, D., Linick, M., Jabbar, H., & Lubienski, C. (2014). Using Bibliometric and Social Media Analyses to Explore the "Echo Chamber" Hypothesis. *Educational Policy, 28*(2), 281–305. https://doi.org/10.1177/0895904813515330
Gulson, K., Lingard, B., Sellar, S., Takayama, K., & Lubienski, C. (2017). Policy Mobilities and Methodology: A Proposition for Inventive Methods in Education Policy Studies. *Critical Studies in Education, 58*(2), 224–241. https://doi.org/10.1080/17508487.2017.1288150
Henig, J. (1994). *Rethinking School Choice: Limits of the Market Metaphor*. Princeton, NJ: Princeton University Press.
Jabbar, H., LaLonde, P. G., DeBray-Pelot, E., Scott, J., & Lubienski, C. (2015). How Policymakers Define "Evidence": The Politics of Research Use in New Orleans. In L. Miron, B. Beabout, & J. Boselovic (Eds.), *Only in New Orleans: School Choice and Equity Post-Hurricane Katrina* (pp. 285–304). Rotterdam, NL: Sense Publishers.
Kuttner, R. (1997, March/April). The Limits of Markets. *The American Prospect*, 28–37.
Layton, L. (2014, June 7). How Bill Gates Pulled Off the Swift Common Core Revolution. *Washington Post*. Retrieved from http://www.washingtonpost.

com/politics/how-bill-gates-pulled-off-the-swift-common-core-revolution/2014/06/07/a830e32e-ec34-11e3-9f5c-9075d5508f0a_story.html
Lubienski, C., Brewer, T. J., & Goel La Londe, P. (2016). Orchestrating Policy Ideas: Philanthropies and Think Tanks in US Education Policy Advocacy Networks. *Australian Education Researcher, 43*(1), 55–73.
Lubienski, C., Scott, J., & DeBray, E. (2011). The Rise of Intermediary Organizations in Knowledge Production, Advocacy, and Educational Policy. *Teachers College Record*, http://www.tcrecord.org/ ID Number: 16487
Lubienski, C., Scott, J., & DeBray, E. (2014). The Politics of Research Production, Promotion, and Utilization in Educational Policy. *Educational Policy, 28*(2), 131–144. https://doi.org/10.1177/0895904813515329
Lubienski, C., Scott, J., & DeBray-Pelot, E. (2015). Producing "Evidence": Overcoming the Limitations of the Market, Competition and Privatization. In F. English (Ed.), *Sage Guide to Educational Leadership and Management* (pp. 455–470). Thousand Oaks, CA: Sage.
McDonnell, L. (2004). *Politics, Persuasion, and Educational Testing*. Cambridge, MA: Harvard University Press.
Meyer, J. W., & Rowan, B. (1992). The Structure of Educational Organizations. In J. W. Meyer & W. R. Scott (Eds.), *Organizational Environments: Ritual and Rationality* (updated ed., pp. 71–97). Beverly Hills: Sage.
Ramirez, F. O. (2012). The World Society Perspective: Concepts, Assumptions, and Strategies. *Comparative Education, 48*(4), 423–439. https://doi.org/10.1080/03050068.2012.693374
Sabatier, P. A., Hunter, S., & McLaughlin, S. (1987). The Devil Shift: Perceptions and Misperceptions of Opponents. *Western Political Quarterly, 40*(3), 449–476.
Sabatier, P. A., & Jenkins-Smith, H. C. (1999). The Advocacy Coalition Framework: An Assessment. In P. A. Sabatier (Ed.), *Theories of the Policy Process* (pp. 117–166). Boulder, CO: Westview Press.
Sandel, M. J. (2012). *What Money Can't Buy: The Moral Limits of Markets*. New York: Farrar, Straus and Giroux.
Scott, J., DeBray, E., Lubienski, C., La Londe, P. G., Castillo, E., & Owens, S. (2016). Urban Regimes, Intermediary Organization Networks, and Research Use: Patterns Across Three School Districts. *Peabody Journal of Education, 00-00*. https://doi.org/10.1080/0161956X.2016.1264800
Scott, J., Jabbar, H., Goel, P., DeBray, E., & Lubienski, C. (2015). Evidence Use and Advocacy Coalitions: Intermediary Organizations and Philanthropies in

Denver, Colorado. *Education Policy Analysis Archives, 23.* https://doi.org/10.14507/epaa.v23.2079

Scott, J., Lubienski, C., DeBray, E., & Jabbar, H. (2014). The Intermediary Function in Evidence Production, Promotion, and Utilization: The Case of Educational Incentives. In K. S. Finnigan & A. J. Daly (Eds.), *Using Research Evidence in Education: From the Schoolhouse Door to Capitol Hill* (pp. 69–92). New York: Springer.

Steiner-Khamsi, G. (2012). Policy Borrowing and Lending in Education. In G. Steiner-Khamsi & F. Waldow (Eds.), *Understanding Policy Borrowing and Lending* (pp. 3–17). Abingdon, UK: Routledge.

Verger, A. (2014). Why Do Policy-makers Adopt Global Education Policies? Toward a Research Framework on the Varying Role of Ideas in Education Reform. *Current Issues in Comparative Education, 16*(2), 14–29.

Weiss, C. H. (1979). The Many Meanings of Research Utilization. *Public Administration Review, 39,* 426–431.

Weiss, C. H. (1980). Knowledge Creep and Decision Accretion. *Knowledge: Creation, Diffusion, Utilization, 1*(3), 381–404.

Williams, J. (2014, October 10). Tulane's Cowen Institute Retracts New Orleans Schools Report, Apologizes. *Times-Picayune.* Retrieved from http://www.nola.com/education/index.ssf/2014/10/tulanes_cowen_institute_retracts_new_orleans_schools_report_apologizes.html

# 5

# UNESCO, Education, and the Private Sector: A Relationship on Whose Terms?

Natasha Ridge and Susan Kippels

## Introduction

Over the past 25 years, there has been a steady increase in the involvement of the private sector[1] in the global education landscape (Patrinos, Barrera-Osorio, & Guáqueta, 2009; Reckhow & Snyder, 2014). While studies of what is now referred to as the global education industry have taken a critical look at some of these new private sector actors (Verger, Lubienski, & Steiner-Khamsi, 2016), there has been less attention paid to the role of the United Nations Educational, Scientific, and Cultural Organization (UNESCO) in facilitating their entry and growing influence. As UNESCO seeks to define its role and exert its influence in the post-Millennium Development Goals (MDGs) world, it has increasingly sought new partnerships and revenue streams from the private sector. While the benefits of the relationship with UNESCO for the private sector are very clear, especially in relation to potentially increasing revenues

---

N. Ridge (✉) • S. Kippels
Sheikh Saud bin Saqr Al Qasimi Foundation for Policy Research,
Ras Al Khaimah, United Arab Emirates
e-mail: natasha@alqasimifoundation.rak.ae; susan@alqasimifoundation.rak.ae

© The Author(s) 2019
M. Parreira do Amaral et al. (eds.), *Researching the Global Education Industry*,
https://doi.org/10.1007/978-3-030-04236-3_5

and/or influence, what is much less clear is how much of a benefit, or indeed cost, these partnerships are to UNESCO, and more importantly, to the countries and communities in which they work.

This chapter explores the relationship between UNESCO and various private sector organizations (including philanthropic ones) active in the global education market. It examines how a multilateral donor organization which, in its own words, is committed to education for all (EFA; UNESCO, 2011) is increasingly appearing as a brand for sale, with its commitment to free, universal education being seemingly diluted over time. The chapter begins by examining the development of private sector involvement in the United Nations (UN) in general and in UNESCO in particular. It then explores the possible motivations behind UNESCO's desire to court the private sector, namely to fill funding shortfalls and reassert its importance in the global education sector (Hüfner, 2015; Mingst & Karns, 2016). Next, it examines some of the more recent UNESCO/private sector partnerships and explores the ethical conflicts inherent in some of these relationships. The chapter concludes by considering how the increased involvement and solicitation of funds from the private sector may actually be influencing and driving UNESCO's global education agenda rather than the other way around, thus potentially placing UNESCO's own brand and reputation at risk.

## The Development and Impetus for Private Sector Involvement in the UN and UNESCO

Over the past quarter century or so, there has been a fundamental change in the way in which the UN and its associated agencies engage and interact with the private sector. While, historically, there has always been some private sector involvement, the last decades have witnessed what Bull, Bøås, and McNeill (2004) call a "quantitative increase in joint projects and initiatives as well as qualitatively new forms of cooperation" (p. 482). Bull et al. (2004) outline what they view as four of the key reasons behind this shift: financial issues, an ideological shift, the need to keep up with external changes, and a change in leadership.

While we do not have the time in this chapter to explore each of these in detail, Bull et al. (2004) state that "there is little doubt that the almost permanent financial crisis of the UN system has been an important driving force for making the UN system seek new and creative solutions" (Bull et al., 2004, p. 484). An ideological shift toward favoring market solutions within the UN is viewed to have originated with the appointment of Kofi Annan as UN Secretary-General in 1997. According to Bull et al. (2004), Annan's business degree and private sector experience were influential in his appointment of other pro-private sector UN agency leaders during his term, all of whom shared a more neoliberal approach to running the organization.

Perhaps as a result of this shift, UN engagement with the private sector became more evident from the late 1990s. In 1999, the UN Joint Inspection Unit (JIU) wrote a report entitled *Private Sector Involvement and Cooperation with the United Nations System*, which describes the "increasing frequency and breadth of private sector collaboration between the United Nations system and the private sector" (UN General Assembly, 2000, p. 2). In the report, UNESCO is noted as having identified the "private sector as a vehicle for its campaigns and ideas" (Mezzalama & Ouedraogo, 1999, p. 9). Following the JIU report, at the meeting of the World Economic Forum in Davos in the same year, Kofi Annan, UN Secretary-General at the time, announced the launch of the UN Global Compact, stating:

> This year, I want to challenge you to join me in taking our relationship to a still higher level. I propose that you, the business leaders gathered in Davos, and we, the United Nations, initiate a global compact of shared values and principles, which will give a human face to the global market. (Fall & Zahran, 2010, p. 3)

Since then, the UN Global Compact "has significantly expanded its constituency and outreach activities to the private sector" (Fall & Zahran, 2010, p. 4). Adams and Martens (2015) state that even now, the Compact "urges governments to ensure that the Post-2015 Agenda be designed with business engagement in mind – 'allowing for maximum alignment with corporate strategies and multi-stakeholder partnerships'" (p. 7).

While some may perceive this to be a positive move in that it creates the opportunity for new collaborations and revenue streams for the various UN agencies by uncritically embracing the private sector as a development partner, the Global Compact ignores the many conflicts between public and private sector interests. This is particularly the case in areas that are considered both public and private goods, such as health and education.

Turning to UNESCO, a number of scholars find that the organization has been exploring market-based educational reforms since at least 1990. Draxler (2008, 2014) writes that it was at the 1990 World Conference on Education for All where the private sector was first mentioned in a significant way, as a sector that could help support achieving universal education (Haddad, Colletta, Fisher, Lakin, & Rinaldi, 1990). In 1999, UNESCO produced one of its first formal publications on private sector engagement, the *Guidelines for Mobilizing Private Funds and Criteria for Selecting Potential Partners* (UNESCO, 1999a). This document provided guidance for UNESCO staff on how to engage with the private sector, noting that priority should go to partners/initiatives that increase UNESCO's image and credibility, provide funding, and align with UNESCO's priority areas (UNESCO, 1999b). Building on this, in 2000 at the World Education Forum in Dakar, UNESCO and other participants agreed on *The Dakar Framework for Action*, which also included facilitating private sector partnerships as a means to meet the 2015 Education for All (EFA) goals (UNESCO, 2000).

UNESCO's commitment to engaging in private sector partnerships emerged again in a 2002 UNESCO report written by Belfield and Levin. The report, *Educational Privatization: Causes, Consequences and Planning Implications,* took a very pro-private sector stance and advocated for more privatization of education, stating:

> For many in the education system, 'privatization' has threatening connotations: it conjures up ideas of cost-cutting, making profits from children, and the breakdown of social ethos of education. This is an unhelpful distortion: privatization programmes are varied, and they can be designed to meet many educational objectives. Private schools may promote the social good and public subsidies can be inequitable. (Belfield & Levin, 2002, p. 15)

Belfield and Levin (2002) described how the World Bank and other agencies support privatization in education and implied that increased involvement from the private sector, including from the for-profit sector, could benefit education. The report even offered practical suggestions on how to improve the public's perception of privatization initiatives, such as a recommendation to make school "vouchers" more appealing to the general public by relabeling them "scholarships" (Belfield & Levin, 2002, p. 65).

In 2012, UNESCO released its *Policy Framework for Strategic Partnerships*, which contained a brief on possible reasons why the private sector would want to partner with UNESCO and how UNESCO could benefit from the private sector (UNESCO, 2012b). Alongside this, the 2014–2021 UNESCO Strategy outlines the organization's strategic objectives for education, among which Strategic Objective 3 is, "Advancing Education for All (EFA) and shaping the future international education agenda" (UNESCO, 2014, p. 31). Key to achieving this objective, one of the three areas of expected results is "partnerships for and coordination of education" (UNESCO, 2014, p. 31). More specifically, the strategy details how, due to budget cuts amounting to more than 20 percent in 2011, there is an urgent need to continue to identify "alternative finance sources … including from new emerging donors and *the private sector* [emphasis added]" (UNESCO, 2014, p. 57). In the same strategy document, it states that "the Organization has entered into a series of new partnerships with the private sector, particularly in relation to the initiative on girls' and women's education. These partnerships broaden the education cooperation platform, bringing in new key stakeholders" (UNESCO, 2014, p. 59). Box 5.1 provides an example of some of the marketing language UNESCO uses on its website to attract private sector funding.

---

**Box 5.1 Attracting Private Sector Funding**

WHY PARTNER WITH UNESCO?

- Benefit from a strong image transfer by associating yourself with a reputable international brand and a prestigious UN agency
- Win greater visibility on the international scene
- Gain access to UNESCO's wide and diverse public and private networks

- Benefit from UNESCO's role of a neutral and multi-stakeholder broker
- Turn your social responsibility into reality
- Strengthen your brand loyalty through good corporate citizenship
- Boost your employees' motivation through hands-on experience in UNESCO's activities

HOW?

- Finance UNESCO's activities to achieve common development goals
- Share your core-business expertise
- Dedicate your staff time/second personnel to UNESCO
- Strengthen the project delivery through in-kind contributions
- Sponsor events, high-level conferences, and International Days

(UNESCO, 2017c, p. 1)

At the 2015 World Education Forum, participating countries and organizations, including UNESCO, GEMS Education, Microsoft, Google, and Pearson, ratified the Incheon Declaration for Education 2030. This new global declaration on education continues the trend in advocating for the private sector as a key partner to support nations in meeting the 2030 Sustainable Development Goals (SDGs). The Incheon Education 2030 framework states that "the private sector, philanthropic organizations and foundations can play an important role, using their experience, innovative approaches, business expertise and financial resources to strengthen public education" (UNESCO, UNDP, UNFP, UNHCR, UNICEF, UN Women, World Bank Group, & ILO, 2015, p. 26). As such UNESCO will remain committed to developing private sector partnerships, at least in theory, for the next 15 years. However, while its direction is partially shaped by external declarations and wider UN policy there are also more particular reasons and a history behind UNESCO's commitment to private sector engagement which is explored in the next section.

## Motivations for UNESCO's Engagement with the Private Sector

The increased role of the private sector within UNESCO did not come all at once, or without internal debate within the sizeable organization. Interviews with former staff members revealed a perception that much of the push for increased private sector involvement came from the top down and was met with resistance based on ethical grounds, procedural concerns, and fears of budgetary distortions (A. Draxler, personal communication, April 2017).

However, regardless of consensus within the organization, the motivations behind UNESCO management seeking new partnerships with businesses and philanthropic entities appear to stem from two main factors: funding and relevance. The former stems from the need to address perceived funding shortfalls (Earley, 2016), and the latter to avoid being viewed as irrelevant in the global education community, as the MDGs finish and the SDGs are yet to gain the attention, traction, or the funding hoped for in the global community (Pogge, & Sengupta, forthcoming; UN, 2017a; World Health Organization [WHO], 2017). If UNESCO is not viewed by the international community as a key player in the global education arena, it will become even more difficult for it to attract funding from member states or the private sector and thus ensuring relevance is critical. These two motivations are addressed next.

## Addressing Funding Shortfalls

In the literature, and more often anecdotally, a common reason provided as the impetus for UNESCO's increased engagement with the private sector has been a lack of funding, in particular as a result of member states failing to meet their obligations (Gotev, 2013; Irish, 2012). While UNESCO is funded through a combination of assessed contributions by member states to the regular budget; voluntary contributions by member states, organizations, and others to special programs; and funds provided by partners such as other UN entities, NGOs, and the private sector (Blanchfield & Browne, 2013, p. 4), the majority of their budget still comes from member states and can be withheld at any time.

In the past both UNESCO and the UN more generally have faced funding challenges since their inception in 1945 (Adams & Martens, 2015) (see Timeline 5.1). Funding streams are generally unstable as members are able to withhold contributions in response to various and wide-ranging disputes. For example, the US withdrew its funding in

1984 on the grounds that UNESCO had become politicized and financially irresponsible, only restoring funding in 2003 (Blanchfield & Browne, 2013). Then again, in 2011, the US pulled all of its funding after the General Conference admitted Palestine as a full member. The most recent 2011 US withdrawal of approximately USD 60 million in annual dues represented a loss of approximately 22 percent of UNESCO's core budget (Engle & Rutkowski, 2012). Following this later budgetary loss, between 2011 and 2015, UNESCO accumulated USD 380 million dollars in back fees (Hüfner, 2015). The USD 60 million budget cut in 2011 was described by UNESCO's Director-General as leaving UNESCO in its "worst ever financial situation" (Irish, 2012, p. 1). The US withdrawal resulted in UNESCO cutting back on spending, including costs such as travel, publications, and communications, as well as freezing job hires and reducing programs (Education UNcovered, 2011; Irish, 2012). Irina Bokova, the Director-General, also said of the 2011 budget cuts, "We are coping in very difficult circumstances. We're fundraising this year, but it's not sustainable on a long-term basis…but member states will have to rethink the way forward" (Irish, 2012, p. 1). One of the aspects of "rethinking the way forward" appears to have included a greater role for the private sector.

These types of comments imply that if member states were to fulfill their funding obligations it would not be necessary for UNESCO to seek funding from outside parties, namely the private sector. However, as can be seen in Timeline 5.1, it was in periods where funding had been reinstated, first by the UK in 1998 and second in 2003 by the US, that UNESCO published its substantive 2006 report on public-private partnerships (UNESCO, 2006). However, even with full funding, there is still the perception that poor financial management is the root of budget shortfalls rather than countries' failure to fulfill commitments. There has been heavy criticism levied at UNESCO for failing to responsibly manage its funds, and the initial funding withdrawals from member states in the 1980s were a protest against perceived fiscal irresponsibility (Associated Press, 1984, 1985). Thus, the argument of a lack of funding from member states does not appear to be so convincing and requires closer attention.

UNESCO, Education, and the Private Sector: A Relationship... 95

**Timeline 5.1** UNESCO's funding crises and private sector initiatives

| | |
|---|---|
| 1945 | UNESCO established |
| 1984 | US withdrew UNESCO funding citing politicization and financial irresponsibility |
| 1985 | UK and Singapore withdrew UNESCO funding[a] |
| 1998 | UK reinstated funding |
| 1999 | UN JIU published the report, *Private Sector Involvement and Cooperation with the United Nations System* |
| 1999 | UNESCO adopted the *Guidelines for Mobilizing Private Funds and Criteria for Selecting Potential Partners* |
| 2000 | United Nations Global Compact formed |
| 2000 | World Education Forum agreed on *The Dakar Framework for Action*[b] |
| 2003 | US reinstated UNESCO funding |
| 2006 | UNESCO published, *UNESCO-Private Sector Partnerships: Making a Difference* |
| 2007 | Singapore reinstated funding |
| 2007 | Partnerships for Education (PfE) launched in partnership with the World Economic Forum[c] |
| 2011 | US withdrew funding again[d] |
| 2012 | UNESCO released its *Policy Framework for Strategic Partnerships*[e] |
| 2012 | Global Business Coalition for Education (GBC-Education) established |
| 2013 | *The Smartest Investment: A Framework for Business Engagement in Education* published |
| 2014 | Business Backs Education initiative established |
| 2015 | Incheon Declaration for Education 2030 adopted at the 2015 World Education Forum[f] |

[a]UK and Singapore withdrew UNESCO funding due to dissatisfaction similar to that of the US. The UK described UNESCO as "harmfully politicized" and as using "excessive expenditure," while Singapore claimed UNESCO was expensive and mismanaged (Associated Press, 1984, 1985, p. 1).
[b]*The Dakar Framework for Action* included facilitating private sector partnerships as a means to meet the 2015 EFA goals (UNESCO, 2000).
[c]In 2007, UNESCO and the World Economic Forum launched the PfE which sought to establish a global coalition of multi-stakeholder PfE to help effectively direct private sector contributions to support the EFA objectives (Draxler, 2008). While UNESCO invested substantial staffing resources and funds to this project, the World Economic Forum did not, despite branding as a partner (A. Draxler, personal communication, April 2017). When the demands grew, the World Economic Forum was able to exit the partnership and continue its education work without UNESCO (World Economic Forum, 2011). Today, the PfE is no longer operational.
[d]This represented approximately 22 percent of UNESCO's budget.
[e]The *Policy Framework for Strategic Partnerships* includes rationale for why the private sector would want to partner with UNESCO.
[f]The Incheon Declaration for Education 2030 accepts the private sector as a means to support meeting the 2030 SDGs.

While funding shortfalls may be a questionable explanation for seeking private sector funding the desire for these funds is a reality. One reason why they may be particularly attractive could be the relatively ease with which they can be obtained and disbursed. UNESCO accepts extrabudgetary funds from donors and collaborates with outside entities through entering memoranda of understanding (UNESCO, 2011, 2013; UNESCO & Microsoft, 2004). While extrabudgetary funds are subject to a review process that involves governance mechanisms and oversight, memoranda of understanding are more opaque, easier to enter into, and subject to preferences of the UNESCO Director-General and other senior officials, thus able to bypass more rigorous vetting mechanisms (A. Draxler, personal communication, April 2017; UNESCO, 2012c, 2013). As a result, not only do funds from the private sector boost overall UNESCO funding, but they also come without a lot of oversight and red tape associated with assessed member contributions, although not without their own conditions.

## Maintaining Relevance and Influence in the Post-Millennium Development Goals World

The second and seemingly more compelling argument for UNESCO's courting of the private sector in education relates to the organization's fears about becoming irrelevant. Research indicates that the spread of global norms of education date to the MDGs where UNESCO emerged as a key player in the global education sector after it became the coordinating agency for MDG 2 (Chabbott, 2003; Heyneman, 2003; Jones, 2004; Ridge, 2012; Samoff, 2000). With the end of the MDGs and slow start to the SDGs, the global community appears not be giving the SDGs the same widespread attention and commitment that were attached to the MDGs (Easterly, 2015; The Economist, 2015).

In the post-MDG global education hierarchy, businesses and philanthropic foundations, often attached to individuals, corporations, or nation states, are emerging as key players and financers of education reforms nationally and internationally (Callahan, 2017; Watson, 2015). Collaboration with UNESCO, therefore, provides private sector actors with an avenue to promote their own education agendas, to see their products in classrooms, or to promote the growth of for-profit private charter schools, for example. While there may be repercussions associated with such arrangements, failure to engage with these new and increasingly powerful actors could leave UNESCO on the margins of substantial shifts in both governance and aid flows in the global education sector. UNESCO's engagement with the private sector is thus strategic and rational, but little is documented about the extent and nature of these new relationships.

## Private Sector Engagement with UNESCO: Extent and Rationale

As discussed earlier, there has been a decided effort on the part of UNESCO to become more engaged with the private sector, in particular in terms of funding. During the first six months of 2016, approximately half of UNESCO's overarching funding for projects (USD 553,920,000) across all of its sectors (education, culture, natural sciences, etc.) came from assessed contributions by member states, followed by voluntary contributions from governments (27 percent). However, as shown in Fig. 5.1, the third largest amount, 15 percent of the budget, equivalent to USD 85,060,000, came from "other sources," that is funds primarily given by the private sector (UNESCO, 2016).

While UNESCO works in a variety of areas including culture and natural sciences, education is UNESCO's largest focus area and receives the greatest budgetary proportion (Singh, 2010; UNESCO, 2016). In terms of the types of private sector funding in education, Table 5.1 shows a breakdown of UNESCO funds received from corporations and foundations using data from UNESCO's Transparency Portal. The data include all available private sector projects that were active or ending on January 1, 2016, across all of UNESCO's activities in the education sector. Seventy eight percent of project funding came from philanthropic foundations (USD 48,798,520), while 22 percent (USD 13,682,183) came directly from various corporations.

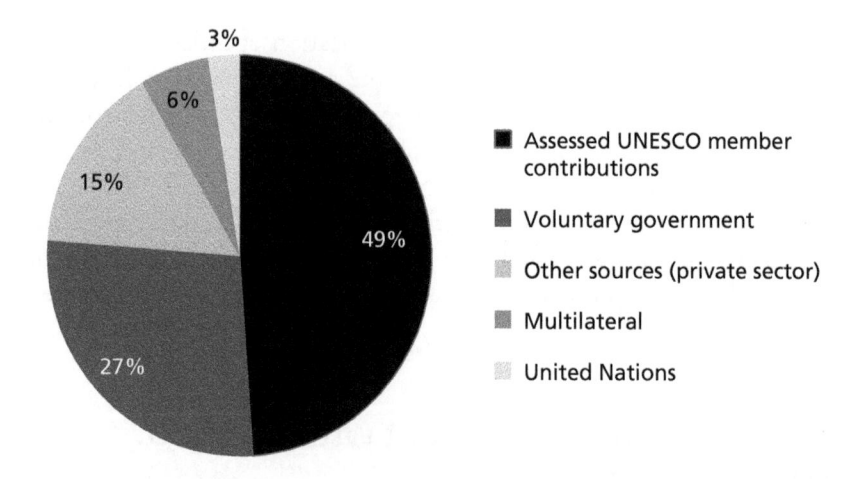

**Fig. 5.1** Sources of UNESCO's funding, January–June 2016 (Source: UNESCO, 2016)

- Assessed UNESCO member contributions: 49%
- Voluntary government: 27%
- Other sources (private sector): 15%
- Multilateral: 6%
- United Nations: 3%

**Table 5.1** UNESCO's private sector education projects broken down by foundations and corporations, as of January 1, 2016[a]

| Category | Amount (USD) |
| --- | --- |
| Foundations | 48,798,520 |
| Corporations | 13,682,183 |
| **Total** | **62,480,703** |

Note and source: The authors categorized these projects[b] (UNESCO, 2016)[c]
[a]The data included in this table represent projects active or concluding on January 1, 2016. These do not directly tie to the sources of funding in Fig. 5.1.
[b]The foundations figure includes "state-funded foundations," which are institutions that are closely tied to a government and to the best of the authors' knowledge receive the majority of funding from a government or royal family member (see Ridge & Kippels, 2017 for more information). State-funded foundations are particularly popular in the Gulf region. USD 37,527,187 of project funding in Table 5.1 came from state-funded foundations. Two examples of state-funded foundations in this context include the Qatar National Research Fund in Qatar and the Al Maktoum Foundation.
[c]This information was collated during the period of December 19, 2016– December 29, 2016 from the UNESCO Transparency Portal. On December 20, 2016, the UNESCO Transparency Portal was relaunched and certain education projects were removed.

When we look more closely at the 49 particular projects funded in 2016,[2] it becomes apparent that private sector organizations were able to benefit from the relationship with UNESCO's in three primary ways: (a) creating opportunities to expand existing market share; (b) providing a means by which to penetrate new markets; and/or (c) improving their organizational image domestically or globally, precisely as advertised on UNESCO's private sector webpage (UNESCO, 2017c). Each of these is explored in more detail below.

## Expand Existing Market Share

*Strengthen your brand loyalty through good corporate citizenship.* (UNESCO, 2017c, p. 1)

Many UNESCO projects receive funding from the private sector for projects that directly link to the consumer products that they sell. This is clearly apparent for some individual companies, such as Procter & Gamble (P&G). P&G supports menstrual hygiene courses tied to its Always products (see Table 5.4). However, the linkages between other projects and some of the business interests of companies only become clearer when looked at in more detail. For example, Table 5.2 shows Pepsi's two-phased project with UNESCO entitled *Strengthening Business Skills for Youth Employment in Myanmar.* After exiting the country in 1997, Pepsi resumed redistributing its products in Myanmar in 2012 as sanctions eased, and it was around this time that the company began its partnership with UNESCO (Barta, 2012; PepsiCo, 2014; UNESCO, 2016). It is hard to believe that the timing of the joint UNESCO project is a coincidence. By positioning itself with UNESCO, the company has been very strategic with its corporate social responsibility (CSR). Pepsi is not only managing to increase its brand in an expanding market, but it is also promoting itself to young consumers. UNESCO, on the other hand, has given its endorsement to a company that is part of the global soft drink industry known to

**Table 5.2** Expand existing market share: Select private sector funded UNESCO projects (January 1, 2016)

| Donor | Project title | Project target country/region | Budget (USD) |
|---|---|---|---|
| Nokia | Mobile technologies and teacher development | Mexico, Nigeria, Pakistan, and Senegal | 361,957 |
| Nokia | Mobiles for reading | N/A | 237,388 |
| Pepsi | Strengthening business skills for youth employment in Myanmar | Myanmar | 500,000 |
| Pepsi | Strengthening business skills for youth employment in Myanmar—phase II | Myanmar | 400,000 |
| William and Flora Hewlett Foundation | Diasporas and grid computing for development in Africa and the Middle East: Towards the creation of an African university grid | Africa and Middle East | 1,673,158 |
| Western Union Foundation | Supporting potential migrant youth in garnering necessary skills and knowledge for employment and life through strengthening vocational training and services in rural areas | China | 150,000 |

Source: UNESCO (2016)

increase the risk of obesity, diabetes, and a host of diseases, and particularly harmful for children (Harvard School of Public Health, 2017).

Table 5.2 also shows that the expansion of market shares also occurs on a wider scale for certain sectors, particularly the technology sector, which, other research has found, also gives generously to education.[3] As of January 1, 2016, information technology (IT) companies or foundations founded by individuals from the IT sector gave almost USD 9 million to 11 UNESCO-private sector projects, all of which promoted IT in education. The companies involved included Ericsson, the David and Lucile Packard Foundation, Nokia (four projects), Samsung, Microsoft, P&G, the Weidong Group, and the William and Flora Hewlett Foundation (see Table 5.2 for more information).

## Penetrate New Markets

*Benefit from UNESCO's role of a neutral and multi-stakeholder broker.* (UNESCO, 2017c, p. 1)

Second, private sector entities utilize their relationships with UNESCO to support their entry into new markets. One case of this is that the highest number of UNESCO-private sector projects in one country are taking place in Myanmar (6 projects out of 49), a country with an attractive emerging market. Following the 2011 presidential election of Thein Sein, which led to liberalizing reforms, the restoring of international relationships, and the easing of sanctions, Myanmar became an important new market for many corporations (Zin, & Joseph, 2012). Companies and foundations that have given to UNESCO Myanmar education projects include Ericsson, Panasonic, Pepsi (two projects, listed under expanding market share), the Open Society Institute, and Microsoft, and in total they committed over USD 3 million (Table 5.3).

In this case, a good example is the UNESCO and Ericsson project. Mobile technology is a core part of Ericsson's business and, in 2015, UNESCO, Ericsson, and Myanmar's Ministry of Education piloted a

Table 5.3 Penetrate new markets: Select private sector funded UNESCO projects (January 1, 2016)

| Donor | Project title | Project target country/region | Budget (USD) |
|---|---|---|---|
| Ericsson | Empowering women and girls through mobile technology in Myanmar | Myanmar | 1,408,466 |
| Open Society Institute | Strengthening capacity for higher education policy reform in Myanmar | Myanmar | 150,000 |
| Microsoft | Mobile literacy for out-school children in Thailand | Thailand-Myanmar border | 500,000 |
| Panasonic | Strengthening schools for education for sustainable development in Myanmar | Myanmar | 250,000 |

Source: UNESCO (2016)

project entitled *Empowering women and girls through mobile technology in Myanmar* in 17 schools. Coincidentally, this was only one year after Ericsson won a contract to work with a mobile communication company in the country (Ericsson, 2014; UNESCO Bangkok, 2015). It could be reasonably argued that this project enabled Ericsson to raise its profile in the country and also to generate goodwill toward its company in order to increase its local presence and market share going forward.

## Improve the Organizational Image at Home and Abroad

> *Benefit from a strong image transfer by associating yourself with a reputable international brand and UN agency.* (UNESCO, 2017c, p. 1)

Finally, private sector entities are able to boost their brand image and gain credibility domestically and abroad through partnering with UNESCO. Table 5.4 shows a few of the organizations that have utilized their relationship with UNESCO to promote their own brand in the education sector, including the Ford Foundation and P&G. There appears to be an increasing interest from private foundations, in particular, those who may be looking to "bluewash" (Karliner, & Bruno, 2000), such as the Varkey Foundation, with its founder based in Dubai, that seek to position themselves as global influencers of education policy.

While the Varkey Foundation (formerly the Varkey GEMS Foundation) has not formally funded any UNESCO education projects as of January 1, 2016, it has developed a close relationship with UNESCO through past projects and current initiatives to promote its own brand as well as that of its parent company, GEMS Education. UNESCO has had a well-publicized relationship with the organization and its founder, Sunny Varkey. Varkey is the head of GEMS Education, a for-profit global school chain based out of Dubai that has annual revenues of nearly USD 700 million (Bouyamourn, 2015). The Varkey Foundation is registered in the UK and was established in 2010 to "improve the standards of education for underprivileged children throughout the world" (Varkey Foundation, 2016b, p. 1). However, when it comes to his own schools operated under

Table 5.4 Improve the organizational image: Select private sector funded UNESCO projects (January 1, 2016)

| Donor | Project title | Project target country/ region | Budget (USD) |
|---|---|---|---|
| Varkey Foundation | The Global Teacher Prize[a] | Global | 1,000,000 |
| Ford Foundation | To support scaling up of comprehensive sexuality education in China | China | 264,934 |
| Procter & Gamble · | Puberty education and menstrual hygiene management | Global | 250,000 |
| Procter & Gamble | Empowerment of girls and women through the use of information and communication technologies (ICTs) in literacy and skills development in Nigeria | Nigeria | 1,000,000 |
| The StratREAL Foundation | Entrepreneurship Education in Arab States | Middle East | 275,000 |
| The Walton Family Foundation | Enhancing life skills of youth affected by the Syrian crisis | Syria | 200,000 |

Source: UNESCO (2016)
[a]This is not a project listed on UNESCO's Transparency Portal. However, it has been included as UNESCO does partner with the Varkey Foundation for the event where the winner of the Global Teacher Prize is announced. The UNESCO Director-General, Irina Bokova, has also publicly endorsed this award (UNESCO, 2017b)

GEMS Education, Sunny Varkey believes you get what you can afford, stating: "We [GEMS Education] adopted the airline model of economy, business, and first class to make top-notch education available based on what families could afford" (Rai, 2014, p. 1). This stance is directly in opposition with UNESCO's constitution, which mandates that the organization works to "advance the ideal of equality of educational opportunity without regard to race, sex or any distinctions, economic or social" (UNESCO Constitution, 1945, p. 3). In spite of these practices and views at odds with EFA, the Varkey Foundation serves on the board of three UNESCO panels: the Girls & Female Education panel, the Teachers Task Force panel, and the Global Alliance of Corporate Partners for Education panel. However, the relationship between the two organizations is much more entangled than just three board positions (Varkey

Foundation, 2016a). The Varkey Foundation has also partnered with UNESCO to run projects in developing countries, organize global networking events, and co-create an alliance encouraging businesses to become involved with education.

One year after the Varkey Foundation was established, in 2011, as part of the UNESCO Global Partnership for Girls' and Women's Education, the Varkey Foundation pledged USD 1 million toward a four-year program in Kenya and Lesotho to support female education in the sciences, mathematics, and technology (UNESCO, 2012d). The same year, UNESCO and the Varkey Foundation publicized that they would partner to run a program to train 10,000 school principals in India, Ghana, and Kenya, and the Varkey Foundation pledged another USD 1 million to this program (Anderson, 2011).[4] When the 10,000 Principals Leadership Program was announced at the Clinton Global Initiative, Irina Bokova, Director-General of UNESCO, commented:

> This partnership between UNESCO and the Varkey GEMS Foundation (including GEMS Education) is an excellent example of the new platforms for cooperation the world needs today. Tackling complex, global challenges requires also innovative and far reaching partnerships between the public and private spheres. GEMS Education works for education as a force for development, for individual realization, for tolerance and dialogue and indeed as a basic human right. (GEMS Education, 2011, p. 1)

Sunny Varkey's appointment in 2012 as a UNESCO Goodwill Ambassador for Education Partnerships therefore comes as little surprise (UNESCO, 2012a).

Private sector motivations for partnering with UNESCO therefore are very transparent, and there is little downside for the private sector organizations in partnering with a prestigious UN agency. However, the benefits for UNESCO are far less clear. In particular, there are questions around how funds are allocated and who decides where and how they are spent. As such, there is the risk that that UNESCO is becoming far less of the policymaker and far more of a policy recipient.

## Private Sector Influence on UNESCO Policies and Priorities

> *The UN's niche is public service not market fitness. Rather than how to be a more efficient competitor in a crowded value-free market place, the challenge it faces is how it can continue to uphold and strengthen internationally agreed norms and standards.* (Adams & Martens, 2015, p. 5)

There is no question that the private sector is influencing and shaping at least some of UNESCO's current education sector activities. While proponents of private sector involvement argue that it enables UNESCO to not only receive more funding but also to be more innovative, there are many other implications to consider when embarking on initiatives that are backed by private sector partners (Gotev, 2013; UNESCO, 2006). In their research into the increasing involvement of the private sector in multilateral institutions, among other concerns, Bull et al. (2004) found that private sector influence may result in complications, such as distortions of policy objectives and an over- or under-focus on certain geographical areas, both of which are applicable to UNESCO today. In addition to these, engaging with the private sector without clear guidelines may result in UNESCO supporting practices at odds with its own education mission and values.

Private sector partnerships could reshape UNESCO and render it an extension of corporate agendas, rather than the other way around. Private sector engagement may result in a distortion of policy aims, and the decision of what education projects to support may become determined by areas that the private sector is willing to fund, instead of what is needed (Bull et al., 2004). While this is evident in individual projects, it is also happening in certain programmatic areas, as seen by the heavy emphasis on IT and girls and women in UNESCO's private sector funded projects. In line with broader issues in global development, over USD 11 million of private sector money was given to UNESCO programs specifically supporting women and girls as of January 1, 2016 with funding received from P&G (three projects), the HNA Group C. Ltd., the Al Maktoum Foundation, Ericsson, and the David and Lucile Packard Foundation.

Conversely, there were no programs with a specific focus on supporting the educational achievement of boys, despite a growing reverse education gender gap in many countries (Ridge, 2014). There is a risk of fashionable initiatives taking precedence over foundational work aimed at building capacity in national education systems. When the private sector dictates the programmatic focus, educational areas in real need may be overlooked, such as support for at-risk boys, and there may be an overemphasis on other, perhaps less pressing areas, such as on new technologies, even though the benefits to student learning from technology may not be so clear (OECD, 2015).

The second result of the growing private sector involvement may be that the geographical priorities of UNESCO and their private sector partners do not align. Companies often prefer to direct their philanthropy to countries/places where they do business, which leads to a risk of overserving or underserving the populations most in need of support (Bull et al., 2004). As touched upon earlier in the chapter, Myanmar became a popular country for the private sector to fund UNESCO projects as they tried to establish their own market presence there. However, in terms of need for programs supporting education, it is not clear whether Myanmar is at the top of list, as there are countries across the world that are perhaps facing more critical development challenges.[5]

A third result of private sector involvement is that it may, in some cases, even lead to UNESCO working with private sector organizations that are partaking in activities that are in direct opposition to UNESCO's education mission to "promote education as a fundamental human right, to improve the quality of education and to facilitate policy dialogue, knowledge sharing and capacity building" (UNESCO, 2017a, p. 1). This is demonstrated by the case of the Varkey Foundation, which receives its funding from a for-profit education conglomerate that uses an ethnicity-based teacher pay scale in its UAE schools and insists that students and their families should receive only the quality of education that they can afford (Ridge, Kippels, & Shami, 2016). In terms of UNESCO's relationship with P&G, not only are there inherent conflicts of interest regarding P&G's education programs, but P&G has also been linked to companies using child labor in palm oil plantations which supply the raw material for their detergents and shampoos (Davis, 2016). Child labor is at odds with UNESCO's mission of EFA and promotion of education as a human right, not to mention various UN initiatives more widely that are trying to end child labor (UN, 2017b; UNESCO, 2017a). Through its partnership with P&G, UNESCO risks endorsing a company profiting from human rights violations of children. While there are vetting processes for partnerships within UNESCO that depend on the type of cooperation agreement, there should be measures in place across all levels to prevent relationships with organizations that may be directly or indirectly causing harm to children.

Ultimately, the private sector influence has implications for UNESCO and the wider UN system. Bull et al. (2004) highlight the issue of how private sector engagement can lead to organization fragmentation, which is applicable to both the UN and UNESCO. The increased influence of the private sector may lead to fragmentation within UNESCO, as new subunits/initiatives are created to support various private sector initiatives (i.e., Business Backs Education), and within the wider UN system (i.e., the Global Compact). As UNESCO establishes entities to cater to the private sector, such fragmentation may contribute to the overshadowing of the UN and UNESCO's wider missions. While funding shortages may indeed hamper activities or call for a more focused approach, this is no justification to essentially sell the UNESCO brand to the highest bidder. Private sector engagement should be on UNESCO's terms and, as of now, there is not much evidence to support that it is. With the election of a new Director-General in 2017, and fresh allegations of corruption during the election cycle, it remains to be seen what direction UNESCO will take next. Whether the engagement with the private sector will continue in the same way or whether some more comprehensive internal guidelines will be established to ensure a balanced partnership driven by recipient needs rather than donor preferences.

# Notes

1. According to UNESCO's website, the private sector includes "business enterprises, including small and medium-size firms, national, international and multinational corporations, philanthropic and corporate foun-

dations, financial institutions and private individuals" (UNESCO, 2017c, p. 1). This definition is used throughout the paper. It is important to note that this definition is broad and private individuals and philanthropists can have different motives than for-profit corporations.
2. Some of these projects are listed in Tables 5.2, 5.3, and 5.4. However, they are not all listed.
3. In a study of Fortune 500 companies, the technology sector was the second largest contributor to education, giving USD 10 million annually and more in-kind donations than any other sector (Van Fleet, 2012).
4. In the March 31, 2014 Financial Year End report that the Varkey Foundation filed with the UK Charity Commission, it is noted that the Varkey Foundation decided to discontinue the 10,000 Principals Training in Kenya, Ghana, and India commitment (Varkey GEMS Foundation, 2015, p. 7). There was no reason given for the discontinuation in the report.
5. These projects occurred before and are completely separate to the 2017 developments related to the mass exodus of Rohingya from Myanmar.

# References

Adams, B., & Martens, J. (2015). *Fit for Whose Purpose? Private Funding and Corporate Influence in the United Nations*. New York, Global Policy Forum.
Anderson, J. (2011, September 22). UNESCO in Partnership to Train School Principals in 3 Nations. *The New York Times*.
Associated Press. (1984, December 28). Singapore Says it Plans to Leave UNESCO. *The New York Times*.
Associated Press. (1985, December 5). Britain Following Lead of U.S., Will Withdraw from UNESCO. *Los Angeles Times*.
Barta, P. (2012, August 10). Bringing Pepsi Back to Myanmar. *The Wall Street Journal*.
Belfield, C. R., & Levin, H. M. (2002). *Education Privatization: Causes, Consequences and Planning Implications*. Paris, France: UNESCO, International Institute for Educational Planning.
Blanchfield, L., & Browne, M. A. (2013). *The United Nations Educational, Scientific, and Cultural Organization (UNESCO)*. Congressional Research Service.

Bouyamourn, A. (2015, June 15). GEMS Bottom Line Benefits from School Seat Shortage. *The National.*

Bull, B., Bøås, M., & McNeill, D. (2004). Private Sector Influence in the Multilateral System: A Changing Structure of World Governance? *Global Governance, 10*(4), 481–498.

Callahan, D. (2017, June 30). As Government Retrenches, Philanthropy Booms. *The New York Times.*

Chabbott, C. (2003). *Constructing Education for Development: International Organizations and Education for All.* New York: Routledge.

Davies, R. (2016). Firms Such as Kellogg's, Unilever and Nestlé 'Use Child-labour Palm Oil'. *The Guardian.*

Draxler, A. (2008). *New Partnerships for EFA: Building on Experience.* Retrieved from www.unesco.org/iiep/PDF/pubs/Partnerships_EFA.pdf. Accessed 03/01/2018.

Draxler, A. (2014). International Investment in Education for Development: Public Good or Economic Tool? *International Development Policy | Revue internationale de politique de développement.* doi: https://doi.org/10.4000/poldev.1772.

Earley, K. (2016, September 30). More Than Half of All Businesses Ignore UN's Sustainable Development Goals. *The Guardian.*

Easterly, W. (2015, September 28). The SDGs Should Stand for Senseless, Dreamy, Garbled. *Foreign Policy* 28.

Education UNcovered. (2011, November 11). *UNESCO Funding Cuts – Highlighting Internal Inefficiencies.* Retrieved from https://eduncovered. wordpress.com/2011/11/11/unesco-funding-cuts-highlighting-internal-inefficiencies/. Accessed on 03/01/2018.

Engel, L. C., & Rutkowski, D. (2012). *UNESCO Without U.S. Funding? Implications for Education Worldwide.* Retrieved from webcache.googleuser-content.com/search?q=cache; http://ceep.indiana.edu/pdf/SP_UNESCO.pdf. Accessed 03 Jan 2018.

Ericson. (2014, March 31). *Ericsson Named a Network Supplier and Managed Services Provider for Telenor in Myanmar.* Retrieved from https://www.ericsson.com/news/1772778. Accessed on 03/01/2018.

Fall, P. L., & Zahran, M. M. (2010). *United Nations Corporate Partnerships: The Role and Function of the Global Compact.* JIU/REP/2010/9.

GEMS Education. (2011, September 22). UNESCO and Varkey GEMS Foundation Announce Program to Train 10,000 School Principals at Clinton Global Initiative. *PR Newswire.*

Gotev, G. (2013, March 5). *UNESCO Chief: Millions Can Benefit from Partnerships with Private Sector.* EURACTIV.

Haddad, W., Colletta, N., Fisher, N. Lakin, M., & Rinaldi, R. (1990). *World Conference on Education for All: Meeting Basic Learning Needs.* Retrieved from http://unesdoc.unesco.org/images/0009/000975/097552e.pdf. Accessed on 03/01/2018.

Harvard School of Public Health. (2017). *Sugary Drinks and Obesity Fact Sheet.* Retrieved from https://www.hsph.harvard.edu/nutritionsource/sugary-drinks-fact-sheet/. Accessed on 06/20/2017.

Heyneman, S. P. (2003). The History and Problems in the Making of Education Policy at the World Bank 1960–2000. *International Journal of Educational Development, 23*, 315–337.

Hüfner, K. (2015). *What Can Save UNESCO?* (Vol. 9). United States: Frank & Timme.

Irish, J. (2012, October 11). UNESCO Chief Says U.S. Funding Cuts "Crippling" Organization. *Reuters.*

Jones, P. (2004). Taking the Credit: Financing and Policy Linkages in the Education Portfolio of the World Bank. In G. Steiner-Khamsi (Ed.), *The Global Politics of Educational Borrowing and Lending* (pp. 188–200). New York City: Teachers College Press.

Karliner, J., & Bruno, K. (2000, August 10). The United Nations Sits in Suspicious Company. *International Herald Tribune.*

Mezzalama, F., & Ouedraogo, L. (1999). *Private Sector Involvement and Cooperation with the United Nations System.* Retrieved from unesdoc.unesco.org/images/0012/001203/120349E.pdf. Accessed on 03/01/2018.

Mingst, K. A., & Karns, M. P. (2016). *The United Nations in the 21st Century.* Boulder, Colorado: Westview Press.

OECD. (2015). *Students, Computers and Learning: Making the Connection,* PISA. OECD Publishing. Retrieved from https://doi.org/10.1787/9789264239555-en. Accessed on 03/01/2018.

Patrinos, H. A., Barrera-Osorio, F., & Guáqueta, J. (2009). *The Role and Impact of Public-private Partnerships in Education.* Washington, DC: World Bank Publications.

PepsiCo. (2014, March 28). *Pepsi-Cola Bottling Plant Opens in Myanmar.* Retrieved from www.pepsico.com/live/pressrelease/pepsi-cola-bottling-plant-opens-in-myanmar03282014. Accessed on 03/01/2018.

Pogge, T., & Sengupta, M. (Forthcoming). Critique of the Sustainable Development Goals' Potential to Realize the Human Rights of All: Why

Being Better Than the MDGs is Not Good Enough. *Journal of International and Comparative Social Policy*. Retrieved from https://cpb-us-w2.wpmucdn.com/campuspress.yale.edu/dist/6/1129/files/2015/10/SDG-HR_Rev-Jan-25-uugh97.pdf. Accessed on 03/01/2018.

Rai, S. (2014, April 14). Billionaire Education Entrepreneur Varkey Takes His Dubai School Chain Worldwide. *Forbes*.

Reckhow, S., & Snyder, J. W. (2014). The Expanding Role of Philanthropy in Education Politics. *Educational Researcher, 43*(4), 186–195.

Ridge, N. (2012). In the Shadow of Global Discourses: Gender, Education and Modernity in the Arabian Peninsula. In G. Steiner-Khamsi & F. Waldow (Eds.), *World Yearbook of Education* (pp. 291–308). New York: Routledge.

Ridge, N. (2014). *Education and the Reverse Gender Divide in the Gulf States: Embracing the Global, Ignoring the Local*. New York: Teachers College Press.

Ridge, N., & Kippels, S. (2017). The Rise and Role of State Philanthropy in the United Arab Emirates. In M. Thompson & N. Quilliam (Eds.), *Policy-making in the GCC: State, Citizens and Institutions*. London: I.B. Tauris.

Ridge, N., Kippels, S., & Shami, S. (2016). Economy, Business, and First Class Education: The Implications of For-Profit Education Provision in the UAE. In A. Verger, C. Lubienski, & G. Steiner-Khamsi (Eds.), *World Yearbook of Education 2016*. New York: Routledge.

Samoff, J. (2000). Institutionalizing International Influence. In N. Burbules & C. A. Torres (Eds.), *Globalization and Education: Critical Perspectives*. New York: Routledge.

Singh, J. P. (2010). *United Nations Educational, Scientific, and Cultural Organization (UNESCO): Creating Norms for a Complex World*. New York: Routledge.

The Economist. (2015, March 26). *The 169 Commandments*.

UN. (2017a, June 28). *Increased Support for Education Crucial to Reaching Sustainable Development Goals, Speakers Tell High-level General Assembly Event*. Retrieved from https://www.un.org/press/en/2017/ga11925.doc.htm. Accessed on 03/01/2018.

UN. (2017b). *World Day Against Child Labour 12 June*. Retrieved from www.un.org/en/events/childlabourday/resources.shtml. Accessed on 09/19/2017.

UN General Assembly. (2000). *Comments by the Administrative Committee on Coordination on the Report of the Joint Inspection Unit entitled "Private Sector Involvement and Cooperation with the United Nations System."* Retrieved from unesdoc.unesco.org/images/0012/001203/120349E.pdf. Accessed on 03/01/2018.

UNESCO. (1999a). *Communities*. Retrieved from portal.unesco.org/en/files/12695/10545478091unc36e.pdf/unc36e.pdfportal.unesco.org/en/ev.php-URL_ID=12695&URL_DO=DO_TOPIC&URL_SECTION=201.html. Accessed on 03/01/2018.

UNESCO. (1999b). *Guidelines for Mobilizing Private Funds and Criteria for Selecting Potential Partners: Proposals by the Director General*.

UNESCO. (2000). *The Dakar Framework for Action*.

UNESCO. (2006). *UNESCO-private Sector Partnerships: Making a Difference*.

UNESCO. (2011, December 13). *Irina Bokova: Technology Can Be a Powerful Education Multiplier*. Retrieved from www.unesco.org/new/en/unesco/about-us/who-we-are/director-general/singleview-dg/news/irina_bokova_technology_can_be_a_powerful_education_multipl/. Accessed on 03/01/2018.

UNESCO. (2012a, April 26). *Education Entrepreneur Sunny Varkey to be Named UNESCO Goodwill Ambassador*. Retrieved from http://www.unesco.org/new/en/media-services/single-view/news/education_entrepreneur_sunny_varkey_to_be_named_unesco_goodw/. Accessed on 11/22/2018.

UNESCO. (2012b). *Follow-up to the Independent External Evaluation of UNESCO: Work for Strategic Partnerships*. Retrieved from unesdoc.unesco.org/images/0021/002175/217583e.pdf. Accessed on 03/01/2018.

UNESCO. (2012c). *Governance for the Administrative Manual*.

UNESCO. (2012d). *UNESCO Global Partnership for Girls' and Women's Education – One Year on*. Retrieved from www.unesco.org/eri/cp/factsheets_ed/ke_EDFactSheet.pdf. Accessed on 03/01/2018.

UNESCO. (2013). *A Practical Guide to UNESCO's Extrabudgetary Activities*. Retrieved from unesdoc.unesco.org/images/0022/002201/220157e.pdf. Accessed on 03/01/2018.

UNESCO. (2014). *UNESCO Education Strategy 2014–2021*. Retrieved from unesdoc.unesco.org/images/0023/002312/231288e.pdf. Accessed on 03/01/2018.

UNESCO. (2016). *UNESCO Transparency Portal*. Retrieved on December 20, 2016 from https://opendata.unesco.org/projects/list/regions. Accessed on 03/01/2018.

UNESCO. (2017a). *Education: Mission*. Retrieved from www.unesco.org/new/en/education/themes/leading-the-international-agenda/education-for-all/mission/. Accessed on 01/25/2017.

UNESCO. (2017b, March 17). *Director-General to Attend Global Education & Skills Forum in Dubai*. Retrieved from www.unesco.org/new/en/unesco/about-us/who-we-are/director-general/singleview-dg/news/director_general_to_attend_global_education_skills_forum_i/. Accessed on 06/22/2017.

UNESCO. (2017c). *Private Sector*. Retrieved from en.unesco.org/themes/private-sector. Accessed on 01/22/2017.

UNESCO, & Microsoft. (2004). *Cooperation Agreement*. Retrieved from www.unesco.org/fileadmin/MULTIMEDIA/HQ/CI/CI/pdf/strategy_microsoft_agreement.pdf. Accessed on 03/01/2018.

UNESCO Bangkok. (2015). *UNESCO Partners with Ericsson to Launch an ICT for Education Project in Myanmar*. Retrieved from www.unescobkk.org/news/article/unesco-partners-with-ericsson-to-launch-an-ict-for-education-project-in-myanmar. Accessed on 03/01/2018.

UNESCO Constitution. (1945). *Constitution of the United Nations Educational, Scientific and Cultural Organization*. Retrieved from https://www.gov.uk/government/uploads/system/uploads/attachment_data/file/269685/UNESCO.pdf. Accessed on 03/01/2018.

UNESCO, UNDP, UNFP, UNHCR, UNICEF, UN Women, World Bank Group, & ILO. (2015). *Education 2030 Framework for Action*.

Van Fleet, J. (2012). A Disconnect Between Motivations and Education Needs: Why American Corporate Philanthropy Alone Will Not Educate the Most Marginalized. In S. L. Robertson, K. Mundy, A. Verger, & F. Menashy (Eds.), *Public Private Partnerships in Education: New Actors and Modes of Governance in a Globalizing World* (pp. 158–181). Cheltenham: Edward Elgar Publishing.

Varkey Foundation. (2016a). *About Us*. Retrieved from https://www.varkeyfoundation.org/about. Accessed on 12/27/2016.

Varkey Foundation. (2016b). *Changing Lives Through Education*. Retrieved from https://www.varkeyfoundation.org/homepage. Accessed on 12/27/2016.

Varkey GEMS Foundation. (2015). *Trustees' Annual Report*.

Verger, A., Lubienski, C., & Steiner-Khamsi, G. (2016). *The Global Education Industry*. New York: Routledge.

Watson, B. (2015, January 14). 10 Companies Spending Millions on Education. *The Guardian*.

WHO. (2017, April 13). *Radical Increase in Water and Sanitation Investment Required to Meet Development Targets*. Retrieved from www.who.int/mediacentre/news/releases/2017/water-sanitation-investment/en/. Accessed on 03/01/2018.

World Economic Forum. (2011). *Global Education Initiative Retrospective on Partnerships for Education Development 2003–2011*. Retrieved from www3.weforum.org/docs/WEF_GEI_PartnershipsEducationDevelopment_Report_2012.pdf. Accessed on 03/01/2018.

Zin, M., & Joseph, B. (2012). The Opening in Burma. *Journal of Democracy*, *23*(4), 04–119.

# 6

# Embedding Education Research in the European Economic Imaginary?

Marcelo Parreira do Amaral

## Introduction

In this chapter I discuss the role and position of education research in current European policy agendas—the Horizon 2020 research framework program of the European Union (EU), in particular—and deliberate on its implications. While previous Social Sciences and Humanities (SSH) research frameworks included their own funding scheme, the new program stipulated that:

> Social sciences and humanities research will be fully integrated into each of the priorities of Horizon 2020 and each of the specific objectives and will contribute to the evidence base for policy making at international, Union, national, regional and local level. In relation to societal challenges, social sciences and humanities will be mainstreamed as an essential element of the activities needed to tackle each of the societal challenges to enhance their impact. (Horizon 2020 Framework Regulation)

M. Parreira do Amaral (✉)
Institute of Education, University of Münster,
Münster, Germany
e-mail: parreira@uni-muenster.de

© The Author(s) 2019
M. Parreira do Amaral et al. (eds.), *Researching the Global Education Industry*,
https://doi.org/10.1007/978-3-030-04236-3_6

This integration of every program into Horizon 2020 has not only changed the previous disciplinary and thematic structure of funding schemes toward more focused resourcing of research that tackles strategic interventions and instrumental solutions, but has also exacerbated hierarchical disciplinary divisions and created new tensions for SSH. I argue that education research—along with other SSH disciplines—is being reduced to its potential for techno-scientific innovation and its instrumental/practical contribution to tackling societal challenges. This affects not only its relationship to policy, but also has important implications for epistemic governance. Thus, it seems crucial to ask what 'embedding' means for discipline-oriented education research. I consider the impact dominant views have on knowledge generation, particularly in the SSH. More specifically, I look at the implications of thinking about education research as primarily serving the ends of the dominant economic imaginary, that is, the European knowledge-based economy (KBE). This is central to discussions on education economization concerning not only its provision (e.g., through privatization and commodification), its implementation and management (e.g., standards, accountability, and quality systems), but also its research activities that impact both policy and practice in the field. The question is whether education research is not simply being 'embedded' in the technocratic tackling of societal challenges, but rather encased in a dominant regime of knowledge production best suited to the emerging Global Education Industry.

In the following sections I will consider different perceptions of the role of SSH in the European context, highlighting the tensions involved. Next, I briefly deliberate on the policies embedding SSH research in the EU's research agendas by looking at perceptions and roles assigned to SSH research in European research policy. I will illustrate the tensions for education research with a concrete example, and then discuss the main elements of the dominant knowledge regime in which this research is embedded. Next, I ask what changes follow from 'embedding' education research in this regime of knowledge production. Using Germany as an exemplary case, I discuss the impact of the changing knowledge regime of epistemic governance on educational research, as well as on the social epistemology of the field. I conclude the chapter by outlining some concerns about the implications and risks for education research as a field when it is 'fully integrated' into this economic imaginary.

## Tackling Societal Challenges: Embedding SSH

In this section I will first discuss the policies embedding SSH research in the EU agenda and then look into the perceptions of, and roles assigned to, SSH research in the European policy.

Current European research policy gravitates around two main concerns that have direct impact on the activities, funding schemes, and institutional formats of SSH research. *First*, the crucial role assigned to research in shaping Europe's future as not just the "most competitive and dynamic knowledge-based economy in the world capable of sustainable economic growth with more and better jobs and greater social cohesion" (EU Parliament, 2000), but also the 'Innovation Union' (EC, 2011). The *second* concern is the relevance attributed to SSH research both for creating societal acceptance of innovations—that is, creating an 'innovation-friendly climate' (EC, 2011) that will secure economic growth—and for guaranteeing social integration by tackling the 'Grand Challenges' of our times.

Two related and mutually reinforcing arguments are commonly put forward to justify the first concern: One, that new knowledge and technologies are important factors that bring about change to economic life; two, that it is only by taking up the challenge of creating a KBE that Europe can successfully compete with the rest of the world.

Indeed, it seems clear that the concept of the KBE has been crucial in giving meaning and shape to European imaginations of the future. Conceptually, Cultural Political Economy offers a useful lens for viewing the impact of KBE by distinguishing between "'economy,' as an imaginatively narrated, more or less coherent subset" of reality that is discursively construed and constructed in specific ways, versus the "'actually existing economy' as the chaotic sum of all economic activities" (Jessop, 2008, p. 16). Thus, the KBE may be understood as an arbitrary and deliberate imaginary, that is, a semiotic system that gives meaning and form to a particular and preferred view of the economy. In this sense, it provides a dominant representation of the operations of the future economy, from which challenges and requirements for action are derived, establishing a powerful strategic policy frame. As Bob Jessop points out:

[W]hether or not the knowledge-based economy provides the most adequate description of current trends in contemporary economic development, the discourse of the 'KBE' has become a powerful economic imaginary in the last 20 years or so and, as such, has been influential in shaping policy paradigms, strategies, and policies in and across many different fields of social practice. (Jessop, 2008, p. 2)

KBE can be viewed as a collective social resource that derives from an understanding of knowledge as a production factor. Regardless of the interpretation,[1] a preferred definition is evident in European research agendas, which is essential to understanding KBE discourse in the European research framework. This definition appears in terms of rhetorical moves to direct the attention of policy-makers to science and technology to bring about changes in the economy and justify reforms and adaptations. Various specific forms of knowledge, such as tacit learning, learning-by-doing, and user-producer interactions, are described as requiring further consideration. KBE is an umbrella concept (Godin, 2006) that spawns other ideas such as knowledge management, diffusion, and innovation systems, bringing them under a coherent conceptual framework devoid of the ambiguities and complexities that make policy-making more difficult. The appeal of this economic imaginary is its ability to provide a positive, straightforward vision of the future, and how to achieve it. Research and knowledge generation are deemed central to this imagined economic future.

As for the second concern, the main policy embedding SSH research has been the focus on so-called 'societal challenges' since the start of the current research framework, Horizon 2020. In previous frameworks, SSH had its own work program and funding scheme. This changed with Horizon 2020 as budgets became focused on research that tackles certain priorities. Horizon 2020 is structured into three sections—excellent science, industrial leadership, and societal challenges. From the approximately €80 billion in funding available from 2014 to 2020, it is expected that 40% will go to the following: (1) health, demographic change, and well-being; (2) food security, sustainable agriculture, forestry, marine, maritime and inland water research, and the bioeconomy; (3) secure, clean, and efficient energy; (4) smart, green, and integrated transport; (5)

climate action, environment, resource efficiency, and raw materials; (6) Europe in a changing world—inclusive, innovative, and reflective societies; and (7) secure societies—protecting freedom and security of Europe and its citizens (see EC, 2017).

As the European Commissioner for Research, Innovation, and Science who initiated the new program, Máire Geoghegan-Quinn, pointed out, SSH is a means to "provide the necessary knowledge and understanding to tackle the [societal] challenges," and follow the vision assigned to SSH in the Vilnius Declaration to "enhance the effectiveness of technical solutions…enable innovation to become embedded in society [and] realise the policy aims predefined in the 'Societal Challenges'" (Vilnius Declaration, 2013).

In short, the understanding of research in this economic imaginary is limited to what is innovation-driven, which assumes, as van den Hove and colleagues point out, "that innovation leads to more products and services in the market place, which leads to more consumption, hence to growth and more jobs, which in turn leads to increased well-being" (2012, p. 74).

Against the background of these policy agendas and research—especially SSH research—is the idea of a KBE created by innovation through knowledge production and dissemination, translated into globally marketable commodities. As illustrated in the quote below, this is justified with reference to global competition and often pitched with a sense of urgency:

> We need to do much better at turning our research into new and better services and products if we are to remain competitive in the global marketplace and improve the quality of life in Europe.
>
> We are facing a situation of '**innovation emergency**'. Europe is spending 0.8% of GDP less than the US and 1.5% less than Japan every year on Research & Development (R&D). Thousands of our best researchers and innovators have moved to countries where conditions are more favourable. Although the EU market is the largest in the world, it remains fragmented and not innovation-friendly enough. And other countries like China and South Korea are catching up fast. (EC, 2011, emphasis in the original)

It is worth taking a closer look at the perception of the role of SSH research in this imaginary. In this policy-oriented and mission-driven environment the focus of attention is placed on research that yields strategic solutions and instrumental interventions, premised on a problem-solving model that embodies only a small part of the SSH field. For instance, research is solicited to advance the acceptability of particular techno-scientific innovations such as gene manipulation or nanotechnology. For this reason, research that promises solutions to behavioral issues as well as social technologies and interventions—such as social mobility, crime prevention, unemployment, social exclusion, and radicalization—is emphasized. Social integration is to be achieved by research that fosters the engagement and self-activation of individuals and consumers, and strengthens entrepreneurship and social innovation.

Despite public commitment to 'social innovation' and 'responsible research and innovation,' SSH/education initiatives are predominantly perceived as strategic supporters of techno-scientific innovation-driven research. This research is supposed to 'maximise the returns to society from investment in science and technology' that can be quickly translated into marketable outputs, such as "new or significantly improved products, processes, marketing, and organization" (EC, 2013).

Meanwhile, the strengths of SSH research—providing culturally sensitive, contextualized critical perspectives, or alternative views—are undermined. Embedded research is often framed as an obvious mechanism for convincing citizens of the advantages of proposed solutions and innovations, and as a means, as Geoghegan-Quinn stated, to "realise the policy aims predefined in the 'Societal Challenges.'" Rather than respected for possessing its own epistemic traditions, SSH research is often depicted as the junior partner of (real) science and engineering (see Ziman, 2000).

Besides overgeneralizing differences within and across these disciplinary fields, this practice also reproduces a hierarchy in which SSH is most often viewed as lacking clear and measurable standards. In the following section I highlight some tensions that result from this supposed role of SSH in the education field by presenting and analyzing an actual example of what is demanded in the Horizon 2020 program.

# Education in the European Research Policy Agenda

Education is central to the politics of European research and innovation. Like practitioners in other SSH disciplines, educators are constantly assured of their fundamental relevance to the realization of the *Europe 2020 Strategy* and the *European Union*. This has had important implications for education systems and their governance, and fostered preoccupation with large-scale assessments. It has also been accompanied by controversy over how education can best contribute to tackling 'predefined' societal challenges. Central to these debates are controversies as to what kinds of education research are best suited to deliver evidence-based results and solutions. We will return to this topic in the next section (see also Thompson, in this volume).

An important example of the new role of education research may be seen in a Call for Proposals issued in 2014. "*YOUNG-3-2015: Lifelong learning for young adults: better policies for growth and inclusion in Europe*"[2] was pitched to the challenge of "overcoming the economic and social crisis and meeting the Europe 2020 targets on employment, poverty reduction, education, sustainability, innovation." Besides the implication that education research will solve economic and social problems, the call explicitly alludes to its economic relevance by explaining that "[t]he need and markets for adult education are [...] likely to rise in the coming years." It further states that those who "are more in need of adult education, such as young, unemployed, low skilled and vulnerable workers, often third-country nationals, actually benefit less from adult education opportunities than other more advantaged groups," in order to link research on policies targeting so-called 'vulnerable groups' with those aimed at economic growth. In other words, the call assumes that economic and social objectives are harmonious and co-extensive. Although these objectives are complementary, they are not linearly or causally related, and due to distinct orientations, differing objectives and temporal horizons, serious conflicts and ambiguities may arise from policies eliding both aims.

In terms of the expected impact, two central aspects are prominent: *policy learning and transfer* of successful programs that demonstrate improvement of learning outcomes, and policy modeling with *data mining/management techniques* that can be used in education governance. The latter exemplifies the technocratic rationale for why researchers are requested to link impact analysis of education policies to skills forecast in order to develop an, "Intelligent Decision Support System [...] for simplifying the access to information and support policy making."

The call for proposals provides little room for alternative views, such as that the reason for inefficiency is the need to address different issues, such as creating growth and inclusion while preventing social exclusion, with the same policy. The call also ignores the possibility that social problems do not stem from a lack of skills or mismatch of supply and demand, but rather the severe economic crises that have eroded the social and economic status of young adults throughout Europe, putting into question the distributional effects of policies targeting them, especially those in vulnerable positions. Instead, the call for proposals defines the problem as a need for 'better coordination,' or simply having the 'right' information to make intelligent decisions; no unintended side effects are foreseen. This example illustrates the kinds of tensions and ambiguities that ensue from this type of embedded research for SSH in general, and for discipline-oriented education research in particular.

In the following section I consider the implications of this development for epistemic governance of education as a field.

# Education Research in the Changing Knowledge Regime: A Glance on Germany

Debates about what constitutes useful research are not new, and have long been accompanied by questions concerning the relationship between science and society. In his essay, 'Science as a Vocation' (1946 [1922]), Max Weber deliberated on the impact of the capitalist, bureaucratized organization of science, on the 'spirit,' or 'inner vocation,' of scholarly work (Weber, 1946 [1922]). Weber also inquired into the impact of high social expectations of science in general, and scholarly work in particular. Weber's position was that the duty of those involved was to uphold an 'intellectual integrity,' and make the scope and limitations of scientific and technical knowledge visible. In other words, the scholars' role was to confront naïve (political) optimism with scholarly (rational) deliberation on the purpose and means of specific courses of action (see also Carney, in this volume). Despite well-known ambivalence in the social sciences, the distinction of roles proved important, since it points to different forms of rationality, as well as to the discrimination of facts and values as central elements shaping our understanding of natural and social realities. According to Weber, natural science's ability to generate knowledge to 'master life technically' leaves aside the question as to whether it is desirable and sensible to do so. A vision of social science research derived ex-negativo to provide reasoned judgment by producing argumentative/interpretative knowledge of our material and social worlds has been constitutive of education research since at least the end of the World War II. Social science and education research have been expected to generate knowledge that provides orientation and justification to legitimize decisions. These are, according to Radtke (2012, p. 291), not only articulated in contrast to the natural sciences, but have also been addressed at the university level in general since the Renaissance.

Social, political, and economic expectations have left indelible marks on the different types of knowledge, and the various approaches to its production in the various social science disciplines in general—education research in particular—during the course of their development. After extended—and often controversial—debates on what constitutes the field, theoretical and methodological pluralism have become widely accepted. However, as I will discuss below, more recent political and economic developments have altered the disciplinary, institutional infrastructure of education research, and have the potential to transform its epistemic governance. Before turning to this question I will briefly examine larger, more profound changes influencing contemporary knowledge generation activities.

Since the mid-1990s, fundamental changes in the production and application of knowledge have been continually reinterpreted in context with changing *knowledge regimes*. Knowledge regimes are the dominant rules and structures affecting and governing the management of knowledge in a society during a specific time period. They represent the interrelationships between different forms of power, management, guidance, governance, cooperation, and organization, which determine how knowledge is handled and regulated. Knowledge regimes are "the structured and (more or less) stabilized relation of practices, rules, principles, and norms with knowledge and different forms of knowledge, usually related to a specific action and problem area" (Wehling, 2007, p. 704ff.). In this context, recent changes in knowledge regimes have been debated mainly in reaction to two developments. First, a pluralization and competition among different forms of and claims to knowledge within the so-called KBEs. Second, the far-reaching changes in the relations between scientific-academic knowledge production and an altering public awareness that influences the process as a whole (ibid.).

Michael Gibbons and colleagues made an enduring and controversial contribution to the debate on these paradigm changes in 1994 when they pointed to a "distinct set of cognitive and social practices [was] beginning to emerge," constituting a "new production of knowledge" (Gibbons et al., 1994, p. 3f.). In distinguishing between what they called *Mode 1* and *Mode 2* knowledge production, they argued that the difference lay in: (a) the contexts of application in which research is carried out; (b) transdisciplinarity, entailing the mobilization of diverse theoretical perspectives and practical approaches; (c) heterogeneity among an enlarged network of producers and sites of knowledge production beyond the academy and university; (d) the heterarchical and transient nature of an environment where academic research could no longer claim exclusive authority, and ideas quickly became obsolete; (e) reflexivity and accountability toward society, reflecting the multiple interests and implications involved; and (f) to multiple new quality control sources and forms (ibid.).

The book provoked vocal debates,[3] and more recent research has addressed changes in the field by asking to what extent education research has become more *Mode 2* than *Mode 1* (Zapp & Powell, 2017; Zapp et al., 2018).[4] Germany is a good place to examine the impact and implications of a changing knowledge regime on the field of education because it exemplifies the tradition of discipline-oriented research that is being challenged by these developments. Education research (*Erziehungswissenschaft*) in Germany has traditionally drawn alternately from humanities and hermeneutics, and on different qualitative and quantitative approaches from social sciences, to provide scholarship that reflects and critiques both policy and practice (see Tröhler, 2014). In the wake of what Germans called 'PISA shock' (Gruber, 2006), this tradition was deemed insufficient, ineffective, expensive, and concerned only "with the fringes of world events," rather than "what really moves people in the schools and the classrooms" (Weiler, 2003, p. 182f). This resulted in an overhauling of German education research—influenced by a powerful alliance of policy-makers and administrators, international organizations, and experts (Radtke, 2016; see also Zapp & Powell, 2017; Gogolin, Baumert, & Scheunpflug, 2011)—that aimed at rendering it more effective, (cost) efficient, and responsive to social and, most importantly, economic needs.

I have two concerns with the idea that education research can be fully integrated into this economic imaginary. I assume that the changes education research is undergoing will not only have institutional but—more importantly—epistemological implications. Because power, politics and knowledge are interlinked (Foucault, 1980), we should be concerned not only with the changing *epistemic governance of education* research, but also with the changing *social epistemology of education*. While related, the former refers to the type of knowledge and how it is produced—which is important in terms of the role of education research in struggles between power and politics. The latter is the rationales, technologies, and strategies of subjectification and identity formation, which relate to deeper political, social, and ethical dimensions.

Different things converged to change the *epistemic governance of education* research in Germany. The movement toward this new knowledge production regime was in large part prompted by international debates in the wake of PISA and TIMSS, and promoted by policy-makers (KMK, WR),[5] public funding agencies (DFG, BMBF),[6] and professional associations (GEBF).[7] Recent well-funded initiatives calling for 'empirical,' 'evidence-based' research (*Empirische Bildungsforschung*) were decisive in shaping German knowledge production. It was assumed that such research would focus on what was applicable to policy priority topics and provided 'evidence for policy' and 'knowledge for action' (BMBF, 2008). It would also utilize specific preferred methodologies, such as those common in school effectiveness research or large-scale assessments. These include randomized control trials, as well as correlational or experimental approaches (see Radtke, 2015; Zapp & Powell, 2016, 2017; Zapp et al., 2018; Normand, 2016). Zapp and Powell argued that in Germany education research "displays key features that indeed characterize 'Mode 2' science" (2017, p. 2), and concluded: "The field reflects strong applicability to its context, is explicitly trans- and multidisciplinary, exhibits organizational diversity, reflexivity and accountability, and has started to integrate novel quality criteria" (ibid., p. 8).

The notion of 'evidence-based policy-making' has also intensified changes in German knowledge production by shifting massive research funding to non-university centers such as the German Institute for International Educational Research (Deutsches Institut für Internationale Pädagogische Forschung, DIPF), the Max Planck Institute for Human Development and Education (Max-Planck-Institut für Bildungsforschung, MPIB), and the Institute for Science and Mathematics Education (Institut für die Pädagogik der Naturwissenschaften und Mathematik, IPN), to name but a few. The German Federal Ministries paid €1 billion to outside consultants between 2009 and 2013, with the Federal Ministry for Education and Research (BMBF) accounting for almost half of that total, which gave further momentum to this process (Zapp & Powell, 2017, p. 7).

In sum, both the European framework program for research Horizon 2020 and the German policy-induced shift to *Mode 2* research in Germany point to a changing regime of knowledge production. This regime assumes education research can solve problems, reducing its ability to produce critical, culturally sensitive, and contextualized knowledge. It also narrows epistemic choice by focusing on evidence-based strategies that rely on quantification and measurement to identify benchmarks and best practices for policy learning and transfer. Education research occupies a subordinate position both in relation to other disciplinary fields, and to policy-making that determines the scope to be produced. This knowledge regime largely emphasizes a utilitarian, neopositivist view of educational knowledge that is seamlessly linked to economic principles of competition, efficiency, and effectiveness. As for how education research embedded in an economic imaginary prompts change in the *social episte-*

*mology of education*, though it is assumed that changes in knowledge are not restricted to academics, they also relate to shifting social and cultural norms, social change, and, ultimately, democracy.

Thomas Popkewitz argued decades ago that education research displays specific types of systems of reasoning important for various social, political, and epistemological grounds. Educational and social scientific research were originally entangled with the politics of social planning and reform. The social epistemology of education, Popkewitz argued, results from education sciences' inscription in the 'modernizing projects' of the late nineteenth and early twentieth centuries that, somehow paradoxically, linked the 'register of personal freedom' to the 'register of social administration.' This implied that educational knowledge was involved in shaping a new relationship between individuals and the state (1997, p. 19).

On the one hand, since social science research coproduces the descriptions, definitions, theories, measurements, and relationships of social reality,[8] it helps constitute the objects it examines. Beyond being entrusted to analyze the physics of political and social mechanics, it was also committed to critiquing injustices, ideology, and domination. In other words, social scientific and educational research, rather than being completely subservient to dominant political narratives and imaginations of modernity, played a problematizing role by disrupting, denaturalizing and questioning hegemonic projects of progress and salvation, that always come in 'alternative-less' guises.

Embedding education research in the normalized, problem-solving research model of the imagined European KBE substantially reduces the scope for scholarship that questions the quest for the measured, standardized, and normalized educational identities it presupposes. Embedding education research eliminates the distinction between reason and rationality which is central to it. In everyday parlance, 'rationality' (ratio) usually refers to technically controlled, causally determined processes—of which the education field is almost devoid. Education is more concerned with reasoned decisions (logos) which, in contrast, are based in purpose and prescriptively bound to judgment, experience, negotiation, consultation, and compromise (cf. Radtke, 2016), resulting in argumentative justifications and moral-political qualities.

## Conclusion

In this chapter I discussed recent policy developments with a focus on the European research framework program Horizon 2020 and on Germany's changing knowledge regime. Both contexts show how research provides strategic interventions and instrumental solutions to socially predefined priorities. Education research is being reduced to its potential for techno-scientific innovation, and its practical contribution to tackling societal challenges. I also examined the policies that have embedded SSH research in the EU agenda, and inquired into the perceptions and roles assigned to it in research policy. These developments have been driven to strategically focus on policy-oriented and mission-driven research to yield strategic solutions and instrumental interventions that advance particular techno-scientific innovations. Social science research that offers behavioral knowledge for social technologies and interventions illustrates the tensions and ambiguities for education research embedded in the European imaginary, and its predefined challenges and solutions.

I also discussed the main elements of the dominant knowledge regime in Germany, and questioned the impact of changing knowledge regimes in relation to the epistemic governance of educational research, as well as the social epistemology of the field, which encase education research in a problem-solving model. Because education research is embedded in the technocratic tackling of societal challenges its ability to produce more critical, culturally sensitive and contextualized, alternative knowledge is reduced. This narrows epistemic choice by focusing on evidence-based strategies that overly rely on quantification and measurement, problematizing the validity of education research as a social, political, cultural, and public good.

I have also reflected on the impact dominant views have in knowledge generation activities concerning the rationales, processes, and impact of the emerging global education industry. The role of this economic imaginary goes well beyond mere political rhetoric summoning a distinctly European—or even global—education space, and has become dominant in providing common definitions, setting hegemonic objectives, and legitimizing specific logics of intervention to shape education research, policy, and practice.

I will conclude by outlining some concerns for the autonomy and intellectual integrity of the field if it is to be fully integrated into this economic imaginary. Weber's view of the role and function of the social sciences shows that 'embedding' education research closes the critical distance necessary for knowledge generation and critical reflection. This undermines the capacity to provide alternative views or critique imbalances and grievances, leading to a research which is always *for* and never *of* social reality.

The consequences of embedding education research in the European economic imaginary can be found in journalism. When journalists were 'embedded' as war correspondents during the 2003 US invasion of Iraq they were criticized for signing contracts promising not to report information the Pentagon deemed 'sensitive.' The consequences are summed up in a quote attributed to US Senator Hiram Johnson, who in 1917 stated that "The first casualty when war comes is truth" (quoted in Knightley, 1975). As for what this means for journalism, the words of Charles Lynch, a Canadian, who was embedded with the British army for Reuters during World War II, provide another warning to education researchers: "It's humiliating to look back at what we wrote during the war. It was crap […]. We were a propaganda arm of our governments. At the start, the censors enforced that, but by the end we were our own censors. We were cheerleaders. […] It wasn't good journalism. It wasn't journalism at all" (Lynch, quoted in Knightley, 1975, p. 332f.).

If research is embedded in a dominant regime of knowledge production, how can it preserve its autonomy from particular interests and political preferences? To what extent does a research policy agenda obsessed with evidence and impact entail an encroachment of academic freedom? What is the effect of shifting quality control from more structural aspects (e.g., academic procedures and peer review) to compliance with predefined priorities? In the same line, if funding shapes the rationales of research projects, what is the impact on education in terms of research agenda setting and specific knowledge technologies to produce (new) subjectivities? What are the implications for organizational and management structures and their impact on academic careers if strong program, project-based funding is unsustainable in the long run? Risks loom large for aggravating the tensions between research and non-scientific stakeholders if undue hope for serving the interests of different groups is unfulfilled. Researching the emerging global education industry will require further deliberation on the oblique implications of its activities, rationales, and dynamics.

## Notes

1. Jessop (2008) terms them 'theoretical paradigms.' See Godin (2006) for a review of different definitions and measurements of KBE.
2. All quotes from the *YOUNG-3-2015* call can be found online at: http://ec.europa.eu/research/participants/portal/desktop/en/opportunities/h2020/topics/young-3-2015.html (retrieved April 19, 2018).
3. See, for instance, Weingart (1997); Ziman (2000); Nowotny, Scott and Gibbons (2001); Weingart, Carrier and Krohn (2007); Crompton (2007); Nordmann, Radder and Schiemann (2014).
4. See also Normand (2016); Fenwick, Mangez and Ozha (2014); with focus on higher education: Bleiklie and Henkel (2005).
5. The acronyms stand for 'Kultusministerkonferenz' (KMK), that is, the Standing Conference of the Ministers of Education and Cultural Affairs of the Länder in the Federal Republic of Germany, and 'Wissenschaftsrat' (WR), the German Council of Science and Humanities.
6. DFG stands for 'Deutsche Forschungsgemeinschaft'(German Research Foundation) and BMBF is the German acronym of the Federal Ministry of Education and Research (Bundesministerium für Bildung und Forschung).
7. GEBF stands for 'Gesellschaft für Empirische Bildungsforschung' or 'Society for Empirical Educational Research.'
8. Well beyond the social constructivist conception of the argument, this latter aspect has been prominently developed in Foucault's work on the role of the social and human sciences, especially in *The Order of Things*, but also in *Madness and Civilization* and *Discipline and Punish*.

## References

Bleiklie, I. & Henkel, M. (2005). *Governing Knowledge. A Study of Continuity and Change in Higher Education.* Dordrecht et al.: Springer.

BMBF (Bundesministerium für Bildung und Forschung) (Ed.). (2008). *Wissen für Handeln – Strategien für eine evidenzbasierte Bildungspolitik.* Bonn/Berlin: BMBF.
Crompton, H. (2007). Mode 2 Knowledge Production: Evidence from Orphan Drug Networks. *Science and Public Policy, 34/3,* 199–211.
EC. (2011). *Europe 2020 Flagship Initiative Innovation Union. SEC(2010) 1161.* Online at: http://ec.europa.eu/research/innovation-union/index_en.cfm. Retrieved 18 Apr 2018.
EC. (2013). *Innovation Union – A Pocket Guide on a Europe 2020 Initiative.* Luxembourg: Publications Office of the European Union.
EC. (2017). *Topics for Social Sciences and Humanities. Research and Innovation.* Participant Portal. Online at: http://ec.europa.eu/research/participants/portal/desktop/en/opportunities/h2020/ftags/ssh.html#c,topics=flags/s/-SSH/1/1&+callStatus/asc. Retrieved 18 Apr 2018.
EU Parliament. (2000). *Presidency Conclusions. Lisbon European Council, 23–24 March 2000.* Online at: http://www.consilium.europa.eu/en/uedocs/cms_data/docs/pressdata/en/ec/00100-r1.en0.htm. Retrieved 18 Apr 2018.
Fenwick, T., Mangez, E. & Ozga, J. (2014). *Governing Knowledge: Comparison, Knowledge-based Technologies and Expertise in the Regulation of Education* (World Yearbook of Education 2014). London/New York: Routledge.
Foucault, M. (1980). *Power/Knowledge: Selected Interviews and Other Writings by Michel Foucault, 1972–1977.* New York: Pantheon.
Gibbons, M., Limoges, C., Nowotny, H., Schwartzman, S., Scott, P., & Trow, M. (1994). *The New Production of Knowledge.* London: SAGE.
Godin, B. (2006). The Knowledge-based Economy: Conceptual Framework or Buzzword. *Journal of Technology Transfer, 31*(1), 17–30.
Gogolin, I., Baumert, J., & Scheunpflug, A. (Eds.). (2011). *Transforming Education. Large-scale Reform Projects in Education Systems and their Effects.* Wiesbaden: VS Verlag für Sozialwissenschaften.
Gruber, K.-H. (2006). The German 'PISA-Shock': Some Aspects of the Extraordinary Impact of the OECD's PISA Study on the German Education System. In H. Ertl (Ed.), *Cross-National Attraction in Education: Accounts from England and Germany* (pp. 195–206). Oxford: Symposium Books.
Jessop, B. (2008). A Cultural Political Economy of Competitiveness and its Implications for Higher Education. In B. Jessop, N. Fairclough, & R. Wodak (Eds.), *Education and the Knowledge-based Economy in Europe* (pp. 11–39). Rotterdam/Taipei: Sense Publishers.

Knightley, P. (1975). *The First Casualty. From the Crimea to Vietnam: The War Correspondent as Hero, Propagandist, and Myth Maker.* New York/London: Harcourt Brace Javanovich.

Nordmann, A., Radder, H., & Schiemann, G. (Eds.). (2014). *Strukturwandel der Wissenschaft. Positionen zum Epochenbruch.* Weilerswist: Vellbrück Wissenschaft.

Normand, R. (2016). *The Changing Epistemic Governance of European Education. The Fabrication of the Homo Economicus Europeanus.* Cham: Springer.

Nowotny, H., Scott, P., & Gibbons, M. (2001). *Re-thinking Science: Knowledge and the Public in an Age of Uncertainty.* Cambridge: Polity Press.

Popkewitz, T. S. (1997). A Changing Terrain of Knowledge and Power: A Social Epistemology of Educational Research. *Educational Researcher, 26*(9), 18–29.

Radtke, F.-O. (2012). Tatsachen und Werte. Erziehungswissenschaft zwischen Expertise und Kritik. *Vierteljahreschrift für wissenschaftliche Pädagogik, 88*(2), 290–308.

Radtke, F.-O. (2015). Methodologischer Ökonomismus. Organische Experten im Erziehungssystem. *Erziehungswissenschaft, 26*(50), 7–16.

Radtke, F.-O. (2016). Konditionierte Strukturverbesserung. Umbau und Neuformierung der deutschen Erziehungswissenschaft flankiert von der Deutschen Forschungsgemeinschaft unter Anleitung der OECD verwirklicht von der Kultusministerkonferenz. *Zeitschrift für Pädagogik, 62*(5), 707–731.

Tröhler, D. (2014). Tradition oder Zukunft? 50 Jahre Deutsche Gesellschaft für Erziehungswissenschaft aus bildungshistorischer Sicht. *Zeitschrift für Pädagogik, 60*(1), 9–31.

van den Hove, S., McGlade, J., Mottet, P., & Depledge, M. H. (2012). The Innovation Union: A Perfect Means to Confused Ends? *Environmental Science and Policy, 16*(1), 73–80.

Vilnius Declaration (2013). *Vilnius Declaration – Horizons for Social Sciences and Humanities.* Online at: http://horizons.mruni.eu/wp-content/uploads/2014/02/ssh_mru_conference_report_final.pdf. Retrieved 18 Apr 2018.

Weber, M. (1946 [1922]). *From Max Weber: Essays in Sociology* (pp. 129–156), translated and edited by H.H. Gerth and C. Wright Mills. New York: Oxford University Press.

Wehling, P. (2007). Wissensregime. In R. Schützeichel (Ed.), *Handbuch Wissenssoziologie und Wissensforschung* (pp. 704–712). UVK: Konstanz.

Weiler, H. N. (2003). Bildungsforschung und Bildungsreform — Von den Defiziten der deutschen Erziehungswissenschaft. In I. Gogolin & R. Tippelt (Eds.), *Innovation durch Bildung. Schriften der Deutschen Gesellschaft für Erziehungswissenschaft (DGfE)* (pp. 181–203). Wiesbaden: VS Verlag für Sozialwissenschaften.

Weingart, P. (1997). From "Finalization" to "Mode 2": Old Wine in New Bottles? *Social Science Information, 36/4*, 591–613.

Weingart, P., Carrier, M., & Krohn, W. (2007). *Nachrichten aus der Wissensgesellschaft. Analysen zur Veränderung der Wissenschaft.* Weilerswist: Vellbrück Wissenschaft.

Zapp, M., Marques, M., & Powell, J. J.W. with Contributions by Biesta, G., & Helgetun, J. B. (2018). *European Educational Research (Re)Constructed. Institutional Change in Germany, the United Kingdom, Norway, and the European Union.* Bristol: Symposium Books.

Zapp, M., & Powell, J. (2016). How to Construct an Organizational Field: Empirical Educational Research in Germany, 1995–2015. *European Educational Research Journal, 15*, 537–557.

Zapp, M., & Powell, J. (2017). Moving Towards Mode 2? Evidence-based Policy-making and the Changing Conditions for Educational Research in Germany. *Science and Public Policy, scw091*, 1–11. https://doi.org/10.1093/scipol/scw091

Ziman, J. (2000). *Real Science: What it is, and What it Means.* Cambridge: Cambridge University Press.

# 7

# The Global Education Industry, Data Infrastructures, and the Restructuring of Government School Systems

Bob Lingard

## Introduction

This chapter focuses on a largely hidden dimension of the privatization and commercialization of government schooling systems, namely the role of edu-businesses in the creation of data infrastructures that are central to the structuring of these systems. Data infrastructures today have an important function in structuring what have been referred to as 'systemless systems' of schooling (Lawn, 2013). Large, private ed-tech companies are central in the provision of these structuring data infrastructures. The chapter thus contributes to the emerging literature on data infrastructures in schooling linked to privatization (Anagnostopoulos, Rutledge, & Jacobsen, 2013; Sellar, 2017; Hartong, 2018) and the emerging Global Education Industry (GEI) (Verger, Lubienski, & Steiner-Khamsi, 2016). It is also situated against the literature on data infrastructures more broadly (Williamson, 2017) and the 'extrastatecraft'

---

B. Lingard (✉)
School of Education, Australian Catholic University, Brisbane, QLD, Australia
e-mail: r.lingard@uq.edu.au

© The Author(s) 2019
M. Parreira do Amaral et al. (eds.), *Researching the Global Education Industry*,
https://doi.org/10.1007/978-3-030-04236-3_7

135

(Easterling, 2014) endemic in new modes of educational governance that have emerged with extensive edu-business participation in the work of the state.

Anagnostopoulos and colleagues (2013) have argued that we do not as yet know enough about the 'contours' and 'consequences' of these data infrastructures. There are both technical and social aspects to these contours of data infrastructures. Drawing on the work of Anagnostopoulos and colleagues, Hartong (2018, p. 135) acknowledges both technical and social aspects and as such defines data infrastructures as 'networks of objects' (data, software, computational capacities, algorithmic codes) and 'subjects' (technicians, administrators, school actors, intermediary agents, etc.). (Also see Sellar, 2017, pp. 344f; and Williamson, 2017, p. 80, for helpful definitions.) She adds again utilizing the work of Anagnostopoulos and colleagues that, "data infrastructures are understood as (the transformation of) governmental constellations constituted by (digital) data flows that, however, are more than computer-based hard- and software, but networks of people, technologies and polices" (Hartong, 2018, p. 136). Important in this definition is the inclusion of networks of people and policies, which extends the definition beyond a technological one as proffered by Kitchin and Lauriault (2015), who suggest that data infrastructures are "a digital means for storing, sharing and consuming data across networked technologies" (p. 467). The next section of this chapter shows how this technological plus people conceptualization of data infrastructures is an expression of the new mode of network governance in schooling (Ball, & Junemann, 2012).

This chapter focuses specifically on two case studies of data infrastructures in schooling: one Australian and the other in the USA. The Australian case describes and analyzes the development of the National Schools Interoperability Program (NSIP), which functions in a networked governance mode through collaboration between governments and ed-tech companies. This important aspect of privatization and commercialization of public schooling is largely hidden and goes on behind the backs of educators. The second case documents and analyzes the *InBloom* data infrastructure initiative across nine US states funded by the Gates Foundation (2011–2014). *InBloom* sought to provide a single platform for the sharing of data about schooling across these states and was set against President Obama's *Race to the Top* legislation that demanded school systems develop 'data systems to support instruction'. This case demonstrates how effective parental opposition to this initiative saw it fail. Teacher concern about these developments in Australia is also briefly documented.

This chapter is derived from research funded by and conducted for the New South Wales Teachers Federation, the largest teacher union in Australia, on commercialization in government schooling in Australia (Lingard, Sellar, Hogan, & Thompson, 2017) and from an Australian Research Council funded project, *Data infrastructure, mobilities and network governance in education*.[1] It also draws on publications to date derived from this research (Sellar, 2017; Hogan, Thompson, Sellar, & Lingard, 2018). In outlining two cases of edu-business involvement in the creation of data infrastructures in Australian and US schooling, some attention is also given to opposition to this mode of privatization. As such, the chapter also contributes in a small way to the emerging literature on successful resistance to the GEI and privatization in schooling and the role of teacher unions (Verger, Fontdevila, & Zancajo, 2016, pp. 158–176) and parents (Lingard et al., 2017; Hursh, McGinnis, Chen, & Lingard, 2018) in such opposition.

In what follows, extrastatecraft evidenced in ed-tech companies' provision of data infrastructures to structure government schooling systems, as part of a new networked mode of educational governance, is first considered. Next, the nature of and enabling conditions and strategies of the GEI are outlined. Then the involvement of Bill Gates and Microsoft in the creation and adoption of a Systems Interoperability Framework (SIF) is considered and seen to be necessary to the enabling of national and global infrastructures in schooling. This is followed by two case studies. As already noted, the first deals with the network governance evidenced in the creation in Australia of the NSIP and the second case documents the failure of the *InBloom* project in the USA, also sponsored by the Gates Foundation. Teacher union and parental resistance and opposition to these two developments of data infrastructures are then considered. A summative account draws the chapter to a close.

# Data Infrastructures, Extrastatecraft, and Restructuring of Government Schooling Systems

Much has been written about the privatization of schooling on a global scale and the growth of what has been called the GEI (Burch, 2009; Ball, 2012; Au, & Ferrare, 2015; Verger et al., 2016; Ball, Junemann, & Santori, 2017). The context for this growth has been the seeming dominance globally of neoliberal policy frames that have witnessed inter alia restructured state bureaucracies within nations and related, the emergence of new modes of educational governance nationally and on a global scale.[2] The first restructuring was through new public management, which complemented the neoliberal agenda of creating quasi-markets in schooling, emphasizing school choice and test-based competition between schools and a test-based mode of educational accountability that steered schools at a distance often through performance indicators (Lingard, Martino, Rezai-Rashti, & Sellar, 2016). The subsequent state restructuring has been called 'network governance' (Ball, & Junemann, 2012) and has witnessed private sector involvement (edu-businesses and philanthropies) with and within the state in multiple kinds of activities across the policy cycle. Koppenjan and Klijn (2004, p. 25) describe this network governance in the following way: "[g]overnment is understood to be located alongside business and civil society actors in a complex game of public policy formation, decision-making and implementation". Aphoristically, Steiner-Khamsi (2018) has encapsulated this new mode of network governance in her discussion of 'businesses seeing like a state' and 'governments calculating like a business' (Steiner-Khamsi, 2018).

Data and data infrastructures have become central to constituting schooling systems under this mode of network governance. As Ozga (2009) noted, "Data production and management were and are essential to the new governance turn; constant comparison is its symbolic feature, as well as a distinctive mode of operation" (p. 150). Testing, both national and of the International Large Scale Assessment (ILSAs) (PISA, TIMSS, PIRLS) kind, are central to this governing through comparison underpinned by the datafication of schooling. Data infrastructures enable this comparison and facilitate datafication of schooling systems (Williamson, 2017).

It is the argument of this chapter that data infrastructures are central to the structuring of schooling systems today, imbricated with the new mode of network governance and are an example of hidden privatization and what Easterling (2014) calls 'extrastatecraft'. In this context, Lawn (2013) has spoken of the emergence of a 'systemless system', when talking about the restructuring of schooling in England. Here he is referring to the post-bureaucratic structure and new governance of schooling, including the weakening of Local Authority involvement and strengthening of the central hand of Westminster. He is also referencing the marketization of government schooling evident in multiple modes of provision of government schools in England (academies, free schools, grammar schools, streamed comprehensives), linked to the "dissolution of the comprehensive system" (Reay, 2017, p. 43). Specifically, Lawn observes:

> The tendency of New Public Management to focus on efficiency, productivity targets and strategic capacities allows the system to be re-imagined through data and, indeed, allows the centre to shape, direct and steer a system that only it fully determines and views as a single system. (2013, p. 232)

This 'systemless system' is constructed around data and data infrastructures, with heavy edu-business, ed-tech company involvement in the latter. While Lawn is speaking specifically about the situation in England, these developments are also evident in path dependent ways in other schooling systems in the developed nations. This will be readily seen in the two cases documented below, one in Australia, the other in the USA.

In terms of 'extrastatecraft', Easterling (2014) suggests that it is linked to the work of private businesses (e.g., edu-businesses, ed-tech companies) in the creation of infrastructures of various kinds that are central to the functioning of contemporary nation-states and their post-bureaucratic structures, but also to global modes of governance. She suggests, "infrastructure is now the overt point of contact and access between us all" (2014, p. 11) and defines it:

As a site of multiple, overlapping, or nested forms of sovereignty, where domestic and transnational jurisdictions collide, infrastructure *space* becomes a medium of what might be called *extrastatecraft* – a portmanteau describing the often undisclosed activities outside of, in addition to, and sometimes even in partnership with statecraft'. (Easterling, 2014, p. 1)

This extrastatecraft is an important mode of largely hidden commercialization and privatization in education. It is also linked to the new mode of network governance involving the private sector; here for-profit entities help to constitute infrastructures central to the workings of the contemporary state—thus extrastatecraft. Standardization is also central to the functioning of extrastatecraft through data and data infrastructures. In schooling, this standardization is evident in the constituting of nations and the globe as commensurate spaces of measurement of school and system performance through national and international testing (Lingard, & Rawolle, 2011). Ball and Junemann (2012, p. 133) see this as the '*isomorphism of measurement*' globally. This standardization and related datafication are also pivotal to the emergence of the GEI and broadening of markets for it.

It has been implied to this point that the new network governance works globally as well as nationally. Indeed, Sassen (2007) has argued that globalization is really the creation of global infrastructures that facilitate and constitute the postnational and global. So what we have seen is the involvement of edu-businesses in educational governance and the new mode stretched globally. In relation to contemporary policy analysis in education in the context of globalization, network governance, and extrastatecraft, Ball (2012) has presciently observed:

> [E]ducation policy analysis can no longer sensibly be limited to within the nation state – the fallacy of methodological territorialism [...] policy analysis must also extend its purview beyond the state and the role of multinational agencies and NGOs to include transnational business practices. (p. 93)

This insight applies to considerations of the GEI that are the focus of this collection and of this chapter.

## The GEI

Verger and colleagues (2016) argue that the GEI refers to the ways edu-businesses with for-profit motives and new philanthropies are today heavily involved in all aspects of education from agenda setting, policy production, and implementation, through to provision of goods and services. They also note that the Organization for Economic Co-operation and Development (OECD) is using this nomenclature, but in a narrower way to refer specifically to ed-tech companies. Verger and colleagues (2016) demonstrate how the GEI has developed in relation to education as a sector for profit making on a global scale and was worth approximately US$4.3 trillion in 2014. Pearson, the world's largest edu-business, argued in its 2012 Annual Report that, "education will be the biggest growth industry of the 21$^{st}$ century" (p. 8).

While Steiner-Khamsi (2018) has documented the core business strategies of edu-businesses on a global scale, with her colleagues Verger and Lubienski (Verger et al., 2016) she has also considered the global conditions that have enabled the growth of the GEI. According to Steiner-Khamsi, the core business strategies of edu-businesses in education include "lowering production and delivery costs in education", "creating an economy of scale by means of standardization", "establishing long-term service and sales contracts", "introducing a fee structure", and "scandalizing public education" (Steiner-Khamsi, 2018, pp. 384ff). Hursh (2016) has written in depth about the latter strategy in respect of the corporate reform agenda to privatize schooling. It is the economy of scale through standardization, however, that is central to edu-business involvement in the creation of data infrastructures in school systems and the constituting of national and global markets.

In terms of the conditions enabling the growth of the GEI, the argument has been made to this point that the restructuring of the bureaucratic state under two iterations (new public management and network governance) has been central. In addition, Verger and colleagues (2016) list the following as enabling conditions, the globalization of the economy and human capital construction of education, the commodification of schooling as a positional good, the financialization of the education sector, changes in the governance of education globally, the emergence of an 'evidence-based' policy paradigm, and perceived links between new technologies and learning (Verger et al., 2016, pp. 6–11). All of these have been important enabling factors for the GEI. Changes in governance structures and the evidence-based paradigm are intimately related to the emergence of data infrastructures. Indeed, they are necessary to both, as has been argued in the introduction to this chapter. However, this chapter argues that Verger et al. underplay the specific significance of datafication beyond evidence-based policy and the necessity of data infrastructures to the new network governance and underplay as well their importance in the expansion of the GEI.

It is interesting to note here the OECD's policy stance on the GEI, which they define more narrowly as the ed-tech industry. The OECD organized the first global summit on the GEI in October, 2015 in Helsinki in collaboration with the Finnish Minister for Education; a subsequent GEI summit was held in Jerusalem in September, 2016. Participants in Helsinki included Education Ministers or their representatives, ed-tech companies (EdTech Industry Network, EduCloud Alliance, Learn Capital, Intel Corporations, Samsung Electronics), academics, and representatives of Education International, the international federation of teacher unions. A central topic for the summit was, 'Schools need a physical and digital infrastructure through which improved teaching and learning products can be delivered'. The Director of the Education and Skills Directorate at the OECD, Andreas Schleicher, in his dinner speech at the first summit, stated there was a pressing need for 'collaborative networks' between Ministries and ed-tech companies and also for 'dialogue between Ministers and the Education Industry'. He concluded by observing, 'the OECD stands ready to support and facilitate' these. The summary notes from summit Rapporteurs also stated that there was a strong consensus concerning the need for such co-operation between 'industry, schools and authorities'.

A couple of things are important here in this OECD work. First, the OECD can be seen to be supporting network governance and extrastatecraft, encouraging the involvement of the GEI in the work of ministries of education. Additionally, two usages of the data that flow through data infrastructures are implied: one the management and interoperability of a data for policy purposes, the other going to the core work of teachers and schools, namely, pedagogy and evaluation practices. On the latter, it is significant that Schleicher in his dinner speech stressed the failure to date of computers in classrooms to have had any positive impact on quality learning outcomes.

## The Systems Interoperability Framework (SIF)

Sellar (2017) has written about the development of a number of 'interoperability standards'[3] in relation to data infrastructures. Most significant here is the development of the Schools Interoperability Framework (SIF) in the USA under the sponsorship of Bill Gates of Microsoft and which he launched at the US School Administrators' Annual Conference in early 1999. At this launch, Gates talked about the necessity for all school systems to develop what he called 'digital nervous systems'. As Sellar (2017) notes, SIF was developed by Microsoft with support from 18 software companies and the Software and Information Industry Association (SIIA). It should be pointed out that SIF is an open, not proprietary standard. Gates' involvement in SIF and the work of the philanthropic, Bill and Melinda Gates' Foundation,[4] must also be situated against their broader role in the corporate reform of schooling in the USA (Hursh, 2016), for example, the Foundation's support for the Common Core State Standards and related testing regime for all students in years 3–8 in US schools.

The first SIF specification was released late in 1999, a more developed form in 2003, when the federal US Department of Education joined the project; an example of network governance. SIF Associations were subsequently created in the UK in 2006 and the Intergovernmental Council in Education in Australia, consisting of all the education ministers from state, territorial, and federal levels of government, endorsed the specification in 2009 and committed to creating an Australian version under their jurisdiction. The international Access 4 Learning (A4L) was launched in 2015 and brought together SIF associations in the USA, the UK, and Australia and argued that SIF provided 'the most comprehensive data model and mature interoperability framework in use globally in education'

(A4L, 2015). Sellar (2017) suggests that this naming of the joint organization is indicative of a broader policy agenda beyond simple data management to providing data for parents, teachers, and students with implications for teaching and learning. It becomes very clear here that SIF opens up a potential global market for ed-tech companies, a significant element of the GEI. National and international testing and the related standardization across national systems and the globe are important here as well. Policy, as will be demonstrated in the cases below, is also important in enabling network governance. It is also clear that what we are seeing here is network governance at work through extrastatecraft.

## Case 1: The National Schools Interoperability Program in Australia[5]

Australia has a federal political structure whereby schooling is the Constitutional responsibility of the states and territories, but where the national or federal government has had increasing involvement in schooling since the 1970s, both in funding and policy terms. This involvement was strengthened considerably from 2007 when a federal government created for the first time a national curriculum and national testing at years 3, 5, 7, and 9 in literacy and numeracy (Lingard, 2010). Often in Australian educational federalism, federal school policies are referred to as 'national' policies, as in 'national curriculum' and 'national testing' (NAPLAN—National Assessment Program Literacy and Numeracy). This nomenclature references the way such policy has been developed and legitimated. The Intergovernmental Council in Education, consisting of all the Education Ministers in the nation, is where these national policies are negotiated and agreed upon; the usage of national acknowledges this agreement. This was the case with the NSIP and the endorsement of the Ministers in 2009 of an Australian SIF specification.

This NSIP work has been carried out by a small group located in the Council's offices in Melbourne and overseen by a steering group of the Chief Information Officers of each state and territory schooling system. NSIP has also been supported by all state and territory schooling systems, the federal department, and all Catholic and Independent School systems across the nation. This involvement of all relevant groups is significant in terms of systemic data interoperability and endorsement of NSIP. The Australian SIF association, consisting of 13 government bodies, 9 Catholic and independent bodies, and 16 commercial providers, has been closely involved in the development of NSIP.

The NSIP website provides a description of SIF, which was developed jointly by the Australian SIF Association and the NSIP office under the broader jurisdiction of education ministers. SIF is described in the following way along with an account of who is involved: The Systems Interoperability Framework, widely known as SIF, is an international specification for the exchange of school data. The SIF Association is made up of education providers and software vendors who have a common interest in having software applications interact and share data. Globally, there are 102 vendor organization members and 1082 end user members of the SIF Association.

The creation of the national curriculum and national testing in Australia has established a national market for commercial providers of various kinds and at the same time demand for interoperability of data sets across state and territory borders and across schooling systems (Sellar, 2017). Sellar (2017, p. 347) argues that the logic of these national developments in Australian schooling is that 'student records should also be transferable between systems'. The associated standardization of this testing and curriculum and the emergence of NSIP based on SIF have been very important here. NSIP will also facilitate moves to the online construction of NAPLAN and potential related data analysis and usage. We can also see in the NSIP work network governance at work, as well extrastatecraft.

Sellar (2017) suggests that what we witness with NSIP in Australia is the "creation of opportunities for commercial provision of data-driven products and services to schools and systems" (p. 346). He also talks about NSIP's Hub Integration Testing Service (HITS), which enables private providers to access system data to test potential products for system interoperability (p. 348). Sellar argues persuasively and on the evidence that "the development and adoption of interoperability standards can be understood as a market making process" (p. 348). He relates three dimensions of these market making processes. He asserts first that standardization "reduces the time and cost of product development and enables a shift from particular to generic solutions" (p. 348). The shift to generic solutions flows from the creation of standardized national policies and thus the creation of a potential national market. Secondly, he points out how the policy spaces for standardization, here with NSIP, are 'state-sponsored' and where "suppliers can shape the needs of users" (p. 348). Potentially, this private sector involvement goes to framing the core of schooling. Thirdly, he opines that, "the tools for enabling interoperability expose data to vendors and provide them with new resources for product development" (p. 348). Sellar suggests that, while the corporate players in the data infrastructure work of NSIP in Australian schooling are much less powerful than Microsoft and the Gates Foundation, their participation in NSIP is nonetheless indicative of extrastatecraft at work, and I would also argue these developments are demonstrative of network governance in Australian schooling.

## Case 2: InBloom in the USA

*InBloom* was a US EdTech initiative launched in 2011 and focused on creating data infrastructures for school systems, funded in large part by $100 million from the Gates Foundation, and which was created in 2013 and ended in 2014 because of widespread parental concerns about privacy matters,[6] which will be a focus of the subsequent section of this chapter. *InBloom* built on earlier attempts "to use technology and data techniques to connect and improve educational settings" (Bulger, McCormick, & Pitcan, 2017, p. 9), such as the Achievement Reporting and Innovation System (ARIS) established in New York City in 2007 and developed by IBM and the ed-tech company Wireless Generation for US$80 million. Ninety percent of Wireless Generation was bought by Rupert Murdoch in 2010 for US$360 million, an indication of the view of education as a burgeoning market for the private sector. ARIS was also used for accountability purposes. Subsequently, the ed-tech Wireless Generation worked with the Gates Foundation to develop a technology platform with four component parts, namely, "a data warehouse, a universal lesson bank, a universal item bank, and a learning trajectory map" (Bulger et al., 2017, p. 10f). This morphed ultimately into *InBloom* in the context of *Race to the Top* policy (e.g., the demand for data-based Instructional Improvement Systems) and funding and the sense that statewide data infrastructures for schooling were necessary.

Bulger and colleagues (2017) describe the purposes of *InBloom* as "to improve American schools by providing a centralized platform for data sharing, learning apps and curricula" (p. 3) and this was to be across all system, school and student related data sets across nine states, including New York. *InBloom* was a 'multi-state consortium', "intended to address the challenge of siloed data storage that prevented the interoperability of existing school datasets by introducing shared standards, an open source platform that would allow local iteration, and district-level user authentication to improve security" (Bulger et al., 2017, p. 3). Bulger et al. continue, "Ultimately, the initiative planned to organize existing data into meaningful reporting for teachers and school administrators to inform personalized instruction and improving learning outcomes" (p. 4). Thus, *InBloom* was about more than simply enabling data flows through creating interoperability between multiple data sets; its longer term purpose was to change the pedagogical work of teachers and schools through data use and personalization. This ambition was situated against much talk about US schooling failing, often articulated by influential edu-businesses and philanthropists (Hursh, 2016; Bulger et al., 2017).

The successful opposition to *InBloom* will be traversed later in this chapter. Suffice to say at this point that Bulger and colleagues argue that the development of *InBloom* was too rapid and too ambitious and perhaps should have focused initially on building the 'cloud-based datastore' before extending into these other domains that go to the core of schooling. They also note that the top-down approach of *InBloom*, while partially aligned with *Race to the Top* requirements and expectations, was also disjunctive with the bottom-up mode of governance and administration of US schooling systems; there was misalignment with the ecology of US schooling. Importantly, it is this grassroots mode of schooling governance that also enabled effective parental and community opposition to it.

As noted above, the development of *InBloom* was set against the *Race to the Top* legislative requirement that school systems create 'data systems to support instruction' and the need for the establishment of 'longitudinal data systems' state wide. *Race to the Top* also made large amounts of federal money (US$4.35 billion, 2010–2015) available to the states contingent upon them meeting such policy requirements. Bulger et al. make important points about the timing of *InBloom* in terms of how it was framed, large scale from the start, limited trialing, and top-down in approach, linked to the climate of concern about the putative decline in US schooling and optimism about the potential of data to transform US schools and improve student learning. The policy intentions of *Race to the Top* also supported *InBloom*'s development, but also framed the pace at which it was developed and its character. In addition to vehement opposition to *InBloom*, particularly from parent groups and teacher unions, dealt with below, these additional factors also contributed to its rapid failure. *InBloom* was gone by 2014 as state by state began to withdraw in the face of mounting opposition and demands for privacy legislation about the collection of student data. This opposition was set against broader public concerns at the time about data privacy.

## Resistance and Opposition to Privatization Through Data Infrastructures

Parental opposition to *InBloom* focused around privacy issues, specifically concerns about full sets of student data of multiple kinds being in the hands of private providers and real consternation that some data held about some children might very well harm their futures; data-based recording of student performance and behavior potentially followed them across the life cycle. There were also real parental and community concerns about the possibility of the on-selling of student data to third parties for profit. Such data mining for other than the purposes for which the data were collected became a real concern and remains so. As this opposition built, the states participating in *InBloom* withdrew one by one from the project and considered the necessity of data privacy legislation.

Bulger and colleagues (2017) suggest that parental suspicion of private access to and control of student data around privacy issues was framed against the almost contemporaneous backdrop of the 'WikiLeaks saga of 2010'. Research interviews with NYSAPE and Long Island Opt Out leaders in New York indicated their deep worry that the data infrastructures underpinning schooling systems would potentially be controlled by private for profit interests, including the world's largest edu-business, Pearson (Lingard et al., 2017; Hursh et al., 2018, in press). They expressed deep concerns about privacy issues. The more activist Opt Out leaders had a broader agenda than simply opposing high-stakes testing associated with *No Child Left Behind* and *Race to the Top*; their broader concerns were about the corporate reform agenda in US schooling, which they saw as defacing democratic public schooling (Lingard et al., 2017) and this included opposition to corporate provision of data infrastructures. Opposition to this element of the corporate reform agenda in schooling was very powerful and successful and resonated with broader public concerns about data usage and data mining; issues that came to the fore at present with the Facebook scandal in respect of the Brexit vote and 2016 US Presidential election. The activist success against *InBloom* also indicates the broader policy interest of the parent activist groups and also of the significance of coalitions to successful opposition to proposed reforms. There was teacher union opposition to *InBloom* in New York. Data privacy has become a central concern of these parental and teacher groups.

In recent, lengthy research interviews conducted with Lisa Ridley and Jeanette Deutermann, leaders of the Opt Out movement in New York and New York state, they indicated that they are now broadening their oppositional focus further to non-research-based, ed-tech, computer-based curriculum, pedagogy, and testing and assessment (Lingard et al., 2017, pp. 59–71). In relation to computer-based education, they expressed deep concern that school children were now often spending all day in front of computer screens doing packaged curriculum, pedagogy, and assessment. They were concerned that the only research on these programs had been done by the ed-tech businesses themselves and that there had been no independent evaluations. They were also concerned that local school systems had often paid for these programs and then mandated their usage in schools and classrooms.

Research conducted for the teacher unions in Australia (Lingard et al., 2017) indicated very limited knowledge amongst Australian teachers of NSIP, but a deep concern about privatization and commercialization of Australian government schooling and great worry about schools being run as businesses and using business language (e.g., students as clients, parents as customers). In the questionnaire completed by 2653 teachers across Australia, the quite common use of technology to document and record student behavior was noted, as well as usage by schools of commercial attendance tracking programs. Teacher respondents (74 percent) expressed deep concern about student data being in private hands; a stance similar to parental opposition to *InBloom* in the USA. An open-ended response on the questionnaire from a teacher noted the connections between standardized testing and commercial involvement (see Hogan et al., 2018). This teacher observed:

> Our teaching is to the test with commercial products that track student achievement and predict student scores. Just for whom are these tests conducted? To show student learning growth? School effectiveness? Teacher effectiveness? Effectiveness of a commercial product???? I was recently horrified to see a report into high achieving primary schools detailing commercial products and teaching models used by the schools researched ... then to see the commercial products websites referring to the report! (Open-ended comment on teacher questionnaire, Lingard et al., 2017)

Questionnaire responses seemed to suggest that there was almost as much commercial provision as state provision for schools. It appeared that the state had constituted a market for take-up by edu-businesses. The system-less system was thus constituted through a mix of state and commercial provision. More school autonomy and one-line budgets were seen to be structural policy conditions that enabled this hybridized situation. This is evidence of the reality that state restructuring has been important to commercialization and privatization and the strengthening of the GEI.

Importantly, as with parental and community opposition to high-stakes testing and the corporate reform agenda in the USA, teachers surveyed unequivocally rejected the constitution of them by policy as neoliberal subjects, the top-down objects of policy. The teacher respondents overwhelmingly expressed social democratic politics and such a view of schooling in relation to the state. This is not to suggest that there were not some views expressed that saw some positives in commercial provision (e.g., texts, computer programs) and the like, but the teachers also wanted some quality assurance from the state with respect to such products. Interestingly, there were no demographic differences across the teacher sample (primary, secondary, gender, age, experience, teaching location, principals, other leaders, classroom teachers) in respect of the views articulated and of the sample's social democratic politics. It seems that there is an as yet untapped potential in the teaching profession and amongst the teacher unions to effectively mobilize in opposition to privatization and commercialization and the increased involvement of the GEI in government schooling.[7]

# Conclusion

This chapter has documented and analyzed two cases of the creation of data infrastructures in contemporary schooling. The argument has shown how state restructuring and the move to network governance, nationally and globally, have enabled the growth of the ed-tech element of the GEI. Datafication of schooling and enhanced computational capacities are important in facilitating this growth of the involvement of the ed-tech business component of the GEI in public schooling, underplayed factors in the research literature on the GEI to date (Verger et al., 2016). It has been shown how these infrastructures work through network governance that sees private providers work alongside the state in policy processes and as such, a manifestation of extrastatecraft. This mode of commercialization, including the work of ed-tech companies in the creation of SIF and system data infrastructures, actually structures the systemless systems that are educational bureaucracies today. This situation raises important questions about schooling and democracy and who should determine the provision of public schooling.

Significantly, as outlined, there is opposition to these developments. The case of *InBloom* is important in proffering an account of successful opposition around issues of data privacy and the question of who are legitimate stakeholders in schooling policy formation. The Australian situation is somewhat different with a much more centralized schooling system. NSIP appears to be little known amongst Australian teachers. Nonetheless, it is the case that there are teacher and teacher union concerns about the impact of the datafication of schools and a recognition that the standardization associated with national testing and the national curriculum opens up a larger market for the ed-tech companies, and indeed is important in both enabling and demanding system interoperability and interoperable data infrastructures.

Teacher unions in Australia funded the research on which this chapter is based and this work can be seen as part of the recognition by the teacher unions that research and knowledge production are very important to successful union political strategies today, including in relation to the enhanced significance of the GEI (Verger et al., 2016, p. 165). More research is required on data infrastructures; ongoing questions include who is creating them, in whose interests and with what effects on schooling, the work of teachers, and the learning of students. As Easterling observes, "Contemporary infrastructure space is the secret weapon of the most powerful people in the world precisely because it orchestrates activities that can remain unstated but are nevertheless consequential" (Easterling, 2014, p. 15). It is hoped that this chapter has helped unpack some of that secrecy and opened up a debate that goes to the core of what government school systems ought to be today.

# Notes

1. Australian Research Council Discovery Project, DP150102098. Chief investigators: Bob Lingard, Kal Gulson, Sam Sellar, and Keita Takayama with Christopher Lubienski and Taylor Webb as Partner Investigators.
2. It should be noted though that state restructuring are not the same thing as the neoliberal agendas. Rather, they are complementary and enabling. Furthermore, Ball, Junemann and Santori (2017, p. 1) are right when they stress the need to talk about neoliberalization as a process rather than as an abstract construction as a noun. This emphasis means we need to attend to the empirical realities of neoliberalism at work in particular contexts.
3. This section and the subsequent one draws heavily on Sellar (2017).
4. On the Gates Foundation, see Tompkins-Stange (2017). She sees this philanthropic organization as an outcomes-oriented one that relies heavily on expertise in a top-down way with a stress on measurable outcomes.

5. This narrative and description of NSIP draws substantially on Sellar (2017).
6. The narrative of *InBloom* here draws closely on that provided by Bulger, McCormick and Pitcan (2017). They also provide a very useful account of the successful opposition to this project.
7. It should be acknowledged that Education International, the international federation of teacher unions, has a coordinated global project about the privatization and commercialization of government schooling. The Australian teacher union that funded the research on which this chapter is based has also used this research strategically.

# References

A4L. (2015). *Introducing the Access 4 Learning Community – The SIF Association Matures to Address Not Only Data Management but Data Usage for Learning*. Retrieved from https://www.prlog.org/12457789-introducing-the-access-4-learning-community.html. Accessed on 03/01/2018.

Anagnostopoulos, D., Rutledge, S., & Jacobsen, R. (Eds.). (2013). *The Infrastructure of Accountability: Data Use and the Transformation of American Education*. Cambridge, MA: Harvard Education Press.

Au, W., & Ferrare, J. (Eds.). (2015). *Mapping Corporate Education Reform: Power and Policy Networks in the Neoliberal State*. New York: Routledge.

Ball, S. (2012). *Global Education Inc.: New Policy Networks and the Neo-liberal Imaginary*. New York: Routledge.

Ball, S., & Junemann, C. (2012). *Networks, New Governance and Education*. Bristol: Policy Press.

Ball, S., Junemann, C., & Santori, D. (2017). *Edu.net: Globalisation and Education Policy Mobility*. New York: Routledge.

Bulger, M., McCormick, P., & Pitcan, M. (2017). *The Legacy of InBloom*. Working Paper 02.02.2017: Data & Society. Retrieved from https://datasociety.net/pubs/ecl/InBloom_feb_2017.pdf. Accessed on 03/01/2018.

Burch, P. (2009). *Hidden Markets: The New Education Privatization*. New York: Routledge.

Easterling, K. (2014). *Extrastatecraft: The Power of Infrastructure Space*. London: Verso.

Hartong, S. (2018). Towards a Topological Re-assemblage of Education Policy? Observing the Implementation of Performance Data Infrastructures and 'Centres of Calculation' in Germany. *Globalisation, Societies and Education, 16*(1), 134–150.

Hogan, A., Thompson, G., Sellar, S., & Lingard, B. (2018). Teachers' and School Leaders' Perceptions of Commercialisation in Australian Public Schools. *The Australian Educational Researcher, 45*(2), 141–160.
Hursh, D. (2016). *The End of Public Schools: The Corporate Reform Agenda to Privatize Public Education*. New York: Routledge.
Hursh, D., McGinnis, S., Chen, Z., & Lingard, B. (2018, in press). Resisting the Neoliberal: Parent Activism in New York State Against the Corporate Reform Agenda in Schooling. In L. Tett, & Hamiton, M. (Eds), Resisting Neoliberalism in Education: Local, National, and Transnational Perspectives, Bristol: Policy Press.
Kitchin, R., & Lauriault, T. (2015). Small Data in the Era of Big Data. *GeoJournal, 80*(4), 463–475.
Koppenjan, J., & Klijn, E. (2004). *Managing Uncertainties in Networks*. London: Routledge.
Lawn, M. (2013). A Systemless System: Designing the Disarticulation of English State Education. *European Educational Research Journal, 12*(2), 231–241.
Lingard, B. (2010). Policy Borrowing, Policy Learning: Testing Times in Australian Schools. *Critical Studies in Education, 51*(2), 129–147.
Lingard, B., Martino, W., Rezai-Rashti, G., & Sellar, S. (2016). *Globalizing educational accountabilities*. New York: Routledge.
Lingard, B., & Rawolle, S. (2011). New Scalar Politics: Implications for Education Policy. *Comparative Education, 47*(4), 489–502.
Lingard, B., Sellar, S., Hogan, A., & Thompson, G. (2017). *Commercialisation in Public Schooling: Final Report Summary*. Sydney: New South Wales Teachers Federation.
Ozga, J. (2009). Governing Education Through Data in England: From Regulation to Self-evaluation. *Journal of Education Policy, 24*(2), 149–162.
Reay, D. (2017). *Miseducation: Inequality, Education and the Working Classes*. Bristol: Policy Press.
Sassen, S. (2007). *A Sociology of Globalization*. New York: W.W.Norton.
Sellar, S. (2017). Making Network Markets in Education: The Development of Data Infrastructure in Australian Schooling. *Globalisation, Societies and Education, 15*(3), 341–351.
Steiner-Khamsi, G. (2018). Businesses Seeing Like a State, Governments Calculating Like a Business. *International Journal of Qualitative Studies in Education, 31*(5), 382–392. https://doi.org/10.1080/09518398.2018.1449980

Tomkins-Stange, M. (2017). *Policy Patrons: Philanthropy, Education Reform, and the Politics of Influence.* Cambridge, MA: Harvard Education Press.

Verger, A., Fontdevila, C., & Zancajo, A. (2016). *The Privatization of Education: A Political Economy of Global Education Reform.* New York: Teachers College Press.

Verger, A., Lubienski, C., & Steiner-Khamsi, G. (Eds.). (2016). *The Global Education Industry.* New York: Routledge.

Williamson, B. (2017). *Big Data in Education: The Digital Future of Learning, Policy and Practice.* London: SAGE.

# 8

# The Transformation of State Monitoring Systems in Germany and the US: Relating the Datafication and Digitalization of Education to the Global Education Industry

Sigrid Hartong

## Introduction

Considerable effort has been made in recent years to examine the complex processes of privatization and commodification related to worldwide school reform agendas, including the rise of the so-called *Global Education Industry* (GEI; e.g., Ball, 2012; Verger, Fontdevila, & Zancajo, 2016; Verger, Lubienski, & Steiner-Khamsi, 2016). The Education Technology (EdTech) sector within is a rapidly growing part of an industry which Forbes Media recently forecasted to produce investments worth US$252 billion globally by 2020 (Shulman, 2017), in personalized learning technologies such as online learning, blended learning, adaptive testing, and learning hardware (see also the *Education Week* section *Digital Directions*, www.edweek.org/dd; US Department of Education, 2012).

---

S. Hartong (✉)
Faculty of Humanities and Social Sciences, Helmut-Schmidt-University Hamburg, Hamburg, Germany
e-mail: hartongs@hsu-hh.de

The ways in which manifold manifestations of the EdTech industry have become interwoven into ongoing global-local transformations of education governance have been examined extensively (Roberts-Mahoney, Means, & Garrison, 2016; Williamson, 2016a, 2016b, 2017). Yet instead of assuming a single process of "direct" commodification, or a "takeover" by global EdTech businesses, it seems necessary to closely observe the multidimensional nature of commodification or corporatization. Courtney (2015) recently described this phenomenon as the "embodied colonization" of spaces in education governance where corporatism and corporate actors flourish (see also Hartong, Hermstein, & Höhne, 2018; Heinrich & Kohlstock, 2016). This development is rarely linear or easy-to-follow. It shifts between a heterogeneous network of power relations connecting public (e.g., schools, departments, ministries, and national and sub-national governments) and private actors (e.g., businesses, non-profit organizations, advocacy groups, and philanthropies). It also encompasses global, national, and local policy settings, as well as different modes of commodified interaction, including indirect forms of sponsorship, affiliation, and partnership.[1]

As I will demonstrate, these complex, cross-sectoral, and cross-scalar relations (Ball, 2016) can also be identified within the ongoing datafication and digitalization[2] of school *administration*, particularly regarding education monitoring systems within ministries or state departments of education. This transformation of school administration has also brought about new—often monetized—relations between state, business, private, and philanthropic groups which should be examined. Facing rising pressure to monitor and report on education, as well as early identify students and schools at risk in order to "boost" student performance, departments of education have increasingly demanded "smart" data technology and management services (Hartong, 2016a; Koyama, 2011). These include an increasing market for "[...] tools to analyze and make sense of the growing mass of data becoming available as education is digitized" (Williamson, 2016c, p. 49). As a result, new actor networks have become assembled around technology, discourses, and rationales that not only reframe performance monitoring practices (Koyama, 2011) but ultimately also the very meaning of "good" school administration and state-level leadership.

In this chapter I present some initial findings on how the datafication and digitalization of state education monitoring systems evolved between 2000 and 2017 in a forerunner, the US, as well as a relative latecomer, Germany. My focus is on policy dynamics—the market in particular—as well as actor networks.[3] I will identify crucial similarities and differences to demonstrate how expanding standardization and interoperability have led to monitoring practices that increasingly flow between nationalization, globalization, and personalization.

## Approaching the Transformation of State Monitoring Systems from a Policy Network Perspective

Following Ball and Junemann (2012), policy network analysis maps the relations between specific actors, emphasizing the contents, interactions, and shared meanings between them (as cited in Williamson, 2016a, p. 2). Hereby, policies are not approached as distinct or compact forms, but rather as dynamic assemblages that change with different contexts of policy making at the levels of state and school administration (Ball, 2016, p. 1).

In the past decade this perspective on shifting networks and policy spaces has been found particularly useful for better understanding globalization processes as global-local policy relations and flows (Ball, 2016; Hartong, 2018a; Steiner-Khamsi & Waldow, 2012). This viewpoint transcends trends affecting nation-states to explore how global and national forces continuously interact with sub-national or local processes, institutions, actors, objects (or fragments of objects), and polities, causing unevenness, friction, and different timelines of policy transformation (Ball, 2016, p. 550; Clarke, Bainton, Lendvai, & Stubbs, 2015, p. 35; Savage & O'Connor, 2015, p. 611).

Despite evidence of a worldwide corporate school reform agenda, the rise of a GEI/global EdTech market, and growing influence of international organizations aggressively supporting EdTech development and greater involvement of for-profit education vendors, commodification still flows differently between local spheres of policy making, and depends strongly on *intra-national* policy network dynamics (Ball, 2016).[4]

Datafication and digitalization have also at least partly established deterritorialized relations of governance (Allen, 2011; Lewis & Lingard, 2015) which, as digital and interoperable network structures, have the potential to bridge "[…] the gap erected by the physical barriers of distance" (Allen & Cochrane, 2010, p. 1075). These new digital relations have contributed to an even greater dynamic of global-local and intra-national policy flows (Hartong, 2018a).

I build on this line of argumentation by providing a closer look at the intra-national policy developments and networks framing the recent datafication and digitalization of state monitoring systems in the US and Germany. I follow this transformation by identifying key moments of reform, emerging network relations, and nodal actors such as boundary spanners, to substantiate document analysis and intensive online research (for a more detailed methodological explanation see Ball, 2016, pp. 3–5; Williamson, 2016a, pp. 3–6).

Germany and the US provide useful examples for tracing intra-national policy flows (Ball, 2016), not only because they are at different stages for assessing impact but also due to the fact that both contain federal, multi-level architectures, where sub-national authorities, such as state[5] ministries and departments of education and—in the US—district-level authorities, decide on the implementation, transformation, and use of education monitoring systems. State actors are important members of the intra-national policy networks charged with digitalizing state monitoring systems, and essential liaisons for private actors to promote ideas and sell products. At the same time, until the beginning of the twenty-first century in both the US and Germany, monitoring at the federal, state, and district levels differed, resulting in a hodgepodge of uncoordinated data systems (Breiter, Grönert, & Lange, 2014). Despite reforms that have significantly reduced heterogeneity in the past 15 years, this has remained a central characteristic of both systems.

As I will illustrate, comparative analysis reveals additional similarities, as well as crucial differences, between the US and Germany. For example, the transformation of state-level monitoring systems in both countries has coincided with the rise of supra-state standardization policies, such as the implementation of common educational standards and standardized tests. Actor networks around cross-sectoral, cross-scale partnerships and collaborations have built on such policies to datafy, digitalize, and standardize state monitoring practices, while simultaneously (particularly in the US) creating different markets for private interest. I have traced shifting forms of "meta-governance" (Ball, 2009, p. 3) within these policy networks, revealing different types of collaborative partnership, as well as dominant sets of defined practices to govern collaborative spaces (Hartong, 2015).

Despite this similarity, there so far appears to be a much stronger commodification and market dynamic in the US, where the process has a much longer history. Here several forms of direct or indirect commodification can be identified, including practices like "contracting out," funding through sponsorship, "information assemblages" consisting of data for profit, and data mediation services (e.g., around the "in-formation" of data; Hartong, 2016a; Sellar & Thompson, 2016, pp. 1–5). Such practices are becoming increasingly visible in Germany but seem, at least so far, much less influential at the state level. I will discuss possible reasons for this at the end of this chapter.

## More Data, More Standards, Increasing Commodification: The Transformation of State Education Monitoring Systems in the US Between 2001 and 2017

Even though education performance monitoring, the implementation of standardized test systems in particular, has a comparatively long history in the US (Sacks, 1999), significant policy network transformations can be identified within the last 15 years. These led to an unprecedented expansion of datafication and digitalization processes, as well as a simultaneous standardization of state-level monitoring systems. These network transformations have been framed by a shift toward education policy "nationalization" (Hartong, 2018b; Savage & O'Connor, 2015), featuring growing federal influence either through mandatory regulations (e.g., the 2001 *No Child Left Behind* Act), incentive funding programs (e.g., the 2005 *State Longitudinal Data Systems* program), or voluntary benchmarking initiatives (e.g., those included in the 2002 *Education Science Reform* Act). Such initiatives have come along with an expanding role of supra-state networks acting as national stakeholders, which either consist of state actors themselves, such as the *National Governors Association* (NGA) and the *Council of Chief State School Officers* (CCSSO), or form around intermediary think tanks, advocacy organizations, non-profits, philanthropies, and business coalitions.

The federal *No Child Left Behind* Act (2001) was an important step in the long-term transformation of state monitoring systems because it required states to collect a greater amount of more detailed disaggregated test data, and submit reports to the federal department of education. Guided by an agenda to hold teachers, schools, and districts more accountable to state education standards, the law fostered an output-driven, high-stakes approach to test-based accountability (e.g., Center on Education Policy, 2002; Ravitch, 2010). It also made state agencies more accountable for successful school leadership.

The law had far-reaching consequences not only in terms of a massive implementation of new "infrastructures of accountability" around tests and monitoring (Anagnostopoulos, Rutledge, & Jacobsen, 2013) but also for an expansion of markets for reporting, "information assemblages" of fabricated data, as well as data administration, management, and mediation at the state and district levels (Sellar & Thompson, 2016; see also Koyama, 2011). In other words, *No Child Left Behind* gave rise to a body of service and product providers for monitoring and assessing both for-profit and non-profit EdTech (see also Pietry, 2013, p. 3).

In that same year (2001), a non-profit association of state education agency leaders, the *State Educational Technology Directors Association* (SETDA), was founded, which in the following years initiated strategic partnerships and collaboration to more closely involve EdTech in state-level monitoring practices (www.setda.org/about). A year later (2002), the federal *Education Science Reform Act* gave the *National Center for Education Statistics* (NCES) the authority to determine voluntary standards and guidelines for state education agencies in developing data systems, which was followed by the *National Governors Association*

*Graduation Rate Compact* in 2005, wherein the governors of all 50 states agreed to implement a common formula for calculating high school graduation rates (Data Quality Campaign [DQC], 2017, pp. 18–20).

A crucial milestone was reached three years later when the *Institute for Education Sciences* (IES), advertised as the "statistics, research, and evaluation arm of the U.S. Department of Education" (https://ies.ed.gov/aboutus), launched the *Statewide Longitudinal Data Systems* (SLDS) grant program. Federal agencies continuously defined the requirements for receiving SLDS grants, including the mandatory submission of longitudinal statistics and promotion of cross-state and cross-scale data sharing. Federal initiatives, such as the *American Recovery and Reinvestment Act* and its program *Race to the Top* (2009), further supported the expansion of SLDS, while simultaneously fostering value-added modeling for teacher evaluation. In the same year, the NCES launched the *Common Education Data Standards* (CEDS) initiative to further promote data use and data interoperability. These tools provided "a common vocabulary, data models that reflect that vocabulary, tools to help educational stakeholders understand and use educational data [and] an assembly of metadata from other education data initiatives" (https://ceds.ed.gov/FAQ.aspx). By 2016 the IES had provided more than $500 million to almost every state-level education department to expand and improve their longitudinal data systems.

The link between the gradual expansion of SLDS and supra-state standardization policies also included the implementation of the *Common Core State Standards* (CCSS), as well as supra-state assessments (named PARCC and *Smarter Balanced*), which many states adopted around 2010 (for a more detailed explanation see Hartong, 2016b). Both not only "increase[sed] comparability of [test] results across states, but [...] enable[d] technology developers to build a range of digital media and tools that can be used in larger markets than was possible when each state had its own unique standards" (Pietry, 2013, p. 62).[6] In other words, while the market for digital state monitoring and the number of EdTech vendors exploded, the rise of standardization and interoperability initiatives triggered the creation of networks between EdTech vendors, state actors, and actors who operated as "intermediaries of standardization" (e.g., the NCES in the CEDS initiative).

Philanthropic organizations, such as the Bill and Melinda Gates Foundation as well as the Broad and Dell Foundations, began promoting SLDS in 2005, while also heavily investing in the promotion of EdTech for state monitoring and the development of data interoperability standards. They did so either directly as "venture philanthropists" (Reckhow, 2013) or indirectly by funding think tanks, non-profits, and businesses (as the *Chan Zuckerberg Initiative*, see endnote 1; see also Lubienski, Brewer, & La Londe, 2016, p. 4). In both cases they operated either individually or as part of multi-philanthropy networks.

One organization created through these joint investments was the *Data Quality Campaign* (DQC), which was first run by 14 partner organizations (DQC, 2017, p. 6), before transforming into an independent non-profit in 2011. Using the corporate world as a role model (DQC, 2017, p. 2), the DQC started to systematically invest in "making data sexy" to get "people other than specialists to become passionate champions for the power of data to transform education into a personalized, results-focused endeavor" (DQC, 2017, p. 1). Exemplary DQC initiatives included the so-called 10 State Actions and the "10 Elements of 'good' State Longitudinal Data Systems," which fostered supra-state alignment and stronger digitalization of state monitoring systems. Both programs integrated unique student identifiers and annual disaggregated measurements of student academic growth.

Despite initiatives such as CEDS and DQC, large parts of the growing EdTech market for state monitoring systems remained legally unregulated in the first decade of the twenty-first century. After 2013, this problem of unmonitored profit-making resulted in a number of data misuse scandals affecting student data security in particular, triggering not only a wave of public demands for stronger legal regulations but also the shutdown of providers or programs, such as the cross-state data sharing initiative *InBloom* (see also Lingard, in this volume).[7]

A wave of new state laws and federal initiatives responded to the growing public skepticism of EdTech vendors in the years that followed, resulting not only in stronger market regulation but also more accurate supra-state data and data system standards as an indicator of quality assurance (see also Herman, 2016). While increased public regulation of EdTech providers now successfully restricted certain market practices, the resulting standardization not only led to an expanding market for standards-aligned monitoring tools but also a new sub-market for different standards and interoperability frameworks (for an overview see http://www.setda.org/wp-content/uploads/2013/12/SETDA_standardsandinitiatives_May2013.pdf). Interoperability and standardization for SLDS was further promoted by federal initiatives such as the 2015 reauthorization of the *No Child Left Behind* Act (now named *Every Student Succeeds Act*) and the *National Education Technology Plan* (2016/2017).

This emerging market for standardization is interesting for two reasons. First, it opened up a different, more indirect means for global providers to shape the US EdTech market and compete with national providers such as the *ed-fi Alliance*, funded by the Dell Foundation, www.ed-fi.org.[8] One example of such a provider is the Gates Foundation funded *Access 4 Learning* Initiative (www.a4l.org), formerly known as the *SIF-Association*. *Access 4 Learning* is a non-profit operating in countries such as Australia and the UK, fostering a global standardization and interoperability of data systems in every domestic market it operates.

However, it is even more significant that the market for data standards and interoperability frameworks is itself an *intermediary* market of cross-sectoral networks, simultaneously addressing state actors and EdTech vendors as partners. These vendors, whose number is a subject of competitive interest, market products such as system monitoring tools. The contest between these networks not only resulted in an "allusion of connection to and endorsement from those who are listed as advisors [and partners] of the project" (Hogan, Sellar, & Lingard, 2016, p. 249) but also in various strategies to sell network participation to businesses.[9]

The rising level of standardization has also led to an increase in so-called all-in-one-solutions, sold to state departments by monitoring system vendors. As an example, the for-profit *Infinite Campus* offers a highly interoperable system to state and district departments which includes "tools to track both student and staff data across the state, as well as the nation" (www.infinitecampus.com). As with the DQC, such vendors promote "personalized learning" through maximized interoperability and real-time data exchange (see also Beer, 2017).

# More Data, More Standards, No (Heavy) Commodification (Yet): The Transformation of State Monitoring Systems in Germany Between 2001 and 2017[10]

It was not until the so-called *Konstanz Resolution*, which approved participation in the *Trends in International Mathematics and Science Study* (TIMSS), as well as the *Programme for International Student Assessment* (PISA) in the late 1990s, that Germany started to collect large-scale performance data. German states had traditionally governed education by providing input resources based on long-term requirement planning, which built on very different and often fragmented statistics, excluding any kind of student performance data.

However, as has been covered extensively elsewhere (Hartong, 2015; Niemann, 2010; Tillmann, Dedering, Kneuper, Kuhlmann, & Nessel, 2008), the so-called PISA-shock led to short-term, yet far-reaching, reform programs assembled around a performance-oriented national monitoring strategy led by the *Standing Conference of the Ministers of Education and Cultural Affairs of the Länder in the Federal Republic of Germany* (*Kultusministerkonferenz* [KMK]) (KMK, 2006). The KMK created nationally centralized standards and standardized assessments around the same time as the supra-state *Common Core State Standards* and the PARCC/*Smarter Balanced* assessments in the US (Hartong, 2015).

Like *No Child left Behind* (2001), the German national monitoring strategy categorically shifted the focus toward performance output, which demanded more detailed reporting of what was happening inside different states, districts, and schools. Two KMK resolutions, the so-called *Minimal Data Catalogue* (*Minimalkatalog*) in 2000 and the *Core Data Set* (*Kerndatensatz*) in 2003, urged states for the first time in German history to record and report a defined amount of nationally standardized, partly individualized data on schools, students, and teachers (KMK, 2003).[11] However, unlike the US these reports did not include disaggregated test data, which instead remained in the schools, nor was it accompanied by high-stakes accountability practices.[12]

In 2004 the KMK founded the *Institute for Educational Quality Improvement* (*Institut für Qualitätssicherung im Bildungswesen*, IQB), which in the following years not only implemented the first national comparative study of aggregated, sample-based state performance data but also played a major role in standardizing state-internal testing practices. Since then the IQB has become an increasingly important data collection agency (Hartong, 2018a). Other data platforms followed, including the website *bildungsbericht.de*, hosted by the *German Institute for International Educational Research* (DIPF), which collects information on the educational monitoring reports of every German state and district where data is available.

Despite the KMK's leading role as a national voice for state education ministers, the expansion of monitoring infrastructures through increased datafication and digitalization entailed stronger influence for the *Federal Department of Education* (*Bundesministerium für Bildung und Forschung*, BMBF). This growing engagement included a range of BMBF programs to foster the expansion and standardization of district-level monitoring practices and cross-district data sharing (Wilkoszewski & Sundby, 2014, p. 19). The BMBF operated as reform consultants to foster partnerships between districts and philanthropies, while creating a competitive environment for federal funding.

The BMBF also provided resources to strengthen empirical research networks in the field of large-scale data collection. One example was the 2009 establishment of the *National Educational Panel Study* (NEPS), comparable to the SLDS in the US. The NEPS was nested within a network of more than 20 large German research institutions to track individual competency development from the pre-elementary sector thru adult education. The growing role of the BMBF was given further momentum by two alterations of German federal law in 2006 and 2009 which, while reinforcing states autonomy in the education sector, permitted federal-state (BMBF-KMK) cooperation, while including joint financing of educational monitoring (2006) and digitalization (2009).

Despite a similar policy pattern of datafication, digitalization, standardization, and "nationalization," the German reforms, for now, are less commodity-oriented than the US reforms. Instead data protection has been strict in terms of public access, rankings centralization, and interoperability of databases. Even the majority of data collected in national IQB assessments remains within the states. In an environment of low-stakes accountability, German state departments felt a lot less pressure than their US counterparts to transform their data systems quickly, or turn to for-profit vendors promising fast data management solutions to "boost" student performance (Beer, 2017). Though centralization and expansion of data systems at the state level, including greater amounts of performance data, has developed slowly, it has also proceeded sustainably, particularly since 2013. The result is a growing number of businesses, which traditionally developed school data management systems that now also work with the state to create more efficient monitoring practices to foster interoperability and disaggregated performance data for personalized output-based decision-making[13] (see also Klesmann, 2017).

Though markets for data standards and interoperability have yet to evolve to the extent they have in the US, intermediary organizations, such as *Dataport* (www.dataport.de) or the *IT-Planungsrat* (www.it-planungsrat.de), monitor interstate system transfers, harmonizing network engagement of statistical offices at the state and national level (*Statistisches Bundesamt*; *Statistische Landesämter*).

While the period between 2000 and 2012 was largely characterized by the implementation of a multi-level, partly standardized education monitoring infrastructure, both KMK and BMBF aggressively turned toward educational digitalization after 2013. Once more associated with disappointing assessment results in an international large-scale assessment (the *International Computer and Information Literacy Study*, www.iea.nl/icils), major national programs now foster digital education. One outstanding example is the BMBF-led *Education Offensive for the Digital Knowledge Society* (*Bildungsoffensive für die digitale Wissensgesellschaft*) 2016, which included the *Digital Pact* (*Digitalpakt*) between BMBF and KMK. BMBF has not only taken a leading role in setting up this new agenda, it has explicitly fostered partnerships with businesses. Two examples of businesses which have become directly involved in the new federal agenda setting are *Bitkom*, an association of "more than 2,500 companies in the digital economy, [...] almost all global players" (www.bitkom.org/EN/About-us/index-EN.html), and the *Hasso-Plattner-Institute*, a business-research center founded by SAP-head Hasso Plattner (https://hpi.de/).

Even though these programs have so far been mainly concerned with digitalizing classroom practices, their involvement in shaping policies is a crucial turning point. Another example is the as yet under-researched *Digital Education Pact* (*Digitaler Bildungspakt*, http://digitaler-bildungspakt.de), founded by Microsoft in 2015, which over the past three years has been building a powerful lobbying network around digital businesses and cross-scale public agencies. It remains to be seen how these shifting network structures will develop in the coming years.

## Comparative Conclusions

Comparative analysis reveals both important similarities and crucial differences between the recent datafication and digitalization of state education monitoring systems in the US and Germany (Table 8.1):

In both countries, the transformation of state-level monitoring systems is closely related to the gradual rise of standardization policies, such as the implementation of supra-state education standards, standardized tests, common data system standards, and interoperability frameworks. Even though sub-national heterogeneity of state monitoring systems has remained a key characteristic of both systems, it has dramatically diminished over the past 15 years. Standardization was not only driven by a rising awareness of how data could be used to improve education but also to commodification (Fig. 8.1) of that data through a gradual expansion of global markets for "standards-aligned" (partly globally distributed) products to enhance competitiveness, as well as increasingly competitive cross-scale and cross-sector networks to promote standards.

Particularly in the US, the ongoing transformation of state-level monitoring systems has been framed by several forms of direct or indirect commodification, including outside contracting, sponsorship, information assemblages of for-profit data, as well as data mediation services (Hartong, 2016a; Sellar & Thompson, 2016, pp. 1–5). While such state-level monitoring practices are so far less influential in Germany, they are becoming increasingly prevalent, driven by the new digital agenda. It may very well be that what has already happened in the US will ultimately also take place in Germany.

Table 8.1 Policies around the transformation of state-level education monitoring systems in the US and Germany between 2001 and 2017

| Indicators | US | Germany |
|---|---|---|
| Important laws and initiatives | No Child Left Behind Act (2001), Education Science Reform Act (2002), Statewide Longitudinal Data Systems (SLDS) Grant Program (since 2005), Common Education Data Standards (CEDS) initiative (2009), American Recovery and Reinvestment Act/Race to the Top (2009), Common Core State Standards/PARCC and Smarter Balanced Assessments (around 2010), Every Student Succeeds Act (ESSA) (2016), National Education Technology Plan (2016/2017) | Konstanz Resolution (1997), National Education Standards (2002), KMK Minimal Catalogue and Core Data Set (2001 and 2003), Implementation IQB (2004), National Monitoring Strategy (since 2006), federal law reforms (2006 and 2009), Education Offensive for the Digital Knowledge Society/Digital Pact (2016) |
| Important policy network actors (other than state departments) | Federal Department of Education, National Governors Association (NGA), Council of Chief State School Officers (CCSSO), State Educational Technology Directors Association (SETDA), National Center for Education Statistics (NCES), Data Quality Campaign (DQC), Foundations such as the Gates and Dell Foundation, Access 4 Learning/ed-fi alliance (interoperability frameworks providers) | KMK, Federal Department of Education, Institute for Educational Quality improvement (IQB), IT-Planungsrat, Dataport, statistical offices at the state and national level (+involved in wider digital agenda: Bitkom, Hasso-Plattner-Institute, Digital Education Pact Network) |
| Level of data regulation and drive for interoperability/ transparency | Medium/high data transparency and growing interoperability, many data sources, after 2013 rising level of regulations | Low transparency, (still) few data sources, strict regulations, after 2011 still (slowly) rising level of interoperability and data transparency |
| Level of commodification | High | Low (yet increasing) |

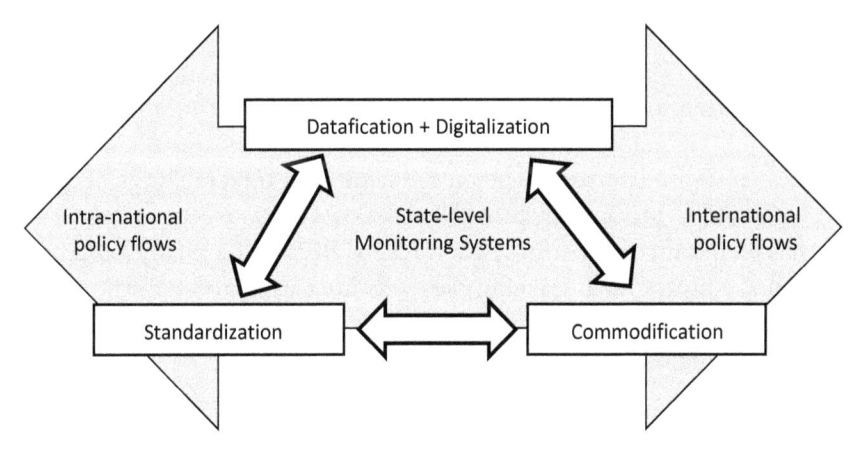

Fig. 8.1 Framing the ongoing transformation of state-level monitoring systems

Or it might not, if we consider the following:

1. While the US system is characterized by a high level of state and district autonomy (Kirst, 2004, p. 16), educational authority in Germany has traditionally been much more state centered. Because districts have less autonomy than the federal government, the federal role is less fragile than in the US where local boards decide where to put funding (see also Niemann, Hartong, & Martens, 2018). Even though powerful supra-state bodies, such as the NGA or the CCSSO, have also emerged in the US, they still operate within complex bargaining networks between national, state, and local actors. Their declarations of intent depend on the willingness to adopt them at the state and district levels. Ultimately, these diverging systems of power decentralization have not only directly affected the regulations around datafication but also questions of funding and, consequently, commodification.
2. Distinct scopes of "intermediary" policy influence by private actors are closely related to these differing finance structures. Whereas the US has checks and balances, as evidenced by continuous bargaining processes and enormous private sector influence (Honig, 2004; Lubienski et al., 2016), education policy in Germany is more hierarchical, characterized by administrative decision-making with major

interest groups institutionally embedded at every stage of law making (Hepp, 2011).
3. In addition to power decentralization and private actor influence, the US and Germany also feature different testing cultures. While in the former we find a strong belief in the value of testing, rankings, and the expertise of private test providers (Sacks, 1999), the latter has been placed its faith more strongly in teachers. Because Germany has established a professional teaching class who are trusted to teach and assess themselves autonomously, Germans are more skeptical of standardized testing and public rankings.

Along with timing, these distinctions explain the distinct modes of datafying, digitalizing, and state-level monitoring in the US versus and Germany, as described in sections "More Data, More Standards, Increasing Commodification: The Transformation of State Education Monitoring Systems in the US Between 2001 and 2017" and "More Data, More Standards, No (Heavy) Commodification (Yet): The Transformation of State Monitoring Systems in Germany Between 2001 and 2017". This contextual embeddedness is highly relevant for explaining relationships that are facilitated within intra-national policy spaces. Even though a growing number of scholars convincingly argue against nationalist, or level- and scale-based policy analysis (e.g., Ball, 2016; Robertson & Dale, 2015), the local differences between the US and Germany are important comparative factors. Alongside the necessity to more closely observe the complex interplay between datafication/digitalization, standardization, and commodification, it is essential to continuously examine the multifaceted meaning of "the national" in an environment of increasingly mobile policy spatialization.

# Final Remarks

Research on educational datafication and digitalization has been criticized for "assuming that technology is neutral," or failing to ask "who has power" (Emejulu & McGregor, 2016, p. 3, as cited in Macgilchrist, 2018, p. 1). Critical policy network analysis is important to better understanding the manifold ways power has become (re-)distributed around datafication and digitalization and fostered the rise of a GEI (Verger, Lubienski, & Steiner-Khamsi, 2016). I have provided only a few insights into the powerful new horizontal and vertical relations which have been emerging around the recent transformation of state-level monitoring systems in the US and Germany, which have opened up different gateways and intensities of direct or indirect commodification.

These changes have rarely been characterized by linear power shifts. Instead, it is difficult to draw a clear line between the public and private sector, or between pedagogic and economic narratives framing current policy network transformations. Building on Macgilchrist's (2018) argument that privatization is not *opposed to*, but *entangled with*, classic conceptions of good education, we need to better understand the transformations of "good" datafied and digitalized education, or school administration and state-level school leadership. In fact, students and teachers have not only become more directly exposed to the observations of EdTech providers but also to the continuous, often nationally obliged intervention of state departments, which are expected to use a maximum amount of data for fast decision-making (Beer, 2017). As a result, in the past 15 years state departments in both countries have massively transformed their institutional structure by increasingly concentrating on efficient data management and effective data mediation. In other words, Fenwick and Edwards' (2016, p. 117) diagnosis that data and the orientation toward data "[...] are increasingly pervasive in the governing, leadership and practices of different professional groups," can be observed in school supervision, which has become gradually rearranged around "practices of sorting, naming, numbering, comparing, listing, and calculating" (Lury, Parisi, & Terranova, 2012, p. 3). The practices in which change has become normalized (Lury et al., 2012, p. 5), active leadership has dominated passive administration, and the power of EdTech is barely called into question.

# Notes

1. As an example, the Bill and Melinda Gates Foundation (related to the Microsoft corporation) recently announced a new collaborate investment in EdTech (total US$12 million) together with the Chan

Zuckerberg Initiative (related to the Facebook corporation), which was given to the venture philanthropy organization *New Profit* (http://www.newprofit.org) as an intermediary investor, which then gave investments (US$1 million each) plus "extensive management advising" to seven organizations "working to promote personalized learning through education technology" (Herold, 2017). However, before launching the new program, the Chan Zuckerberg Initiative had already given money to institutions such as the *College Board* (a non-profit, which in the US is, e.g., administering the *Scholastic Aptitude Test*, SAT), or to networks of state and district leaders that engaged in EdTech reforming. Different from a non-profit, "the organizational structure [of the Chan Zuckerberg Initiative] allows for direct investment in for-profit companies and political lobbying and donations, as well as philanthropic giving. It also limits the extent to which the group is legally required to publicly report on its activities" (Herold, 2017).

2. Building on Mayer-Schönberger and Cukier (2013, p. 78), "datafication" stands for the quantification of things, while "digitalization" refers to the conversion of analog information into a binary computer code.

3. These insights are related to an ongoing project, funded by the *German Research Foundation* (DFG, project number HA 7367/2-1), which seeks to improve the understanding of digital-era governance and the role of data management in education within the federal contexts of Germany and the US. The project includes analyses of (1) policy material, such as monitoring regulations, resolutions or digitalization/datafication programs (ongoing), (2) the actors and institutions involved in performance data management at national and state level (ongoing), (3) the performance data infrastructures and their modes of operation in three selected states per country (scheduled for 2018), and (4) interviews with national- and state-level policy actors, technicians, administrators, and data system companies (scheduled for 2018).

4. Organizations include the *Organization for Economic Co-operation and Development* (OECD), and one example of a vendor can be found at www.oecd.org/education-industry-summit

5. This chapter also uses the term "state" to refer to the German *Laender*.

6. For a more detailed description of the CCSS, PARCC, and Smarter Balanced, see Hartong (2016b).

7. *InBloom* was a nation-wide acting non-profit "[...] that offered a data warehouse solution designed to help public schools embrace the promise of personalized learning by helping teachers integrate seamlessly the number of applications they use in their day-to-day teaching" (Horn, 2014), and which had received over US$100 million from the Gates and Carnegie Foundations. Building on Bulger, McCormick, and Pitcan (2017), p. 2), InBloom ideal typically represented the pent-up clash between Silicon valley style software solutions, which the exploding EdTech market had triggered, and more cautious datafication approaches of state and school districts as well as the wider public.
8. The DQC, for example, decided to work with *ed-fi* and promoting their standards to vendors and state actors.
9. For example, the SETDA promotes business partnerships as a "unique opportunity for meaningful engagement with State Members throughout the year including significant participation in multiple networking events." These include "joint developments of reports and case studies" and "tailored promotions" (www.setda.org/partners/private-sector). Similar to SETDA, the Consortium for School Networking (CoSN), an association for school system technology leaders, offers different sponsorship packages ranging from platinum to bronze, and funds sponsor sessions and leadership initiatives (these sessions and initiatives currently cost $5000 and $12,000, respectively). Even though CoSN claims its initiatives are vendor neutral, it offers sponsors the opportunity to participate in the advisory panel, so that they can participate in "helping to shape direction and focus by identifying best practices, tools, resources, webinars, presentations, and case studies" (CoSN, 2017, p. 8).
10. This section partly builds on online research provided by my project colleague Annina Förschler, whom I would like to thank very much.
11. It seems important to note that only the *Minimal Catalogue* was obligatory for the states, while the *Core Data Set*, which was including individual data, was passed as a recommendation to the states.
12. This, however, may change in the future.
13. See, for example, the provider ISB AG/the edoo.sys system, which is currently used in Rhineland-Palatinate, Bavaria and Baden-Wuerttemberg, for example, www.svp-rlp.de/projektinformationen/hintergrund.html; or ascaion/the product Edunite, www.ascaion.com/download/20140509_Leistungsbeschreibung_edunite.pdf

# References

Allen, J. (2011). Topological Twists: Power's Shifting Geographies. *Dialogues in Human Geography, 1*(3), 283–298.
Allen, J., & Cochrane, A. (2010). Assemblages of State Power: Topological Shifts in the Organization of Government and Politics. *Antipode, 42*(5), 1071–1089.
Anagnostopoulos, D., Rutledge, S. A., & Jacobsen, R. (Eds.). (2013). *The Infrastructure of Accountability. Data Use and the Transformation of American Education.* Cambridge, MA: Harvard University Press.
Ball, S. J. (2009). Academies in Context: Politics, Business and Philanthropy and Heterarchical Governance. *Management in Education, 23*(3), 100–103.
Ball, S. J. (2012). *Global Education Inc.: New Policy Networks and the Neo-liberal Imaginary.* New York: Routledge.
Ball, S. J. (2016). Following Policy: Networks, Network Ethnography and Education Policy Mobilities. *Journal of Education Policy, 31*(5), 549–566.
Ball, S. J., & Junemann, J. (2012). *Networks, New Governance and Education.* Bristol, UK: Policy Press.
Beer, D. (2017). The Data Analytics Industry and the Promises of Real-Time Knowing: Perpetuating and Deploying a Rationality of Speed. *Journal of Cultural Economy, 10*(1), 21–33.
Breiter, A., Grönert, T., & Lange, A. (2014). *Schulverwaltungssoftware in den Bundesländern 2014.* Bremen, Germany: ifib.
Bulger, M., McCormick, P., & Pitcan, M. (2017, February 2). *The Legacy of InBloom* (Data & Society Working Paper). New York: Data & Society.
Center on Education Policy (CEP). (2002). *A New Federal Role in Education.* Washington, DC: CEP.
Clarke, J., Bainton, D., Lendvai, N., & Stubbs, P. (Eds.). (2015). *Making Policy Move: Towards a Politics of Translation and Assemblage.* Chicago: Policy Press.
CoSN. (2017). *Sponsorship Opportunities* (pp. 2017–2018). Washington, DC: CoSN.
Courtney, S. J. (2015). Corporatised Leadership in English Schools. *Journal of Educational Administration and History, 47*(3), 214–231.
Data Quality Campaign (DQC). (2017). *From Hammer to Flashlight. A Decade of Data in Education.* Washington, DC: DQC.
Emejulu, A., & Mcgregor, C. (2016). Towards a Radical Digital Citizenship in Digital Education. *Critical Studies in Education*, 1–17.

Fenwick, T., & Edwards, R. (2016). Exploring the Impact of Digital Technologies on Professional Responsibilities and Education. *European Educational Research Journal, 15*(1), 117–131.
Hartong, S. (2015). Global Policy Convergence Through 'Distributed Governance'? The Emergence of 'National' Education Standards in the US and Germany. *Journal of International and Comparative Social Policy, 31*(1), 10–33.
Hartong, S. (2016a). Between Assessments, Digital Technologies, and Big Data: The Growing Influence of 'Hidden' Data Mediators in Education. *European Educational Research Journal, 15*(5), 523–536.
Hartong, S. (2016b). New Structures of Power and Regulation Within 'Distributed' education Policy—The Example of the US Common Core State Standards Initiative. *Journal of Education Policy, 31*(2), 213–225.
Hartong, S. (2018a). Towards a Topological Re-assemblage of Education Policy? Observing the Implementation of Performance Data Infrastructures and 'Centers of Calculation' in Germany. *Globalisation, Societies and Education, 16*(1), 134–150.
Hartong, S. (2018b). *Bildungsstandardisierung in den USA. Vergessene Ursprünge und aktuelle Transformationen.* Weinheim, Germany: Juventa.
Hartong, S., Hermstein, B., & Höhne, T. (Eds.). (2018). *Ökonomisierung von Schule? Aktuelle Transformationen des schulischen Feldes in nationaler und internationaler Perspektive.* Weinheim, Germany: Juventa.
Heinrich, M., & Kohlstock, B. (Eds.). (2016). *Ambivalenzen des Ökonomischen: Analysen zur „Neuen Steuerung" im Bildungssystem.* Wiesbaden, Germany: VS Verlag.
Hepp, G. F. (2011). *Bildungspolitik in Deutschland. Eine Einführung.* Wiesbaden, Germany: VS Verlag.
Herman, M. (2016, January 13). Data Dashboards a High Priority in National Ed-Tech Plan. *Education Week.*
Herold, B. (2017, June 21). Gates, Zuckerberg Teaming Up on Personalized Learning. *Education Week.*
Hogan, A., Sellar, S., & Lingard, B. (2016). Commercialising Comparison: Pearson Puts the TLC in Soft Capitalism. *Journal of Education Policy, 31*(3), 243–258.
Honig, M. I. (2004). The New Middle Management: Intermediary Organizations in Education Policy Implementation. *Educational Evaluation and Policy Analysis, 26*(1), 65–87.

Horn, M. (2014, December 4). InBloom's Collapse Offers Lessons for Innovation in Education. *Forbes*.
Kirst, M. W. (2004). Turning Points: A History of American School Governance. In N. Epstein (Ed.), *Who's in Charge Here? The Tangled Web of School Governance and Policy* (pp. 14–41). Washington, DC: Brookings Institution Press.
Klesmann, M. (2017, October 21, 22). Handeln nach Zahlen. Schulleiter sollen mit Hilfe interner Daten ihre Schulen besser machen. Jedes Jahr soll die Schulaufsicht die Ergebnisse kontrollieren. *Berliner Zeitung*, p. 11.
KMK. (2003). *Kerndatensatz (KDS) für schulstatistische Individualakten der Länder. Beschluss der Kultusministerkonferenz vom 8. 5. 2003*. Berlin, Germany: KMK.
KMK. (2006). *Gesamtstrategie der Kultusministerkonferenz zum Bildungsmonitoring*. München, Germany: Luchterhand/KMK.
Koyama, J. P. (2011). Generating, Comparing, Manipulating, Categorizing: Reporting, and Sometimes Fabricating Data to Comply with the No Child Left Behind Mandates. *Journal of Education Policy, 26*(5), 701–720.
Lewis, S., & Lingard, B. (2015). The Multiple Effects of International Large-Scale Assessment on Education Policy and Research. *Discourse: Studies in the Cultural Politics of Education, 36*(5), 621–637.
Lubienski, C., Brewer, T. J., & La Londe, P. G. (2016). Orchestrating Policy Ideas: Philanthropies and Think Tanks in US Education Policy Advocacy Networks. *The Australian Educational Researcher, 43*(1), 55–73.
Lury, C., Parisi, L., & Terranova, T. (2012). Introduction: The Becoming Topological of Culture. *Theory, Culture & Society, 29*(4–5), 3–35.
Macgilchrist, F. (2018, forthcoming). Discourse, Digital Education and the Teacher: Driving Change in Educational Technology. *Culture-Society-Education*.
Mayer-Schönberger, V., & Cukier, K. (2013). *Big Data. Die Revolution, die unser Leben verändern wird*. München, Germany: Redline.
Niemann, D. (2010). Turn of the Tide—New Horizons in German Education Policymaking Through IO Influence. In K. Martens, A.-K. Nagel, & M. Windzio (Eds.), *Transformation of Education Policy* (pp. 77–104). Basingstoke, UK: Palgrave Macmillan.
Niemann, D., Hartong, S., & Martens, K. (2018). Observing Local Dynamics of ILSA Projections: A Comparison Between Germany and the U.S. *Globalisation, Societies and Education* (forthcoming).
Pietry, P. J. (2013). *Assessing the Educational Data Movement*. New York: Teacher College Press.

Ravitch, D. (2010). *The Death and Life of the Great American School System: How Testing and Choice Are Undermining Education*. New York: Basic Books.
Reckhow, S. (2013). *Follow the Money: How Foundation Dollars Change Public School Politics*. Oxford: Oxford University Press.
Roberts-Mahoney, H., Means, A. J., & Garrison, M. J. (2016). Netflixing Human Capital Development: Personalized Learning Technology and the Corporatization of K-12 Education. *Journal of Education Policy, 31*(4), 405–420.
Robertson, S. L., & Dale, R. (2015). Towards a 'Critical Cultural Political Economy' Account of the Globalising of Education. *Globalisation, Societies and Education, 13*(1), 149–170.
Sacks, P. (1999). *Standardized Minds: The High Price of America's Testing Culture and What We Can Do to Change It*. New York: Perseus Books.
Savage, G. C., & O'Connor, K. (2015). National Agendas in Global Times: Curriculum Reforms in Australia and the USA Since the 1980s. *Journal of Education Policy, 30*(5), 609–630.
Sellar, S., & Thompson, G. (2016). The Becoming-Statistic: Information Ontologies and Computerized Adaptive Testing in Education. *Cultural Studies? Critical Methodologies, 16*(5), 491–501.
Shulman, R. (2017, May 17). Global Ed-Tech Investments and Outlook: 10 Ed-Tech Companies You Should Know About. *Forbes*.
Steiner-Khamsi, G., & Waldow, F. (Eds.). (2012). *Policy Borrowing and Lending in Education. World Yearbook of Education*. London: Routledge.
Tillmann, K. J., Dedering, K., Kneuper, D., Kuhlmann, C., & Nessel, I. (2008). *PISA als bildungspolitisches Ereignis: Fallstudien in vier Bundesländern*. Wiesbaden, Germany: VS Verlag.
US Department of Education. (2012). *Enhancing Teaching and Learning Through Educational Data Mining and Learning Analytics: An Issue Brief*. Washington, DC: US Department of Education.
Verger, A., Fontdevila, C., & Zancajo, A. (2016). *The Privatization of Education: A Political Economy of Global Education Reform*. New York: Teachers College Press.
Verger, A., Lubienski, C., & Steiner-Khamsi, G. (2016). *World Yearbook of Education 2016: The Global Education Industry*. London: Routledge.
Wilkoszewski, H., & Sundby, E. (2014). *Steering from the Centre: New Modes of Governance in Multi-level Education Systems* (OECD Education Working Papers, 109). Paris: OECD.
Williamson, B. (2016a). Boundary Brokers: Mobile Policy Networks, Database Pedagogies, and Algorithmic Governance in Education. In T. Ryberg,

C. Sinclair, S. Bayne, & M. de Laat (Eds.), *Research, Boundaries, and Policy in Networked Learning* (pp. 41–57). Cham, Switzerland: Springer.

Williamson, B. (2016b). Silicon Startup Schools: Technocracy, Algorithmic Imaginaries and Venture Philanthropy in Corporate Education Reform. *Critical Studies in Education, 59*(2), 1–19.

Williamson, B. (2016c). Digital Methodologies of Education Governance: Pearson Plc and the Remediation of Methods. *European Educational Research Journal, 15*(1), 34–53.

Williamson, B. (2017). Learning in the 'Platform Society': Disassembling an Educational Data Assemblage. *Research in Education, 98*(1), 59–82.

# 9

# International Education Hubs as Competitive Advantage: Investigating the Role of the State as Power Connector in the Global Education Industry

Marvin Erfurth

## Introduction

Public education systems developed in close relationship with modern nation states. Over the past three centuries, education for the masses has been predominantly state-sponsored and became a crucial tool in the nation-building efforts of states competing and collaborating in the international system. Education researchers have long studied different explanations for these developments, the varying shapes national education systems have taken (cf. Archer, 1979; Benavot, Resnik, & Corrales, 2006; Green, 1997; Ramirez & Boli, 1987), as well as their role in bringing about national identity and citizenship (Zajda, 2009; see also Anderson, 1991; Heller, Sosna, & Wellbery, 1986). Today, traveling policy ideas stimulate a global circulation of similar concepts across geographical

---

M. Erfurth (✉)
Institute of Education, University of Münster, Münster, Germany
e-mail: m.erfurth@wwu.de

© The Author(s) 2019
M. Parreira do Amaral et al. (eds.), *Researching the Global Education Industry*,
https://doi.org/10.1007/978-3-030-04236-3_9

regions so that a small number (such as the knowledge-based economy) increasingly undergird education policies in most national education systems (cf. Dale, 2015). This change in the practice of education policy is accompanied by a growing strand of study more recently coined Global Education Policy (GEP) research (cf. Mundy, Green, Lingard, & Verger, 2016). This research focuses on globalizing discourses, agendas, and actors in the study of education policy to investigate the various implications of the changing contextual conditions in which education policy evolves, such as the influence of intricate relationships between domestic and foreign actors on national education policy (cf. Marginson, 2016; Verger, 2016; see also Ball, Junemann, & Santori, 2017).

Amidst the changing contextual conditions for education policy, in which policies are increasingly authored by diverse actors in multiple locales at the same time, particularly business-driven environments for providing mass education seem to prevail. In these environments, the state often only provides seed funding to establish a school or university, but institutions must become self-sustaining to stay in business. The state as a sponsor of mass education slowly but steadily vanishes in some parts of the developed world, having potentially profound implications for education provision and research. In those regions, the historically established monopolies of states providing education for the masses through different varieties of subsidizing, are, for better or worse, slowly disappearing, potentially leading to—and being the result of—an arguably changing role of the state in education.

Instigated by the dominance of concepts informed by economic thinking in education policy circulating in globalizing discourses, GEP research contemporarily shifts attention to the role of education in the world economy. What comes more and more to the fore through *Global Education Industry* (GEI) research as a dedicated perspective within GEP is not only a growing global business in education, but more intriguingly a booming business *with* education. In globalizing policy discourses, education's role in the global economy is constantly portrayed as existential. Indeed, several colleagues have pointed out the relation of this invocation to (selective interpretations of) the knowledge-based economy concept, in which education is often seen as a panacea for pressing issues. At least discursively, education has become a crucial component of the global economy—or, as some scholars would put it, an extra-economic factor, a factor that determines economic competitiveness (cf. Sum & Jessop, 2013, pp. 261–295). Evidence for perceiving education as a direct component of the global economy may be found in the growing use of financial instruments and processes of abstraction for generating profits *with* education and the development of a "globalized economic sector" in education (cf. Verger, Lubienski, & Steiner-Khamsi, 2016). While the state remains the main authority for the governance and regulation of education, these changing policy contexts and a growing business *with* education contest the historical role of the state and its rationales for sponsoring mass education.

Inspired by the increasing number of emerging, undertheorized, and empirically understudied education policy developments in the new millennium, GEP scholars advocate for a re-reading of education policy as a research object (cf. Simons, Olssen, & Peters, 2009a, 2009b). One prominent approach to such a re-reading as part of GEP research examines complex global relations of state and non-state actors in network-like formations, and the effects of those formations on domestic education policy (cf. Ball et al., 2017). Conclusions drawn from applications of this approach for researching GEP often stress the increasing agency inscribed in such networks themselves, hypothetically leveling out power differences between state and non-state actors, with the state potentially losing its historical position as a primus inter pares for governing education. In this chapter, I challenge the belief that the state is becoming less relevant to the dynamics and effects of GEP by arguing that the state is rather changing its roles while remaining central, which makes it imperative to understand the shifting role of the state in new, emerging policy settings.

From this analytical perspective, the processes emphasized in GEI research highlighted in the introduction and conclusion of this volume as, for instance, *economization*, *commodification*, and *financialization* of education as outcomes of a growing business *with* education do not occur in dissociation, but are rather prompted by state finance- and competitiveness-driven reforms (see also: Jessop, 2017; Peters & Besley, 2015; Schwartzman, 2013; Spring, 2015; van der Zwan, 2014). I depart from the observation that the formation of a "globalized economic sector" in education in which corporations, foundations, and networks merge and interact is premised on the changing role of the state as "a key institution in the making, maintenance and modification of industry sectors" (Verger et al., 2016, p. 13). Studying the changing role of the state in education commands more attention to the potentially global dynamics and processes enabling the GEI to flourish, and of which the state may be the genuine enabler/driver.

I will discuss the emergence of International Education Hubs (IEHs) as an example of the changing role of the state in education in the United Arab Emirates (UAE), and deliberate on some of its potentially far-reaching implications for higher education policy. To do so I examine a key policy document for comprehending the UAE as an IEH, *Vision 2021*. As part of a large-scale politico-economic project, the organization of higher education in the UAE contemporarily becomes part of global interconnections of competition, cooperation, and conflict. From the perspective of International and Comparative Education, this phenomenon illustrates the increasing complexity of education policy, which may produce unforeseen, disruptive effects through the interplay between the "global" and "local." In the context of GEP research, IEHs provide an opportunity to study the intricate relations that constitute global discursive policy spaces. Arguably, changing relationships of higher education to society, state, and the (knowledge-based) economy generate far-reaching consequences, with profound implications for higher education policy and governance.

Against this backdrop, I will first elaborate on conceptual considerations for researching the changing role of the state in education by discussing the interplay of ideational and material aspects for analyzing education policy. I will then describe *Vision 2021* and review this policy by applying the conceptual considerations elaborated, illuminating a conception of the role of the state as a power connector for achieving a competitive advantage as an IEH. I conclude with some thoughts for further investigation as part of a continuing research project intended for contributing to ongoing dialogues for researching the GEI.

## Researching the Role of the State in the Global Education Industry: Conceptual Considerations

Changing contextual conditions for policy making in education have recently led to the emergence of GEP research as an analytical tool for understanding education policy in these new settings. In this section, I discuss GEP as an analytical lens for analyzing education policy in connection with changing contextual conditions, and elaborate the conceptual lenses for a sharpening of the categories used to explore it.

GEP sets out to address three different but intertwined analytical dimensions in investigating education policy as a practice in times of global interconnection: (1) contents and agendas; (2) institutional frameworks; (3) processes of coordinating national education systems with their institutions, practices, and effects.[1]

By extending the analytical perspective to account for global interconnections within local spaces, intricate social, economic, and cultural interdependencies can be discussed concerning their relevance to education systems through gradually differently formalized interactions between state and supranational levels. In particular, as an emerging research approach, current analyses in GEP research focus predominantly on discourses, agendas, and not least actors (inter-, trans-, and supranational) with global reach (cf. Mundy et al., 2016).

This particular analytical lens for examining education policy has merit because it addresses the object of study as being increasingly "shaped by social actors in disparate locations who exert incongruent amounts of influence over the design, implementation, and evaluation of policy" (Bartlett & Vavrus, 2017, pp. 1–2). Contemporary social science has more recently focused on topological rather than geographical conceptions and understandings of space to deal with the relationships of processes and developments in "disparate locations" that exert influence on local phenomena. For instance, just as a subway map ignores actual distances to create a schematic map of linked locations on a network, the increasing datafication of the social world provides the necessary information and data that can be linked to present the image of a reality that exists only in terms of the transmission of knowledge and information—

the creation of a rather topological instead of geographical mapping of the world. In relation, seemingly every aspect of our social world can be made "comparable," which, in education, has perhaps become most prominent in Programme for International Student Assessment (PISA) results relating student performance across the world. An analytical understanding of policy as a sociocultural practice is premised on relational conceptions of space, scale, and time (cf. Jessop, Brenner, & Jones, 2008; or more recently Robertson, 2018), wherein states act in a particular mode—or take on a changing role—by governing through relating.

States may arguably always have defined their purpose and justified their existence by achieving success in their territory in relation to other locales or groups, but now increasingly so by reforming education, which is comprehended as an extra-economic factor to achieve competitiveness in the global economy (cf. Jessop, Fairclough, & Wodak, 2008). Debates in the 1990s about the withering of the nation state in light of dichotomous theoretical frameworks such as "the national vs. the international" (Rhodes, 1994; Rosenau & Czempiel, 1992) conceptualized the state as a once vital "power container" whose influence was diminishing, and in particular was limited by its territorial reach (Bekke, Kickert, & Kooiman, 1995). However, more recent state-theoretical research shed new light on contemporary state formations that (analytically) function as the so-called power connectors—social entities managing global relations to provide optimal conditions for businesses and other entities to succeed in the global economy. As connectors rather than containers, states skip the lengthy process of developing entities locally, and may, for instance, instead attract outsiders whose skills and talent are currently valued in relentlessly changing environments (cf. Jessop, 2016). Through such ingenious interplays of public and private spheres, governments relativize their geographical position and developmental stage in the world by extending their opportunity structures (cf. Dale & Parreira do Amaral, 2015) throughout different combinations of territories, places, scales, and networks in strategically relational conceptions of space (cf. Jessop, 2016; Jessop et al., 2008; Jones & Jessop, 2010). Viewing contemporary state formations in these terms analytically enables us to see them as power connectors competing to combine their opportunity structures to achieve global reach and competitiveness, increasingly often pursuing economic growth and competitive advantages by reforming education. In the next section, I will discuss one example of this.

## International Education Hubs as a Social Phenomenon

A paradigmatic example of the effects of states as power connectors in education may be seen in policies pursuing the creation of the so-called IEHs. Several states, predominantly located in East Asia and the Middle East, currently use this label to market themselves as international destinations for learning. Analytically, IEHs are arguably a particular power-connector formation of states pursuing structural competitiveness in connection to their always-individual understandings of what knowledge-based economies are. In the growing body of literature about IEHs as a still relatively new social phenomenon, the vast amount of scientific inquiries too often takes the phenomenon as face value presented in strategy papers and mission statements. Often void of analytical lenses for critically engaging with existing policies, most research on the topic misses to study the phenomenon's potential implications. IEHs are to date mainly categorized in several different ways (for instance, as student, talent, or knowledge/innovation hubs, or also "acropolises" and "archipelagos"; cf. Knight, 2014; Lane & Kinser, 2011), distinguishing what is and what is not a hub, and is investigated as a new best practice model for governing and internationalizing higher education. The implications of the eminent growing business in and *with* education in IEHs, or the changing role of the state in education, are, however, only seldom addressed, and even less researched.

I argue that IEHs as a social phenomenon surfacing in diverse parts of the world provide vital opportunities for investigating the indicated changing role of the state in relation to emerging GEI research, in which states aim to connect global networks of, for instance, finance, manufacturing, research, and education within their territory as a hub. The term hub implies an understanding of the world as being composed of networks. Again, this view is premised on a topological understanding of relationships in the social world elucidated above. Unlike mere nodes on a network, hubs occupy a central position enabling them to be part of several networks simultaneously which they connect, making them more resilient and somewhat more competitive (on this topic, see, for instance, Barabási, 2003, 2014). Prominent education hub strategies position the state as a regional or global magnet for talent, academic excellence, and high-skilled labor, by balancing supply and demand of human capital. In this chapter, I regard IEHs as governmental politico-economic projects aiming at the transformation of selected territories into economically competitive and socially progressive areas by means of reforming education, in particular higher education. Here, the state paradigmatically acts as "a key institution in the making, maintenance and modification of industry sectors" (Verger et al., 2016, p. 13) through collaboration with global players offering expertise, experience, and other diverse factors for success that position such players as valuable, powerfully networked collaborators for the state, thus promising an invaluable competitive advantage.

The transformation of selected territories into economically competitive and socially progressive areas by means of reforming (higher) education involves material aspects, such as finance for the construction of schools and universities, as well as the creation of metrics, league tables, and rankings. However, what often remains disregarded in scholarly work on such reform processes are those practices of power accompanying and conditioning such material aspects. Ideational aspects are therefore co-constitutive to material ones. In her book about the intricate, often veiled relationships between infrastructure and power by investigating economic zones, broadband networks, and quality standards that Keller Easterling (2016) coins as *Extrastatecraft*, she emphasizes that:

> active forms [of infrastructure and power] are also social or narrative forms, and the designer can enhance the spatial consequences [...] with the non-spatial stories that accompany it. Just as the US suburban house was popularized in part through narratives about family and patriotism, a persuasion or ideology attached to a technology may deliver it to a ready audience or a powerful political machine. (ibid., p. 217)

Researching a changing role of the state in IEHs therefore involves exploring how the social phenomena coined IEHs are produced through, for instance, stories being told, generating processes of sense- and meaning-making for interpreting as well as shaping the world.

For such an analytical approach to researching education policy as a sociocultural practice in which material and ideational aspects are comprehended co-constitutively, the theoretical approach *Cultural Political Economy* (CPE) offers some unique features. From a CPE perspective, education policy is an activity that is culturally produced by political actors, market participants, and society at large, although governments usually take on the role of coordination. The so-called cultural turn in political economy is particularly relevant here as it opens the possibility to account for the powerful effects of ideas and concepts (as ideational aspects) in addition to material aspects (such as laws, trade agreements, or money). Sum and Jessop (2013) call the attribution of active power to ideational aspects of sense and meaning "semiosis," while they term their reflection about different forms of material-causality "structuration." Both semiosis and structuration are co-constitutive and equally relevant for analysis when acknowledging that people need to reduce the complexity of their environment to understand it. This process is accomplished through selective attributions of meaning that structure suitable, complexity-reduced environments through different "selectivities." These selectivities, which Sum and Jessop regard as discursive, agential, strategic, and technological, are mutually interdependent with semiosis and structuration. While semiosis and structuration condition selectivities, the selectivities, in turn, also condition semiosis and structuration in an ongoing, circular, emergent, and always dynamic process. The subjectivity of this process gives special recognition to the integration of ideational aspects into politico-economic analyses by conceiving them as co-constitutive with material aspects. Sum and Jessop address these mental processes as ubiquitous in our thinking, pointing to the relevance of dealing with complexity and cultural aspects in analyses of education policy.

Together semiosis, structuration, and selectivities create social, economic, and political imaginaries which reciprocally influence the aspects above (cf. Sum & Jessop, 2013). Social imaginaries are discursive-semiotic spaces of complexity reduction created in discourses, which consciously attribute particular importance to specific social, material, and temporal-geographical scopes for action. For instance, a political imaginary guiding organization might frame a "global education sector," just as new ideas about the way science influences business in a knowledge-based economy might create an economic imaginary impacting the organization of higher education. Although social imaginaries are mainly produced in discourses, they constitute theoretical and political frameworks for objectives, which thus become action-guiding outside such discourses as they are translated into somewhat formalized social structures such as policies. If a social imaginary is retained as a mechanism of "selection," "variation," and "retention" in CPE, it usually guides future political decisions; its retention, in turn, is also already influenced by prior decisions. Therefore, imaginaries are both path-dependent and path-shaping: though they are discursive-semiotic spaces created in discourses, their retention impacts physical spaces. Against this background, a CPE perspective provides a kind of circulatory lens for researching processes of understanding and shaping the world as inter-related, for which the co-constitutiveness of material and ideational aspects is key.

## Envisioning the United Arab Emirates as a Global Hub for Business Through Knowledge and Innovation: The Making of an International Education Hub

The elaborated conceptual framework provides one possibility for exploring the changing role of the state related to GEI research and may arguably be a contribution to the field for theorizing (global) education policy. From a CPE perspective, an increasing body of work focuses on the above explained material aspects of education hubs (cf. Fox & Al Shamisi, 2014; Mok & Bodycott, 2014; Sidhu, Ho, & Yeoh, 2014), and only a smaller portion on the narratives and relevance of ideational aspects. Due to the focus and scope of this chapter, I will only focus on the UAE as one prominent education hub by engaging with Vision 2021, launched in 2010, a central policy in its creation as a hub on which the elaborated framework will be applied in the next section. While some scholars would argue there is no underlying strategy for transforming the UAE into an

IEH, I will review the publicly available policy with a focus on laying this intention open. By using a discursive approach for investigating the policy (cf. Fairclough, 1992; Wodak, 2004; Wodak & Fairclough, 1997), it will provide insight into selective understandings of the world through sense- and meaning-making ("semiosis" and "selectivities"), revealing the changing role of the state in governing education as a power connector in the GEI.

*Vision 2021* has a traditional structure of reform strategies. The policy identifies certain developments as problematic and constructs specific aspects as issues before offering modifications to existing programs and the launch of additional initiatives for improvement of the current situation, as well as the achievement of overall goals (cf. Jungmann & Besio, 2018). The policy is divided into four themes beginning with a preface recounting the UAE's remarkable progress in recent decades, and the historical roots of this success. Its purpose is to unfold a vision for the UAE's Golden Jubilee in 2021, the achievement of which is described as potentially difficult due to challenges regarding the fabric of society, economic competitiveness, national identity, as well as "health, education, environment and well being." The policy's relevance is emphasized by stating that an "ambitious nation like ours cannot achieve its goals by relying on its past achievements. We must work harder, be more innovative, more organised, and more vigilant in examining the trends and challenges that will face us." Hence, the preface promises a problem analysis, but only provides this in one of the four themes—United in Knowledge—which I will cover in more detail later. As an overall goal of the policy, the preface describes the method of the policy as proactive for "bequeath[ing] to future generations a legacy worthy of the pioneers who founded our great nation, a legacy defined by prosperity, security, stability, and a life filled with dignity and respect." The overall slogan of the policy reflects this goal by stating "United in Ambition and Determination."

The following four themes of the policy share the same structure: First, a vision summary composed of a slogan and a short description. Second, a subdivision of leitmotifs with short descriptions, followed by vision statements elaborating the original hopes for the year 2021. The first theme is "United in Ambition and Responsibility," accompanied by the slogan, "An ambitious and confident nation grounded in its heritage."

Here, the focus is on the state and the society, while its leitmotifs cover the individual (confident and socially responsible Emiratis), the family (cohesive and prosperous families), the community (strong and active communities), and culture (vibrant culture) as a sort of fabric uniting individuals and families as a nation. Although a problem analysis is promised in the preface, it is interesting that this aspect is missing—not only in the first, but also in the following themes. What the themes do is describe in detail how the future is envisioned, such as "Ambitious and responsible Emiratis will successfully carve out their future, actively engaging in an evolving socio-economic environment, and drawing on their strong families and communities, moderate Islamic values, and deep-rooted heritage to build a vibrant and well-knit society" in theme one. In this aspect, the structure of the policy deviates from how it is outlined in its preface.

The second theme is "United in Destiny," whose slogan is "A strong union bonded by a common destiny." This theme focuses on the relationship between the seven Emirates and the national government, aiming for success through unity and cooperation. The leitmotifs address the centrality of the seven Emirates to the federation (upholding the legacy of the nation's Founding Fathers), the role of the national government (safe and secure nation), as well as their interrelationships for achieving unity while remaining open to the world (enhanced international standing). The third leitmotif emphasizes that the "UAE will enhance its pivotal role as a regional business hub whose essential infrastructure and institutions provide a gateway linking our neighbourhood to the world, serving as a role model for the region." It promises to "not slow the pace of its improvement. In the economic and government sphere, our nation will build on sectors of excellence to export its model abroad, while constantly evolving to create new competitive advantages." What comes to the fore is a competition-state as a connecting entity—a gateway to the world and regional business hub—that is being envisioned as one united nation composed of seven Emirates achieving this goal through cooperation.

The third theme, "United in Knowledge" with the slogan "A Competitive Economy Driven by Knowledgeable and Innovative Emiratis" is one that commands some deviation when describing it. The reason for this is that the accompanying website for *Vision 2021* presents a basic form of problem analysis for this theme, although the website as such resembles the actual policy. As a sort of added problem definition to the policy, one is informed that the "global economy will witness significant economic changes in the coming years and the UAE Vision 2021 National Agenda aims for the UAE to be at its heart."[2] This selective understanding of the world through sense- and meaning-making, leading to the perception of significant economic changes needing to be anticipated, explains better the slogan of this third theme as the modification/initiative of the policy for existing programs to achieve the overall vision. Hence, the theme is summarized by envisioning a "diversified and flexible knowledge-based economy [that] will be powered by skilled Emiratis and strengthened by world-class talent to ensure long-term prosperity for the UAE."

The focus of this theme complements the second one, outlining how the economy of the global business hub is envisioned for the year 2021. Its three leitmotifs emphasize the economy's different facets. The first leitmotif entitled "Harness the full potential of National human capital" states that "Knowledgeable and Innovative Emiratis" provide indispensable "human capital" as a somewhat solid foundation for a "knowledge-based economy" by "attracting and retaining the best talent." The next leitmotif, "Sustainable and Diversified Economy," describes a "knowledge-based economy" as diversified and expanded to "new strategic sectors to channel our energies into industries and services where we can build a long-term competitive advantage." As a connecting entity and business hub, the UAE "will forge ever stronger international partnerships and capitalize on them to boost trade and commerce." Leitmotif three, "Knowledge-Based and Highly Productive Economy," complements the previous by stating that "[i]nnovation, research, science and technology will form the pillars of a knowledge-based, highly productive and competitive economy, driven by entrepreneurs in a business-friendly environment where public and private sectors form effective partnerships." The discussed third theme can be seen as the cornerstone of *Vision 2021*, indicating that its achievement will be accomplished by investing in "science, technology, research and development throughout the fabric of the UAE economy." This is particularly interesting from the analytical perspective of GEI research because the policy here, as in other passages, reiterates the necessity of entrepreneurial and business-driven environments in partnership with private sectors. Although higher education is not directly addressed, it is implied as a guarantor for achieving *Vision 2021* when speaking of innovative and knowledgeable Emiratis, research, and science.

The slogan of theme four, "United in Prosperity," is "A nurturing and sustainable environment for quality living." The focus of this theme is divided into four dimensions of living that interdependently bring about the "knowledgeable and innovative Emiratis" envisioned in theme three. The leitmotifs address medical care ("long and healthy lives"), education ("first-rate"), access through infrastructure ("well-rounded lifestyles"), and the environment ("well-preserved natural"). The leitmotifs covering first-rate education and well-rounded lifestyles are particularly important with regard to the focus of this chapter: The first presents a vision of "well-rounded individuals [who] enhance their educational attainment, and achieve their true potential, contributing positively to society." The implied focus is again human capital: "The UAE will successfully encourage Emiratis to maximise their potential by remaining in school and reaching higher levels of education. […] [U]niversity enrolment will rise, and more Emiratis will climb higher up the ladder of learning into post-graduate education." The latter of the two leitmotifs outlines the policy's conception of the UAE as a global hub:

> An excellent standard of infrastructure and utilities will satisfy the fundamental needs of citizens and businesses while also boosting our nation's economic competitiveness as a leading global hub. As a symbol of mobility and interconnectivity, the UAE will reap the benefits of truly nationwide, user-friendly business and technical systems including transport and communication networks. High-quality utilities will deliver the reliable supplies of energy and water that we require.

The policy ends by stating "[a]nticipating the problems of tomorrow is the only reasonable way to preserve and enhance our way of life, acting with initiative in full awareness of our collective responsibility."

# The Discursive Construction of an International Education Hub as a Competitive Advantage

This section will adopt the elaborated conceptual framework for reviewing the presented policy by using a discursive research approach. From the analytical lens of GEP research, a first insight when engaging with the policy is the particular composition of the visions and their leitmotifs presented. Though expressed with the aim of transforming the UAE locally, they are influenced by concepts circulating in globalizing policy discourses, such as the knowledge-based economy. Although the exact workings of the UAE's understanding of the knowledge-based economy are not described further, the solution to future economic change is. This involves increasing higher education attainment and provision and attracting global talent—key aspects of any of the many IEH definitions. Furthermore, investment in research on subject areas directly contributing to defined goals and visions is seen as crucial. Among these are improvement of physical infrastructure—such as transport and communication—throughout the UAE, as well as fostering business and innovation. This to some extent also explains the multiplication and dominance of such programs in UAE university portfolios.

The policy's preface presents a particular understanding of the world, the complexity of which—from a CPE perspective—has been reduced through semiosis and structuration. The world is understood as posing specific challenges to the development of society, the economy, and national identity in the UAE. As for the individual, the challenges are to health, education, environment, and well-being. Derived from such challenges is the need for proactive change to secure the future success of the nation. The policy unfolds a social imaginary rooted in this selective understanding, creating a simplified version of the world with a central role for science, learning, and research, some core aspects of higher education, and their close coordination with the economy for a prosperous future. This is described as the knowledge-based economy, necessitating, as presented in theme three (United in Knowledge), leitmotif one, that more "Emiratis will enter higher education, where they will enrich their minds with the skills that their nation needs to fuel its knowledge economy. Universities will listen closely to the needs of Emiratis and of their future employers, and will balance their teaching to the demands of the workplace."

The solution to the identified social and economic challenges is selectively assessed in connection with a selective understanding of the knowledge-based economy and its requirements. The question of how "to solve the diagnosed problems and to realize socially constructed objectives" is answered by the creation of a global hub (as a so-called *knowledge brand* in CPE research; cf. Sum & Jessop, 2013, p. 6). This social imaginary functions as the fabric binding and uniting the society and its government in their efforts to create the conditions necessary for success in the knowledge-based economy through the transformation of the UAE into a global hub. Although the hub is described as one for business and innovation, higher education implicitly appears in several sections of the policy, such as, for instance, theme three, leitmotifs one and three. Higher education is also implied as an extra-economic factor determining competitiveness by providing science, research, and opportunities for learning. The stunning growth in the number of higher education institutions in the UAE may serve as a material causality constituted by those ideational aspects, facilitated by the model of free zones to attract foreign institutions and improve national universities.

The semiotic-discursive space created by *Vision 2021* is, on the one hand, dependent on the UAE's legacy regarding trade and business. On the other hand—and perhaps of greater interest for researching the changing role of the state in education in relation to GEI research—is how the policy also shapes the path for future development. The changing role of the state—or, arguably, its changing mode for governing higher education—is perhaps best described by quoting directly from *Vision 2021* where it states that the "UAE will enhance its pivotal role as a regional business hub whose essential infrastructure and institutions provide a gateway linking our neighbourhood to the world, serving as a role model for the region." The state functions as a guarantor of success, a guardian in a time of complex change, and—as the themes "United in…" induce—a uniting and "power connecting" entity to link "the economic and government sphere, […] build[ing] on sectors of excellence to export its model abroad, while constantly evolving to create new competitive advantages." Furthermore, as stated in theme three, leitmotif two, this IEH connects economic advantages by relating research and education to the economy, "forg[ing] ever stronger international partnerships," in order to "capitalize on them to boost trade and commerce." The powerful narrative, which unfolds throughout the policy relating it to globalizing discourses about economic and social challenges, presents the transformation of the UAE into a hub as the solution to those pressures and for achieving competitive advantages.

## Conclusion

In this chapter, I explored the changing role of the state by example of reviewing *Vision 2021* as a key policy for comprehending the UAE as an IEH. IEHs as governmental projects aiming at the transformation of selected territories into economically competitive and socially progressive areas by means of reforming education, in particular higher education, are regarded as paradigmatic examples of competition-states, analytically viewed as power connectors in connection to theorizing space as strategically relational. While IEHs have been illuminated as a social phenomenon in relation to the growing body of literature, conceptual considerations for one possible approach to researching a changing role of the state were elaborated and applied to *Vision 2021*. By reviewing this policy with a discursive research approach and the presented conceptual framework, the discursive construction of the state as a global hub for achieving competitive advantages in the knowledge-based economy has been discussed, and the role of higher education for achieving those visions has been stressed. The scope and focus of this chapter, however, only allow for a brief discussion of a changing role of the state in education, for the further study of which the method of comparison and the conception of GEP as a sociocultural practice may be particularly insightful.

In connection to the topic of this edited volume, the deliberations above contribute to GEI research by elucidating IEHs as large-scale politico-economic projects through which the organization of higher education becomes part of global competition, cooperation, and conflict.

In those new policy settings, it is the state that creates business-driven environments in higher education enabling a "global economic sector" in education to flourish. Attempts to research those changes in GEP research often abstain from theory for guiding scientific inquiry within policy studies in education. However, the expressed need of re-reading education policies due to ongoing, complex change (cf. Simons et al., 2009a, 2009b) may highly profit from this, for the reason of which CPE has been discussed as a vital theoretical approach that may open up new vistas for the study of GEP. Using this approach, I was able to highlight that—although often approached as diminishing in power in relation to global players—at least discursively, the state in the investigated IEH contrarily envisions its role as a primus inter pares that foresees and directs change processes. In education, this changing role of the state arguably challenges the state's monopoly on sponsoring/providing mass education, while the state in turn seeks to strengthen the monopoly on its regulation as a power connector. The implications of this changing mode of governing (higher) education, however, remain a seldom studied but imperative area to the study of contemporary challenges in education.

The discussion above aims at contributing to international and comparative education by highlighting the growing complexity of researching education policy, and also by discussing some disruptive effects through interplays of global influences and local visions. While I provide evidence for the changing relationship between society, the state, and the economy in the context of higher education policy in the UAE, further research is necessary to better understand the role of the state and the implications of its change in relation to GEI research. Here, the gray literature often disregarded by researchers may provide interesting insights into the business-driven environments of IEHs. For instance, the impact of market research produced by local players should be taken seriously due to the expertise that the growing number of specialists in higher education as a business has, and the weight their assessments play in the strategies of universities setting up shop. With regard to emergent comparative research designs, capturing their views might be crucial for tapping research potential when researching IEHs.

In concluding, researching the implications of IEHs for higher education policy and governance will benefit highly from comparison as a method of knowledge generation, which in turn also entails epistemological, ontological, and conceptual realignments of our analytical tools. In any case, this will surely offer new ways of seeing both challenges and achievements, enabling us to appraise IEHs as an analytical concept for analysis *of* instead of just *for* policy.

## Notes

1. For instance, find an informative discussion about those three traditional analytical dimensions of policy (*policy, polity,* and *politics*) in Jessop, 2016, p. 17.
2. The website is publicly accessible via http://www.vision2021.ae, while the indicated problem analysis can be found via https://www.vision2021.ae/national-agenda-2021/list/economy-circle

## References

Anderson, B. (1991). *Imagined Communities. Reflections on the Origin and Spread of Nationalism.* London: Verso.
Archer, M. S. (1979). *Social Origins of Educational Systems.* London/Beverly Hills, CA: Sage.
Ball, S. J., Junemann, C., & Santori, D. (2017). *Edu.net. Globalisation and Education Policy Mobility.* London: Routledge.
Barabási, A.-L. (2003). *Linked. How Everything Is Connected to Everything Else and What It Means for Business, Science, and Everyday Life.* New York: PLUME.
Barabási, A.-L. (2014). *Network Science.* Mountain View, CA: Creative Commons.
Bartlett, L., & Vavrus, F. (2017). *Rethinking Case Study Research. A Comparative Approach.* New York: Routledge.
Bekke, H. A. G. M., Kickert, W. J. M., & Kooiman, J. (1995). Public Management and Governance. In J. Kooiman & F. A. van Vught (Eds.), *Public Policy and Administrative Sciences in the Netherlands* (pp. 201–218). London: Harvester-Wheatsheaf.
Benavot, A., Resnik, J., & Corrales, J. (2006). *Global Educational Expansion. Historical Legacies and Political Obstacles.* Cambridge, MA: American Academy of Arts and Science.

Dale, R. (2015). Conjunctions of Power and Comparative Education. *Compare: A Journal of Comparative and International Education, 45*(3), 341–362.
Dale, R., & Parreira do Amaral, M. (2015). Discursive and Institutional Opportunity Structures in the Governance of Educational Trajectories. In M. Parreira do Amaral, R. Dale, & P. Loncle (Eds.), *Shaping the Futures of Young Europeans: Education Governance in Eight European Countries* (pp. 23–41). Oxford: Symposium Books.
Easterling, K. (2016). *Extrastatecraft. The Power of Infrastructure Space*. London/New York: Verso.
Fairclough, N. (1992). *Discourse and Social Change*. Cambridge, UK: Polity Press.
Fox, W. H., & Al Shamisi, S. (2014). United Arab Emirates' Education Hub: A Decade of Development. In J. Knight (Ed.), *International Education Hubs. Student, Talent, Knowledge-Innovation Models* (pp. 63–80). Dordrecht, The Netherlands: Springer.
Green, A. (1997). *Education, Globalization and the Nation State*. New York: Palgrave.
Heller, T. C., Sosna, M., & Wellbery, D. E. (1986). *Reconstructing Individualism. Autonomy, Individuality, and the Self in Western Thought*. Stanford, CA: Stanford University Press.
Jessop, B. (2016). *The State. Past, Present, Future*. Cambridge, UK: Polity Press.
Jessop, B. (2017). Varieties of Academic Capitalism and Entrepreneurial Universities. On Past Research and Three Thought Experiments. *Higher Education, 73*, 853–870.
Jessop, B., Brenner, N., & Jones, M. (2008). Theorizing Sociospatial Relations. *Society and Space, 26*, 389–401.
Jessop, B., Fairclough, N., & Wodak, R. (Eds.). (2008). *Education and the Knowledge-Based Economy in Europe*. Rotterdam, The Netherlands: Sense Publishers.
Jones, M., & Jessop, B. (2010). Thinking State/Space Incompossibility. *Antipode, 42*(5), 1119–1149.
Jungmann, R., & Besio, C. (2018). Semantiken des Sozialen Wandels. Zur diskursiven Gestaltung von Innovation. In S. Bosančić, S. Böschen, & C. Schubert (Eds.), *Diskursive Konstruktion und schöpferische Zerstörung* (pp. 11–42). Weinheim, Germany: Julius Beltz.
Knight, J. (2014). *International Education Hubs. Student, Talent, Knowledge-Innovation Models*. Dordrecht, The Netherlands: Springer.
Lane, J. E., & Kinser, K. (2011). The Cross-Border Education Policy Context: Educational Hubs, Trade Liberalization, and National Sovereignty. *New Directions for Higher Education, 155*, 79–85.

Marginson, S. (2016). The Global Construction of Higher Education Reform. In K. Mundy, A. Green, B. Lingard, & A. Verger (Eds.), *The Handbook of Global Education Policy* (pp. 291-311). Chichester, UK: John Wiley & Sons, Ltd.

Mok, K. H., & Bodycott, P. (2014). Hong Kong: The Quest for Regional Education Hub Status. In J. Knight (Ed.), *International Education Hubs. Student, Talent, Knowledge-Innovation Models* (pp. 81-99). Dordrecht, The Netherlands: Springer.

Mundy, K., Green, A., Lingard, B., & Verger, A. (Eds.). (2016). *The Handbook of Global Education Policy*. Chichester, UK: John Wiley & Sons.

Peters, M. A., & Besley, T. (2015). Finance Capitalism, Financialization, and the Prospects for Public Education. In M. A. Peters, J. M. Paraskeva, & T. Besley (Eds.), *The Global Financial Crisis and Educational Restructuring* (pp. 21-49). New York: Peter Lang.

Ramirez, F. O., & Boli, J. (1987). The Political Construction of Mass Schooling: European Origins and Worldwide Institutionalization. *Sociology of Education, 60*(1), 2-17.

Rhodes, R. A. W. (1994). The Hollowing Out of the State. *The Political Quarterly, 65*, 138-151.

Robertson, S. L. (2018). Spatialising Education (or, the Difference that Education Space Make). In E. Glaser, H.-C. Koller, W. Thole, & S. Krumme (Eds.), *Räume für Bildung – Räume der Bildung* (pp. 43-54). Opladen, Germany: Barbara Budrich.

Rosenau, J. N., & Czempiel, E.-O. (1992). *Governance without Government: Order and Change of World Politics*. Cambridge, UK: Cambridge Studies in International Relations.

Schwartzman, R. (2013). Consequences of Commodifying Education. *Academic Exchange Quarterly, 17*(3), 1-7.

Sidhu, R., Ho, K.-C., & Yeoh, B. S. A. (2014). Singapore: Building a Knowledge and Education Hub. In J. Knight (Ed.), *International Education Hubs. Student, Talent, Knowledge-Innovation Models* (pp. 121-143). Dordrecht, The Netherlands: Springer.

Simons, M., Olssen, M., & Peters, M. (2009a). Re-reading Education Policies. Part 2: Challenges, Horizons, Approaches, Tools, Styles. In M. Simons, M. Olssen, & M. A. Peters (Eds.), *Re-reading Education Policies: A Handbook Studying the Policy Agenda of the 21st Century* (pp. 36-95). Rotterdam, The Netherlands: Sense Publishers.

Simons, M., Olssen, M., & Peters, M. A. (2009b). Re-reading Education Policies. Part 1: The Critical Education Policy Orientation. In M. Simons,

M. Olssen, & M. A. Peters (Eds.), *Re-reading Education Policies: A Handbook Studying the Policy Agenda of the 21st Century* (pp. 1–35). Rotterdam, The Netherlands: Sense Publishers.

Spring, J. (2015). *Economization of Education. Human Capital, Global Corporations, Skills-Based Schooling*. London: Routledge.

Sum, N.-L., & Jessop, B. (2013). *Towards a Cultural Political Economy. Putting Culture in Its Place in Political Economy*. Cheltenham, UK: Edward Elgar.

van der Zwan, N. (2014). Making Sense of Financialization. *Socio-Economic Review, 12*, 99–129.

Verger, A. (2016). The Global Diffusion of Education Privatization: Unpacking and Theorizing Policy Adoption. In K. Mundy, A. Green, B. Lingard, & A. Verger (Eds.), *The Handbook of Global Education Policy* (pp. 64–80). Chichester, UK: John Wiley & Sons, Ltd.

Verger, A., Lubienski, C., & Steiner-Khamsi, G. (2016). The Emergence and Structuring of the Global Education Industry. Towards an Analytical Framework. In A. Verger, C. Lubienski, & G. Steiner-Khamsi (Eds.), *The Global Education Industry* (pp. 3–24). New York: Routledge.

Wodak, R. (2004). Critical Discourse Analysis. In C. Seale, G. Gobo, J. F. Gubrium, & D. Silverman (Eds.), *Qualitative Research Practice* (pp. 197–213). London: SAGE Publications Ltd.

Wodak, R., & Fairclough, N. (1997). Critical Discourse Analysis. In T. A. van Dijk (Ed.), *Discourse as Social Interaction* (pp. 258–284). London: SAGE Publications Ltd.

Zajda, J. (2009). Globalisation, and Comparative Research: Implications for Education. In J. Zajda & V. Rust (Eds.), *Globalisation, Policy and Comparative Research* (pp. 1–12). New York: Springer.

# 10

# The Globalized Expert: On the Dissemination and Authorization of Evidence-Based Education

Christiane Thompson

## Introduction

*Pearson is 100% focused on global education and helping learners to progress around the world. Having a strong brand is fundamental to building our reputation and our success as an education business.* (Pearson in The Bookseller, 2016)

The multi-national media corporation Pearson presents itself as "the world's learning company." With more than 5 billion Euros in sales in 2016, Pearson is among the largest companies in the educational sector worldwide. When it comes to textbooks and preparation materials for school performance tests, Pearson is the market leader, and as such has profited significantly from the advancement of test culture in the United States ushered in by the No Child Left Behind Act. In 2015, Pearson took over the task of test development within the context of the Programme for International Student Assessment (PISA) Study and

C. Thompson (✉)
Theory and History of Education, Goethe-University Frankfurt am Main, Frankfurt am Main, Germany

contributed to the digital implementation of the Organization for Economic Co-operation and Development (OECD) Study. Meanwhile, Pearson has also expanded by acquiring education businesses in several different countries (see Ball, 2012).

In my opening quote, Pearson emphasizes its self-image as an "educational business" and major global player in education. Its market position is treated as a product of scientific advancement and innovation. The company's self-description of its position may not initially seem unusual. However, it does give one pause when this depiction and the company's dominant position are viewed in terms of the increasing expansion of the paradigm of evidence-based educational research.[1] The latter is of particular importance regarding the way in which educational innovation has become increasingly an issue of the market and policymaking.

In this chapter, I examine the way in which companies like Pearson use "evidence-based educational research" to position themselves in the market as a "scientifically proven" success in education.[2] The fact that the comparative results of large-scale empirical research of education performance are becoming more common serves as my point of departure. I will use Pearson to show how *everyone* is encouraged to think in terms of evidence-based educational research. My thesis is that under the heading of "global expertise" a new form of subject-formation is emerging. In this context, individuals are increasingly asked to use and consider output supported, digitally available data sources for educational purposes. By promising an evidential basis, large companies succeed in marketing their products to gain insights and acquire knowledge on how to further develop them, consolidating new regimes of learning which increasingly draw on databases (Ozga, Dahler-Larsen, Segerholm, & Simola, 2011; see also Hartong, in this volume). This outcome, along with the establishment of transnational actors and companies, is highly significant for the globalization of the education sector (see Spring, 2009).

My aim is to trace the dissemination of evidence-based education research and knowledge by asking what strategies and forms are used to *convince* individuals that they are *dependent on* this knowledge and that they should engage with it thoroughly. This question directs our attention to issues of "authorization," that is, practices and strategies to present knowledge as legitimate and reasonable (Jergus & Thompson, 2017;

Thompson, 2017). I will develop this perspective on the constitution of authority in the first part of the chapter. First, however, I will emphasize that though evidence-based knowledge is typically regarded uncritically, it still *has to be presented as valuable at different locations and in different contexts*. I will cover important crossing points and trajectories within the dissemination of evidence-based knowledge, and the ways it entices individuals to engage with it.

In order to research practices of authorization, I draw on different empirical materials that show an interest in spreading or circulating evidence-based educational knowledge and research. These are a TED Talk by Andreas Schleicher, coordinator of the PISA study and director of the education department at the OECD, Pearson's data hub "The Learning Curve," and Pearson's learning platform "Revel." I will analyze these materials in terms of the ways they promote an evidence-based perspective within education to show how Pearson uses this to improve its market position. As for methodology, I use discourse analysis (Jergus & Thompson, 2017) with a particular focus on how individuals are addressed or enticed "to become global experts." My analysis also focuses on how individuals are encouraged to join Pearson's global project of evidence-based education innovation.

I will begin with the notion of authorization and its analytical relevance for education policy research. By drawing on the work of German sociologist Heinrich Popitz (2004), as well as Max Weber's work on social power, I describe how "network connectivity" is formed in the context of evidence-based research. In the second part of the chapter, I will use Schleicher's TED Talk (2012) to illustrate the enlistment of a "global expert." Schleicher's talk is not only about disseminating the results of evidence-based education research; it also refers to a specific role vis-à-vis this knowledge. In the third section, I look at "The Learning Curve," Pearson's data platform designed to *make* users researchers. After that I turn to "Revel," Pearson's learning platform for getting users to engage and invest in product development. I summarize my results in the final section to affirm the emergence of a "digital education laboratory" wherein a company like Pearson consolidates its market position and its status as scientific actor in the field of education.

## Researching Practices of Authorization

Research on authorization departs from the viewpoint that concepts and ideas are not authorized or justified in and of themselves (Schäfer & Thompson, 2009). As mentioned above, the manifestation of authority is related to social and discursive practices: Evidence-based knowledge is not self-evident. Rather, it has to be presented as valuable and indispensable (Thompson, 2013).[3] In other words, authority relations are dependent on the demonstration and confirmation of authorizing practices. Authority is a matter of recognition.

The complexity of social power and its realization is an important focus within education policy research. It is reflected in various network analyses that demonstrate the differentiations and interrelationships of various actors and participants. Ball, for example, analyzes how neoliberal imaginaries circulate in new networks and sites of philanthropy, business and government (Ball, 2012). Lubienski (in this volume) has examined the significance of intermediaries between research production and policymaking who promote evidence-based research within the decision-making processes. Along these lines, the chapter will turn toward the ways evidence-based educational knowledge is distributed and anchored in different locations, as well as digitally connected or framed. I examine the shapes and forms of network connectivity in terms of the German sociologist Heinrich Popitz's theory describing four forms of social power (2004).

The first form of power is the "power of action" (ibid., p. 22). This power resides in the possibility of enforcement, mostly based on corporeal superiority. From an anthropological point of view, the power of action is based on human vulnerability. Popitz's second form of power is control of behavior by threats and promises. Here, social power rests on instrumental superiority and institutional control. The third form of power is "authoritative power," which is based on the need and longing for social coordination and orientation (e.g., by values). Authoritative power rests on the possibility of providing a common view of further action, that is, the construction of a coherent future. Because authoritative power creates shared value commitments, it reinforces recognition and identification with specific knowledge forms. This will be of particular importance for the following analysis.

The fourth form of social power is related to what Popitz calls "data constitution" (*datensetzende Macht*; Popitz, 2004, p. 29). Data-setting authority is related to the prescribing nature of materiality. Artifacts are constructed so that users can only handle them in one way. Take, for example, a fence along a busy street to keep pedestrians from crossing at a certain point. The data constituting power can also mean the release of new tasks on a learning platform only after the former tasks have been performed successfully. In both cases, human action is "determined" by a materialized authority, an authority that is not thematized in any significant way. In a digital age when the architects of decision-making direct and influence choice,[4] the importance of the data constituting power cannot be overestimated.

The field of education and educational policy is permeated with various power formations and constellations. Despite the values and beliefs of humanism and Enlightenment, educational practices and policymaking still draw on "power of action." Think of the various forms of situational superiority exerted in the classroom by particular forms of corporeal presence, or in stock market battles of education businesses. The second form of social power can, for example, be located in the threats and promises of high-stakes testing, which result in budget gains or losses.

Whereas the first two forms have a disciplinary and regulating quality, the third form stimulates and motivates, while the fourth form conceals social power. In the following, I will show how evidence-based knowledge can be defined as authoritative power when considered as the basis for a "global project of educational innovation." I will demonstrate not only how education policymakers and researchers, but every knowledge consumer is addressed and connected to this "global project." I will describe the forms of identification and orientation in terms of the formation of "global experts." Special attention will be given as to how Pearson strategically uses the power of data constitution to spread "evidence-based knowledge."

*Belief of legitimacy*, a concept which stems from Max Weber's sociology (2000), is particularly helpful to complement Popitz' theory of social power.[5] Weber argued that social power *relies* on the *belief* that the given power arrangements are adequate and legitimate. In the following, I use this idea to ask how evidence-based knowledge is presented to the audience so that it appears valuable, fair and even self-evident. I emphasize digital presentations and frameworks because they provide the network connectivity for endowing evidence-based education research with authority. First, I will examine Schleicher's advocacy of PISA in terms of its constitution as "authoritative power." From here I chart a trajectory of global expertise to Pearson's "The Learning Curve" and its learning platform "Revel."

## The Popularization of a "Global Expertise" on Education

The significance of PISA has continually risen since its initial publication. While only 32 countries took part during the first round, that number is expected to climb to 80 in 2018. In many countries, the study is widely publicized—and considered an indispensable reference point to estimate competitiveness. Thanks to PISA, the OECD has quickly been able to expand and consolidate its status as a global leader in education.[6]

Media presence and global expansion are interrelated: The results of the study compelled the participating countries to compete. This, in turn, affirmed the OECD's identity as the transnational actor that oversees this competition. How the PISA study was pitched to the public makes sense in terms of Andreas Schleicher's expression "to bring into position" (2012), referring not only to how knowledge resulting from PISA is made available to a broader audience but also how this knowledge creates a particular "addressee," that is, an individual who is not a policymaker or researcher but believes in "global expertise."

Andreas Schleicher gave a talk, "Use Data to Build Better Schools," at the TEDGlobal meeting in July 2012. Schleicher discussed the PISA study, particularly its "direct measurement" approach to competencies as "problem-solving abilities." He presented the results from the then current 2009 investigation and the long-term positive educational-political changes that have been carried out, based on the study, since 2000 were reported. Schleicher not only described a narrative of increasing educational success but also the reduction of social disparities and inequalities within the educational system. He ended his talk with several references to the factors which make for a "first-class system" of education (Schleicher, 2012, 17:24, the transcript of the talk can be found at TED, 2012).

Based on the content of Schleicher's presentation, we can break the popularization and spread of expertise down to three aspects: (1) The assumed *improvement of the scientific research* via a global or international perspective. In the accompanying notes, Schleicher wrote: "Education is generally thought of as a domestic policy issue. But what can we learn by looking at education on the global scale?" (see TED-Blog, 2012). Here, Schleicher assumes the prevalence and superiority of a global standpoint.

Schleicher makes the possibility of learning plausible in two ways. First, a *detached* perspective, absent national biases, made possible by comparing countries. Throughout his talk, Schleicher portrayed the OECD as an alternative to the limitations imposed by a local perspective (see Schleicher, 2012, 12:45). The global perspective of PISA allows for a "systematic" approach that first makes it possible to define "education quality" and equal opportunity. Schleicher presents PISA as an innovative educational laboratory where, for the first time, the major questions in education can be investigated scientifically.

(2) In addition to "global expertise" as a means to improve research, Schleicher also described a *standardization of education*. According to Schleicher, PISA is not merely about reproduction in learning, but rather the ability to apply knowledge to new situations (Schleicher, 2012, 2:30). In doing so, Schleicher challenges the critique that PISA ignores the content of the respective school lessons. Schleicher argues:

> But if you take that logic, you know, you should consider life unfair, because the test of truth in life is not whether we can remember what we learned in school, but whether we are prepared for change, whether we are prepared for jobs that haven't been created, to use technologies that haven't been invented, to solve problems we just can't anticipate today. (3:00)

For Schleicher, education must be conceptualized in terms of change and productivity that transcends national contexts and preferences. He presents "global expertise" as a perspective that—free of national and cultural limitations—casts its unbiased view, as it were, on the enabling of innovation. It is precisely in this sense, Schleicher states, that PISA *directly* measures student knowledge and ability (Schleicher, 2012, 2:24). Schleicher establishes the authoritative power of PISA in terms of its neutrality, validity and orientation toward the future. The educational researcher's authority is a feature of the standardized global education to come, which will enable people to keep pace with what the future holds. Whoever wishes to follow this innovation-oriented conception of education must endorse PISA-instituted comparison and competition.[7]

(3) Schleicher's reference to the global expertise underpinning PISA points to the increasing significance of *self-responsibility and individualization*. When comparing different educational systems, the less successful are characterized as "bureaucratic," inundating teachers with rules and guidelines (Schleicher, 2012, 15:50). In a successful system, "[t]he teachers can themselves find out what they teach their students" (ibid). Schleicher distinguishes administrative responsibility and bureaucratic control from self-organization and independent working, to "enable … teachers to make innovations in pedagogy" in a given system (Schleicher, 2012, 16:50). In the PISA model, inventiveness and innovation play a significant role in the authorization of individualized global expertise.

Toward the end of his presentation, Schleicher challenges his audience to adopt PISA's perspective in order to make the improvement in education *their own project*. His closing statement cites the need for change in education administration: "If we can help every child, every teacher, every school, every principal, every parent see what improvement is possible, that only the sky is the limit to education improvement," he states, "we have laid the foundations for better policies and better lives" (Schleicher, 2012, 19:20). PISA's "global expertise" is relevant to everyone—it addresses each individual in terms of his or her responsibility.[8] Carvalho (2014) also described cooperation between various actors, so that a comprehensive implementation of this kind of thinking becomes possible, as one of PISA's central concerns, (in general terms see Jergus & Thompson, 2015). Following Popitz (2004), PISA can be viewed as a globalizing knowledge system that bases its authoritative power in a rhetoric of innovation transcending national views and traditions of education and educational policy.

In other words, PISA claims the position of "global expertise." It requests everyone to work to improve education and commit themselves to innovation based on the evidence of educational research. It is the latter, according to Schleicher, that determines the aim of the endeavor as well as its empirical achievement. Those who do not follow this path will be left behind. The danger lies in the prejudices and limitations of "national debates." When Schleicher[9] insinuates that PISA research is unaffected by these concerns he is establishing the authority of PISA, which adopts the perspective of "global expertise," consolidating the power of evidence-based education.

## Global Expertise in Pearson's "The Learning Curve"

The increasing expansion and popularization of PISA results exert a power beyond the public recognition of league tables. Beyond educational policy, PISA addresses individuals in terms of an evidence-based and innovation-oriented project. A global "value basis" for education is constructed by affirming the importance of global expertise. In this section, I will look at Pearson's "The Learning Curve" to show how the newest forms of data storage and processing have led to a further expansion of this expertise in that all addressees become "experts."

"The Learning Curve" is an online platform where users select relevant data from the educational field to represent it in terms of national comparisons. The project's website invites its audience to, "[e]xplore nearly 70 indicators from 50 countries over 25 years to understand what affects education performance, and the link to the wider socio-economic environment" (Pearson, 2017b). "The Learning Curve" calls upon its users to work with the available data to gain insights into the operation of educational systems. In this way, they are no longer just recipients of the results of the educational research. Rather they, as Schleicher suggests, make this research their own and adopt its terms.

Ben Williamson (2016)—building on Beer (2013)—coined the term "prosumer" to describe this. The users are both consumers and producers—active participants constructed as interactive agents who are, "solicited to perform independent analyses by tweaking variables, adjusting statistical weightings and generating new visualizations" (Williamson, 2016, p. 132). The *prosumer* transcends the distinction between popular and expert knowledge. Meanwhile, the governing knowledge of the education field is being reconfigured. Other scientific paradigms have been omitted; reference to statistical analyses has become normalized (ibid., p. 133) because it is both user-friendly and activating.

Williamson attributes great significance to how data is presented in "The Learning Curve," which he says shows the OECD and Pearson "are now increasingly becoming centers of visualization with the technologies and techniques to render dynamic educational data visualizations and to mobilize the interactivity of users to ensure their consensus" (ibid., p. 134). Seeing is believing, and statistical numbers can be related and aggregated in various ways to generate new perspectives and "visions" of education (ibid.). What makes this platform special is not maintaining informational knowledge regarding statistically relevant numbers on "education," but rather user-generated overviews and maps. These institute users as knowledge generators who take part in and induce educational innovations. Users become researchers who are able to try out their own ideas and investigative designs.

The number columns and graphics disseminated via the platform change the authoritative structure of knowledge. The data is viewed as a kind of "raw material," which is then made available by international actors or large companies (OECD, World Bank, etc.).[10] Companies and institutions present the evidential basis, and users are tasked with generating knowledge. Authorship and authority are shifted to users who are then enlightened by their role as knowledge generators. At least, that is what the website claims:

> Here's where you can really get to grips with all the data we've collected. Our range of tools below helps you understand the links between education inputs, outputs, and the wider socio-economic environment. *Explore, and make your own conclusions.* (Pearson, 2017b, my emphasis)

This view reflects Kant's essay on Enlightenment where he demands that everyone use their own reason. However, this authorization strategy, where users work with a platform to generate knowledge-based authority, contrasts with the fact that "The Learning Curve" becomes a data-setting authority by virtue of its programming (Popitz, 2004). If every possible operational step in the platform is determined by the programming, and cannot be changed by the users, then whose "learning" is being "curved?"

Though it is true that this restriction is a general feature of the "culture of digitality" (Stalder, 2016) in which participants have to accept the interpretative framework in which they move (e.g., the prescribed maximum length of a tweet), this overlooks the fact that the "programming limitations" are affirmed and advocated aggressively. As Michael Barber, Pearson's educational advisor responsible for the platform states (2017a), "*The Learning Curve* is a contribution to the growing evidence base." "The Learning Curve" is a "meta-resource," which gathers evidence-based knowledge from a multitude of scientific studies.[11] Similar to "What Works Clearinghouse," an initiative of evidence-based educational research in the United States (cf. Jornitz, 2008; Thompson, 2014), Pearson refers to the value of evidence-based knowledge. They also emphasize that there are no concrete instructions or policies suggested by the operating company, and that even education ministers themselves would have "to learn" from the data. The data-setting authority presents the platform as a neutral, scientific meta-resource that users use as they see fit; however, it is significant that the limits of the knowledge presented, as well as the existence of alternative research approaches to "education," are never referred to.

In Barber's introduction to "The Learning Curve" we learn that, "Pearson itself is committed to efficacy – demonstrating the impact on learning outcomes of all its products and services – to ensure it too contributes to the improved performance of education systems that is required for the 21st century" (Barber, 2017). As this quote reveals, the platform must be conceived as a product of the company's broader marketing strategy. The link between providing scientific knowledge and selling education products is presented in the accompanying materials in terms of a specific media format.

## Working with "Revel"

In addition to its data platform, "The Learning Curve" also contains short videos featuring well-known scientists and politicians considered experts in education who support it and, at the same time, discuss to what extent their own work is part of *the larger shared project*, that is, realizing innovations through education and in the field. Here we see network building and construction: Among the videos is one featuring Andreas Schleicher who, as in his TED Talk, demands the audience to learn from PISA in order to improve education and schools. Another video features Osama Manzar, founder of the "Digital Empowerment Foundation" in India. Manzar describes the significance of digitalization to emancipation, without referring directly to Pearson or "The Learning Curve." Nevertheless, because they appear side by side they are effectively presented as a common, coordinated effort.

The juxtaposition of narratives shows that "The Learning Curve" does not just gather data, it also establishes a global network where actors become visible thanks to their local educational innovations. This embedding of regional contexts within global perspectives is labeled "Stories" on "The Learning Curve" menu. Individuals, institutions and countries are presented as "lessons" about education, covering topics such as "Space to learn" or "Education and entrepreneurship" (see Pearson, 2017c). The format "best practice presentation" is produced by interweaving local and global perspectives. On the basis of this presentation, a number of different individuals and groups are jointly addressed via "The Learning Curve." It is not just the education policymakers and planners who are the primary recipients of the platform; the data is also loaded with references to concrete pedagogical action demonstrating the importance of "The Learning Curve" for educational practice.[12]

With just two clicks, the user is taken from "The Learning Curve" to Pearson's range product lines like another digital platform, "Revel." "Revel" is presented in a similar way, containing short videos of observations from education researchers, as well as short statements from professionals who have used the platform successfully. The students who benefit also appear to sing the praises of "Revel." Marketing and utility are tied together in the "Revel Efficacy Report," which can be downloaded under "Results." In the initial description "About Revel" we read:

> Revel is designed to make a measurable impact on defined learner *outcomes* related to access, completion, competence, and progression. It is the first product at Pearson to have an *efficacy framework* built in from the very beginning. Every step of product development has an embedded learner-focused, evidence-based process, ensuring that instructors and students are driving product decisions and that these decisions have a positive impact on results. (see Revel, 2015)

As this quote makes clear, product marketing has become more flexible, encompassing not just evidence-based educational research, but also an appeal to users as experts. Simultaneously, the learning platform is developed and made more efficient.

The efficacy report is composed according to this requirement, featuring "research reports" from university lecturers who have worked with "Revel." These texts appropriate the scientific language of quasi-experimental research. Important background information on the application of "Revel" is given in the beginning of the text. Under the section "Settings," we find information about the university where Revel was used ("4-year public research university") or information about the student body ("average age of undergrads"). Further information refers to the challenges and goals that the lecturer wanted to target with Revel, for example, using Revel as a tool for students' course preparation or for testing. This is followed by "Results and Data," a section on "Student Experience," and finally the sections "Conclusion" and "References." The central result or finding of or recommendation results from the implementation is recorded in a reminder box. As Shawn Olson from Utah State University says in his report:

> REVEL assignments prepared students to engage in class discussions and writing assignments that required them to analyze their own beliefs and opinions. The correlation between overall REVEL scores and final course grades was very strong. (Revel, 2015, p. 8)

The reports on "Revel" are full of illustrations and depictions quantifying the results and investigations. A report from the University of Dallas features the following illustration (Fig. 10.1):

Here the instructor compares the average course results before and after "Revel" and presents significant improvement. The accompanying text also specifies the statistical dispersion of outcomes, and compares them across semesters. In this sense "Revel" users become education researchers who scientifically investigate and evaluate themselves with the platform.

By launching "Revel" as an educational program designed for further development and innovation, Pearson intertwines research and marketing. The company's belief in this process is demonstrated by their initiative to design a "Results Library," which is "an online repository of more than 600 data-driven case studies quantifying the impact of Pearson's digital learning solutions on learning outcomes, retention, and subsequent success" (Revel, 2015, p. 2). By recording their experiences with "Revel," users effectively become its collaborators and proponents. They are not only involved in spreading "Revel" but also become part of the program's innovation and convince themselves and others of its innovative power.

By addressing individuals as "global experts," "Revel" links the authorization of knowledge and the professionalization of teachers with its own product development. Teachers present themselves as working scientifi-

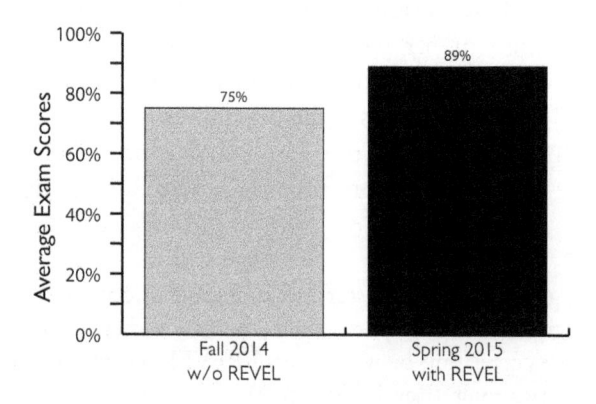

**Fig. 10.1** Result depiction in one of the reports. (Revel, 2015, p. 7)

cally, experts participating in the global innovation of teaching and learning. Pearson can then claim the successes that teachers achieve with "Revel" as its own. Case studies presented on "Revel" highlight problems typically encountered by teachers so that the program appears to be supporting them.[13] One example is students' disinterest in reading course material. Pearson offers advice and tools to overcome this:

> Consider assigning Revel reading to be due before the students come to class. You can assign the entire chapter in just a few clicks. Throughout the chapter, quizzes and journaling opportunities help students retain the information they have read. (Revel, 2015, p. 21)

This statement shows how Pearson uses "Revel" users to further market their product. "Revel" can be the solution to any problem. Pearson can then turn around and use this user-generated data to analyze its customers' usage behavior, creating a feedback loop where the product markets and develops itself. The importance of this cannot be overstated in terms of what it means for the "datafication" of "education businesses" and the possibility of structuring and evaluating large amounts of information via algorithms. Williamson (2017, p. 45) argues that while datafication seems to emancipate users, it is in fact the platforms and programs that become more powerful and free to direct and exploit them. The better companies become at performing real-time analyses to predict behavior, the more efficient and, ironically, user-friendly they become. In this light, the criteria of scientific research and evidence-based analysis remain central to strategies for improving the market position. This is also evident in the case studies that Pearson lists on its website—each of which fails to mention something significant—how learning platforms also limit learning.

## The Digital Education Laboratory

Above I have shown how the popularization and spread of evidence-based educational research have interwoven scientization and marketization as a global project of innovation. I asked how evidence-based knowledge of educational research has become an authority for a considerable number of individuals. I began with a talk by Andreas Schleicher to analyze how PISA results could be considered relevant for all of the actors involved. I emphasized how motives of "individualization" and "self-responsibility" came to override the importance of bureaucratic administration. Education as innovation occurs when educators think they have taken ownership of it.

Next, I used Pearson's "The Learning Curve" to show how users were turned into "education researchers" working with the platform. The data on "The Learning Curve" is presented as accurate and authentic information to be analyzed and evaluated by users motivated by the Enlightenment motto to arrive at one's "own conclusions." Users are addressed as "global experts," thereby becoming part of a research narrative pitched as a vital contribution to educational innovation. In fact, Pearson's products are generally marketed as innovations in which consumers can help creating. The blurred lines between scientization and marketization are especially evident in the "Revel Efficacy Report," which contains short research endorsements from lecturers who speak the language of evidence-oriented educational research and spread it through the promoted learning platform.

This internet-based promotion is particularly suitable for the construction of an "education laboratory" enveloped by an aura of exacting experimental science. When Pearson positions "The Learning Curve" as a "meta-source," the company links the strategy of authoritative power with the power of data constitution (Popitz, 2004). Scientization and datafication are fused together and offered to the general public as a "service." Following Weber's theory (2000), one comes to see how the company generates belief in the legitimacy of its actions. Pearson appears less like another market participant, and more like a quasi-public, official educational ambassador. The quasi-public is constituted via the accessibility of the educational laboratory: On "The Learning Curve," anyone can work with the data and come to their own conclusions. With "Revel," users are also invited to provide evidence-based feedback *to* Revel, which becomes an evidence-based working *with* Revel. Program development and professionalization of one's own educational practice become intertwined. This reflects

Stephen Ball's claim that Pearson expands its influence by operating across various educational "message systems": pedagogy, curriculum and assessment (Ball, 2012, p. 127).

How university teaching and schooling change under the influence of the strategies utilized by large companies like Pearson, which are able to establish successful "educational laboratories" because they possess the necessary infrastructures for data storage and analysis, is a question that awaits further attention. From what I have presented we can conclude that authoritative power depends upon the notion of an innovation-oriented laboratory of education, along the lines of what Ben Williamson describes in terms of public policy labs as the imaginary of the "innovation ecosystem for education" (Williamson, 2014, p. 221).

We should also consider the consequences of exploitation and monitoring by means of the expanding education laboratory which no doubt gives companies like Pearson deep insight into educational institutions.

According to Gert Biesta (2011), as well as Fenwick and Edwards (2014) who also follow Bruno Latour's analysis, PISA is a powerful global network Pearson uses to further its commercial interests. Products are advertised in such a way that consumers are incorporated into the language game of educational research and transformed into its proponents. By such means the network extends the reach of the scientific community to previously unreachable local educational practices. Above and beyond the websites and programs that function as mediators and translators within this laboratory (Fenwick & Edwards, 2010), the multiplication and distribution of global experts will further the project of a marketized evidence-based education. This is where Weber's concept the "belief of legitimacy" unfolds further research perspectives for education policy studies, by showing how individuals participate in establishing this network, and identify with the global project of evidence-based innovation. Further research should follow the extension and infusion within educational institutions, and the far-reaching changes of "education" and "learning" (see Amos, in this volume), to ask under what conditions the "global experts" can distinguish themselves from the valuations and significance of an evidence-oriented perspective.

# Notes

1. See, for instance, Bellmann and Müller (2011) for the discourse on evidence-based education.
2. Here, I am referring to previous results, which have been published in German with a focus on "educational research on subject-formation" (Thompson, 2018). In this chapter, I am focusing on the practices of legitimation and authorization.
3. The case of non-compliance in medicine is a good example that medical knowledge is not in and of itself authorizing. It has to become a part of the doctor-patient-relation in such a way that it can shape the medical treatment.
4. The behavioral-economic approaches of "nudging" have been implemented in numerous areas of life. In this context, the power of data constitution is justified via libertarian paternalism.
5. Weber (2000) has differentiated traditional, rational, as well as charismatic forms of domination or authority thereby bringing into view how they depend on different strategies of authorization within the social order: for example, the bureaucratic structure within rational domination or the extra-ordinary self-presentation in the context of charismatic domination.
6. For presentation of the OECD regarding the guidelines for the economization of test results, see Spring (2015). Lingard and Sellar (2016) have recapitulated the development of the OECD toward its establishment in terms of epistemological as well as infrastructural governance.
7. Gert Biesta (2015) described the "psychological way of thinking" connected with PISA (social psychology) as addressing the "fear of being left behind." PISA would equally address the fears and worries of the nations and individuals to be "left behind" or "fall back" in response to the social and economic transformations. The numbers and statistics would be turned into a superficial observation and tempt everyone to accept the simplicity and order presented in the scale (Biesta, 2015, p. 351). One is tempted to take part, even if one were to admit that the quality of the educational system cannot be determined solely in terms of the PISA results.
8. The singularization of responsibility can be illustrated with a heading that Schleicher used together with Zoido (2016, p. 374): "In the Dark, All Schools and Education Systems Look the Same."

9. The TED Talks are precisely addressed toward the broader public. The motto of the talks are: "Ideas worth spreading" (TED, 2017).
10. Pearson presents itself as an instance whose understands its data services as achievements and services for the community.
11. Barber (2014, p. 76) articulates his educational-political self-conception in a different context as follows: "I think that a lot of my personal work in government was about bringing data to the point of decision. And good data."
12. Here the analysis deviates from the other studies, which emphasize that the digital preparation, above all, the investigation of pedagogical institutions and spaces take place from a removed perspective (see Decuypere, Ceulemens, & Simons, 2014).
13. See also the "Pearson Community" to Revel (Revel, 2017).

# References

Ball, S. J. (2012). *Global Education Inc.* Abingdon, UK: Routledge.
Barber, M. (2014). Data Work (Conversation with Jenny Ozga). In T. Fenwick, E. Mangez, & J. Ozga (Eds.), *Governing Knowledge: Comparison, Knowledge-Based Technologies and Expertise in the Regulation of Education* (pp. 75–85). London: Routledge.
Barber, M. (2017). Introduction 'The Learning Curve' by Michael Barber. Retrieved from http://thelearningcurve.pearson.com/about. Accessed 13 Oct 2017.
Beer, D. (2013). *Popular Culture and New Media: The Politics of Circulation.* London: Palgrave.
Bellmann, J., & Müller, T. (Eds.). (2011). *Wissen, was wirkt. Kritik evidenzbasierter Pädagogik.* Wiesbaden, Germany: VS Verlag.
Biesta, G. (2011). Welches Wissen ist am meisten wert? Zur Veränderung des öffentlichen Status von Wissenschaft und Wissen im Feld der Erziehung. In A. Schäfer & C. Thompson (Eds.), *Wissen* (pp. 77–98). Paderborn, Germany: Schöningh.
Biesta, G. (2015). Resisting the Seduction of the Global Education Measurement Industry: Notes on the Social Psychology of PISA. *Ethics and Education, 10*(3), 348–360.
Carvalho, L. M. (2014). The Attraction of Mutual Surveillance of Performances: PISA as a Knowledge-Policy Instrument. In T. Fenwick, E. Mangez, &

J. Ozga (Eds.), *Governing Knowledge: Comparison, Knowledge-Based Technologies and Expertise in the Regulation of Education* (pp. 58–72). London: Routledge.

Decuypere, M., Ceulemens, C., & Simons, M. (2014). Schools in the Making: Mapping Digital Spaces of Evidence. *Journal of Education Policy, 29*(5), 617–639.

Fenwick, T., & Edwards, R. (2010). *Actor-Network Theory in Education.* Abingdon, UK: Routledge.

Fenwick, T., & Edwards, R. (2014). Network Alliances: Precarious Governance Through Data, Standards and Code. In T. Fenwick, E. Mangez, & J. Ozga (Eds.), *Governing Knowledge: Comparison, Knowledge-Based Technologies and Expertise in the Regulation of Education* (pp. 44–57). London: Routledge.

Jergus, K., & Thompson, C. (2015). Innovation im Horizont frühkindlicher Bildung? *Zeitschrift für Pädagogik, 61*(6), 808–822.

Jergus, K., & Thompson, C. (Eds.). (2017). *Autorisierungen des pädagogischen Selbst. Studien zur Adressierung der Bildungskindheit.* Wiesbaden, Germany: VS Verlag für Sozialwissenschaften.

Jornitz, S. (2008). Was bedeutet eigentlich 'evidenzbasierte Bildungsforschung?' Über den Versuch, Wissenschaft und Praxis verfügbar zu machen am Beispiel der Review-Erstellung. *Die Deutsche Schule, 100*(2), 206–216.

Lingard, B., & Sellar, S. (2016). The Changing Organizational and Global Significance of the OECD's Education Work. In K. Mundy, A. Green, B. Lingard, & A. Verger (Eds.), *Global Education Policy* (pp. 357–373). West Sussex, UK: Wiley Blackwell.

Ozga, J., Dahler-Larsen, P., Segerholm, C., & Simola, H. (Eds.). (2011). *Fabricating Quality in Education. Data and Governance in Europe.* London: Routledge.

Pearson. (2017a). *The Learning Curve.* Retrieved from http://thelearningcurve.pearson.com/. Accessed 13 Oct 2017.

Pearson. (2017b). *Data Hub.* Retrieved from http://thelearningcurve.pearson.com/data-hub. Accessed 13 Oct 2017.

Pearson (2017c). *Stories.* Retrieved from http://thelearningcurve.pearson.com/stories. Accessed 13 Oct 2017.

Popitz, H. (2004). *Phänomene der Macht.* Tübingen, Germany: Mohr.

Revel. (2015). *Revel Efficacy Report 2015.* Retrieved from https://www.pearsonhighered.com/revel/educators/results/. Accessed 22 Sep 2017.

Revel. (2017). *Pearson Community Revel.* Retrieved from https://www.pearsoned.com/pearson-community/revel/. Accessed 30 Nov 2017.

Schäfer, A., & Thompson, C. (Eds.). (2009). *Autorität*. Paderborn, Germany: Schöningh.
Schleicher (2012). *TED Talk: "Use Data to Build Better Schools"*. Retrieved from https://www.ted.com/talks/andreas_schleicher_use_data_to_build_better_schools. Accessed 13 Oct 2017.
Schleicher, A., & Zoido, P. (2016). The Policies that Shaped PISA, and the Policies that PISA Shaped. In K. Mundy, A. Green, B. Lingard, & A. Verger (Eds.), *Global Education Policy* (pp. 374–384). West Sussex, UK: Wiley Blackwell.
Spring, J. (2009). *Globalization of Education. An Introduction*. New York: Routledge.
Spring, J. (2015). *Economization of Education. Human Capital, Global Corporations, Skills-Based Schooling*. New York: Routledge.
Stalder, F. (2016). *Kultur der Digitalität*. Berlin, Germany: Suhrkamp.
TED. (2012). *Transcript*. Retrieved from: https://www.ted.com/talks/andreas_schleicher_use_data_to_build_better_schools/transcript. Accessed 13 Oct 2017.
TED. (2017). *Ideas Worth Spreading*. Retrieved from https://www.ted.com/. Accessed 13 Oct 2017.
TED-Blog (2012). *4 Surprising Lessons About Education Learned from Data Collected Around the World*. Retrieved from https://blog.ted.com/4-surprising-lessons-about-education-from-data-collected-around-the-world/. Accessed 13 Oct 2017.
The Bookseller. (2016). *Pearson Rebrand to Reflect 100% Focus on Education*. Retrieved from https://www.thebookseller.com/news/pearson-rebrands-reflect-100-focus-education-319864. Accessed 13 Oct 2017.
Thompson, C. (2013). Im Namen der Autorität: Spielarten der Selbstinszenierung in pädagogischen Ratgebern. In P. Bühler, T. Bühler, & F. Osterwalder (Eds.), *Zur Inszenierung pädagogischer Erlöserfiguren* (pp. 19–35). Bern, Switzerland: Haupt.
Thompson, C. (2014). Autorisierung durch Evidenzorientierung. Zur Rhetorik der Evidenz als Versprechen gelingender pädagogischer Praxis. In A. Schäfer (Ed.), *Hegemonie und autorisierende Verführung* (pp. 93–111). Paderborn, Germany: Schöningh.
Thompson, C. (2017). Wirksamkeit als Motor und Anspruch der Veränderung. In K. Jergus & C. Thompson (Eds.), *Autorisierung des pädagogischen Selbst. Studien zu Adressierungen der Bildungskindheit* (pp. 49–89). Wiesbaden, Germany: Springer VS.

Thompson, C. (2018, forthcoming). Bildung in Zeiten globaler Expertise. In N. Ricken, R. Casale, & C. Thompson (Eds.), *Subjektivierung – eine erziehungswissenschaftliche Theorieperspektive*. Paderborn, Germany: Schöningh.
Weber, M. (2000). *Wirtschaft und Gesellschaft. Grundriß der verstehenden Soziologie*. Tübingen, Germany: Mohr.
Williamson, B. (2014). New Governing Experts in Education. Self-Learning Software, Policy Labs and Transactional Pedagogies. In T. Fenwick, E. Mangez, & J. Ozga (Eds.), *Governing Knowledge: Comparison, Knowledge-Based Technologies and Expertise in the Regulation of Education* (pp. 218–231). London: Routledge.
Williamson, B. (2016). Digital Education Governance: Data Visualization, Predictive Analytics, and 'Real-Time' Policy Instruments. *Journal of Education Policy, 31*(3), 123–141.
Williamson, B. (2017). *Big Data in Education. The Digital Future of Learning Policy and Practice*. London: Sage.

# 11

# Digitization, Disruption, and the "Society of Singularities": The Transformative Power of the Global Education Industry

S. Karin Amos

## Introduction

Digitization and algorithmization—the core of innovation and technology in education—are undoubtedly hot topics. The largest and most influential international organizations like the European Union (EU), the United Nations Educational, Scientific, and Cultural Organization (UNESCO), and the World Bank have all put digital competencies and new technologies to augment and enhance learning at the top of their education agendas. The starting page of the World Bank's website on education and technology, for example, states that "World Bank support for the use of ICTs in education includes assistance for equipment and facilities; policy development; teacher training and support; capacity building; educational content; distance learning; digital literacy and skills development; monitoring and evaluation; and research and development (R&D) activities."[1] The World Bank's blog on education for global development promotes "OLE, Open Learning Exchange"—a digitization

S. K. Amos (✉)
University of Tübingen, Tübingen, Germany
e-mail: karin.amos@uni-tuebingen.de

© The Author(s) 2019
M. Parreira do Amaral et al. (Eds.), *Researching the Global Education Industry*,
https://doi.org/10.1007/978-3-030-04236-3_11

initiative to foster education in disrupted, violence-ridden, poverty-stricken communities.[2] The OLE mission includes another type of disruption I will describe below in which the shift from teacher-centered to student-centered and personalized learning are constitutive elements. Gert Biesta has described this shift with the phrase, "from education to learnification" (2015).

The European Commission (EC), in line with its high aspirations for driving the knowledge economy, also emphasizes digital technologies in education. The EC's Joint Research Center Policy Report on *Digital Education Policies in Europe and Beyond* (EC, 2017) illustrates how the EU observes and stimulates digitization activities in its member countries and throughout the world. EU member states have equally committed themselves to promote digitization and algorithmization. Moreover, one may declare digitization of education not only one of the top trends of international organizations but also of the member states irrespective of the size of the respective educational programs or the state of their implementation.

Algorithmization and digitization are closely linked to the rise of the global education industry (GEI) which, as I will argue in this chapter, is central to the transformation of education from a modern to a late modern institution. As has been frequently emphasized, education as mass schooling organized by age group and different subjects is essentially a product of the nineteenth and twentieth centuries, when it met the requirements of high modernity in an industrial age. As the mode of production and ideas of life development changed, public education was increasingly pressed to adapt to new conditions. What followed was a huge shift to data collection on student-centered, personalized learning, as well as the abovementioned move from education to learnification in the age of globalization. In this chapter I will:

(1) Highlight some of the major aspects of algorithmization and digitization by way of examples at the national and international levels. Digitization and algorithmization as a significant segment of the GEI often have the effect of masking commercialism and profit. Somewhat paradoxically, digitization and algorithmization are as much a characteristic of elite training as they purport to support democratic and

participatory processes. This is the case because, on the one hand, state-of-the-art hardware and software are expensive and parents who do possess the financial means are willing to pay in order to ensure a competitive edge for their children. It is also the case because top educational programs are a priority for parents who invest in enhancement and augmentation in all areas of life. With regard to the latter, for-profit and nonprofit orientations tend to overlap as market-focus is characteristic of any industry, including GEI. Somewhat paradoxically, however, the low costs of distributing learning programs once they are developed together with the easy accessibility and equally low cost of the hardware, such as tablet computers and digitized products, promise to increase access to education in poor countries. Although the focus of the present contribution is a general systematization and contextualization of GEI activities in the area of digitization, I am certain that a comparison of vertical case studies elicits interesting insights into how the global narrative on digitization is translated and broken down nationally, as well as how various multi-level analyses converge to compose a mutually resonating narrative.

(2) To make the relation between digitization, education, and GEI more clear, I will show how economic disruption factors in. To illustrate I draw on Carey (2015) to look at some successful startups in higher education, and show how these technological trends relate to what Reckwitz (2017) has called the singularization of society. Singularization and personalization are related concepts, which show how education is being transformed from a modern to a late modern institution.

(3) Consider adaptive learning and e-advising as widely used tools in tertiary education. The University of Arizona experience highlights how common the use of such tools already is. Although this particular example pertains to higher education, e-advising systems are more and more often introduced at every level. I have chosen University of Arizona because it is among the many major public universities serving a large and diverse student population with limited resources. As one type of disruption digital instruments promise to do more with less, thus making their implementation attractive and cost-efficient. The University of Arizona experience also shows how difficult it is to

separate commercial use from public service. In many ways, the introduction of these digital monitoring/advising/assisting systems follows the mission of personalized medicine to bring out the best in every individual and help each realize his or her potential to the fullest. The prize to pay eventually is full disclosure of oneself—a paradoxical surrendering of autonomy in order to gain autonomy. The aim of personalization moreover supports Reckwitz' theory of "singularization" (2017), while at the same time undermining notions of the "the general," or "the public." The term in German is *das Allgemeine*, and I will discuss the context of this concept later in the chapter. For now it is important noting that thinking of the GEI as a clearly demarcated area where traditional notions of private and public can be smoothly applied will probably miss the broader implications of this industry.

## Digitization and Algorithmization: International and National Examples

Digital competencies of the next generation are an integral component of one of the key EU education strategies, Horizon 2020. The EC's single digital market policy is strongly linked to education in terms of this program by way of "Information and Communication Technologies" (ICT), which purport to help us learn better, more efficiently and creatively, innovate to solve complex problems, and access wider and more up-to-date knowledge. According to the EU webpage, "ICT provides everyone with flexible and accessible learning opportunities, in and outside the classroom."[3] In a similar vein, in 2014 the European Parliamentary Research Service Blog posted that:

> The world of education is currently undergoing massive transformation as a result of the digital revolution. In the European Union (EU), children become active online from the age of 7, and 76% of EU households have access to broadband Internet. However, research shows that early use of digital technologies is not necessarily linked to good digital competencies.

As jobs are becoming more 'knowledge and digital skills-intensive', continued investment in upgrading education and training systems will be instrumental to maintaining the EU's competitiveness and attractiveness. (Posted April 2014, EPRS, 2014)

This same narrative is adopted by the Organization for Economic Co-Operation and Development (OECD), and of particular interest in terms of the relationship between digitization and GEI is a 2016 Centre for Educational Research and Innovation (CERI) report, "Innovating Education and Educating Innovation: The Power of Digital Technologies and Skills." The importance of this report, a compilation of OECD expertise in this area, is evidenced by the fact that its author is CERI director Dirk van Damme. The report serves as background to the second GEI Summit held in September 2016 in Jerusalem, where the proper use of technology was said to promise that:

> Although they cannot transform education by themselves, digital technologies do have huge potential to transform teaching and learning practices in schools and open up new horizons. The challenge of achieving this transformation is more about integrating new types of instruction than overcoming technological barriers. (OECD, 2016, p. 10)

Note the caveat that, "although they [i.e. digital technologies, KA] cannot transform education by themselves digital technologies do have huge potential to transform teaching and learning practices in schools." This clearly adheres to the logic of innovative disruption, which I will explain in further detail below. Innovative disruption is related to Schumpeter's "creative destruction" of economic development and innovation. Innovative disruption similarly addresses issues of efficacy and efficiency, of channeling means to achieve best effects. An example in transportation would be Uber; in photography, digitization has wiped out analogue almost completely; with computing it was PCs. As these examples show, disruptive innovation does not start from the center of a given business practice, but unravels it from the fringes. In education digital technology is now peripheral; however, the shift to personalized learning, strongly supported by digital technologies, bodes profound changes. The message in the quote above is that systems do not merely need to be changed, but transformed. To make this happen, an innovation-friendly environment is a prerequisite. This relies on the collaboration between traditional institutions and stakeholders in public education with those of the emerging education industry. Continuing from the quote above we learn that:

> understanding the education industries better, including their market structures and innovation processes, would help to create a more mature relationship with the education sector. Innovation in the industry – which develops the products and services that could drive innovation in schools – does not happen in isolation from what is happening in the education sector. Only when there is an innovation-friendly culture in education systems, supported by an innovation-friendly business environment and policies, will industries start to engage in risk-intensive research and development. Governments can support this by fostering a climate of entrepreneurship and innovation in education. (ibid.)

This alludes to countries like Estonia,[4] who were pioneers in overhauling their bureaucracies in government, education,[5] and other public sectors, and are posed as models others are encouraged to follow. The message of transformation and system overhaul is also driven home by chief evangelists such as Google's Jaime Casap, who played a key role in launching Google Apps at Arizona State (see Theo Priestly, 2015, on the role of chief evangelists). UNESCO also strongly emphasizes digitization, but does so with reference to democracy, participation, and human rights. As is the case for other international organizations and national policies as well, UNESCO places digitization in a knowledge society context. However, UNESCO's framework emphasizes not only quality of education and universal access to knowledge and information, but also respect for cultural and linguistic diversity—as well as freedom of expression.

These glimpses at the inter- or trans-national level of education policy emphasizing ICT and other forms of digitization illustrate that they are connected to a powerful narrative of progress, improvement, and modernization. They also have to do with redemption, and though this is more hidden it is expressed in the expectation that new technologies make the world more just and equitable by realizing the vision of universal access to education, and furthering industrial innovation to free humans from the toil of labor—something I will discuss further at the end of this chapter. One example of how this transpires at a national level is the German Federal Ministry of Education and Research's strong emphasis on the role of digitization in society at large, as well as specific areas such as tertiary education, medicine, and vocational training. "Bildung digital" (BMBF, 2018) unites a wide range of activities and programs, from early childhood education to every level of formal schooling including tertiary education, to adult education and beyond. As one would expect in a society undergoing profound technological change, Science, Technology, Engineering and Mathematics (STEM) subjects are especially emphasized. Baden-Wuerttemberg, whose tradition in individual entrepreneurship provided many of the key players in today's automobile, turbine, and other industries, is pushing hard for digital transformation at the state level in Germany. Encouraging tinkerers and risk-takers is the spirit of the new century. The underlying rhetoric at all levels of educational policy and institutional settings is the Silicon Valley mission to make humans fit to survive in a high-tech environment.

## Digitization and the GEI

As Antoni Verger emphasized in "The rise of the global education industry: Some concepts, facts and figures" (2016), education has become an important asset in the knowledge economy at every level. This market is inexhaustible, and facilitated by the emergence of a global education regime (Parreira do Amaral, 2011). This industry's market is both deep—for example, lifelong learning—and wide, in that it is easily adaptable to conditions almost anywhere in the world. As indicated in the previous section, governments, international organizations, corporations, education technology evangelists, and venture capitalists, all push this trend and speed its implementation. Commodification, privatization, and digitization are intricately linked.

Whether in the form of educational provision, administration, infrastructure, online degrees, virtual universities, student data processing or the machinery to provide it, GEI has transformed education.[6] The feedback loops of data collection and analysis ensure the datafication trend does not end with how education is organized and carried out, but also affects how it is researched. A general observation illustrating this point is the notable decrease in education chairs specializing in philosophy, concurrent with the rise of empirical research and closely linked to quantitative methods (see also Parreira do Amaral, in this volume).

It is unsurprising that the most common paradigm of business and technology innovation—disruption—is a feature of GEI. Disruption, or more precisely, disruptive innovation, is a term coined by Clayton Christensen which, "describes a process by which a product or service takes root initially in simple applications at the bottom of a market and then relentlessly moves up market, eventually displacing established competitors." Christensen, a professor at the Business School of Harvard University, also founded the Christensen Institute for Disruptive Innovation,[7] as well as a number of other initiatives such as the Forum of Growth and Innovation. He is also heavily involved in pushing the application of the concept in education (Christensen, Horn, & Johnson, 2008). The title of his book, *Disrupting Class*, signals the project of unraveling organized education as age cohorts segregated by social class learning a set program of subjects. Disruption in education again takes its lead from Schumpeter and would, in theory, promote equity along the lines of the World Bank's OLE.

With this in mind, we will now look more closely at GEI. As indicated, the tenet of digitalization and algorithmization is personalized learning to help students to develop his or her potential to the fullest. It is decontextualized and can be broken down into bits and pieces that can be measured, tested, and assessed. So, while personalized learning combats the notion of homogeneity, it still must define some standard and pre-defined outcome so that learning, however personalized or individualized it may be, can be applied to league tables and other forms of comparison. While it looks as if modern digital technologies are just another means of instruction, their revolutionizing potential consists in the fact that instruction in the classical sense is no longer necessary, and may even be an impediment to technology. This is what makes digital technologies different from the blackboard or other "analogue" learning materials such as textbooks that require a teacher to explain, guide, check, and discuss content. As Christensen suggested, do not start at the core—unravel a sector from the fringes to bring about disruptive innovation. Unlike traditional schooling with its limited flexibility to individual needs, this innovation promises to accommodate learning styles and habits of all types to cultivate individual potential to the fullest, while also stimulating collaboration. Whether GEI is more support and service-oriented to education as we know it, or whether it is intentionally disruptive, is often unclear, because while there is a digitization strategy within the traditional framework of education policy, federal or state governments are still key actors who primarily want to implement digitization as part of the development of the established public school system. Conversely, disruptive innovation is an integral part of digitization, and disruption by definition implies a skeptical stance toward established structures. Technology innovators, evangelists, and venture capitalists commonly regard education as they do government, finance, and health—overly bureaucratized, inflexible, inefficient structures that have to be radically changed.

Prominent protagonists who emphasize this view and credit it with authority are influential "movers" and "shakers" such as Peter Thiel, one of Silicon Valley's foremost entrepreneurs and venture capitalists; Sebastian Thrun, computer scientist, robotics specialist, high-ranked Google executive, proponent of Massive Open Online Courses (MOOCSs) (which he used for his own courses), and founder of Udacity; Ray Kurzweil, another prominent Google executive, futurist, and computer scientist mainly associated with the term Singularity, which he also used to name a Silicon Valley University; Elon Musk, another highly prominent entrepreneur (Tesla, SpaceX), who has been outspoken in his critique of the public education system and founded a private school, Ad Astra; and Tim Draper, Silicon Valley venture capitalist and founder of Draper University, a six week course in entrepreneurship and innovative business. Ayn Rand, Wilhelm Reich, Milton Friedman, and Friedrich August von Hayek are among the most frequently cited sources to give expression to the "Silicon Valley" philosophy of enlightened individualism, combined with community-based connectivity, faith in the market, and distrust of big government. The ingredients of this mixture are far from free of tension. Rand's concept of objectivism and her focus on individual interests illustrates that "connectivism" is far from uncontended.

The 2016 OECD report on innovation in education quoted above argues that education policy makers should pay attention to innovation in the education industry and overcome their reservations about the role of private interests. The "key messages for innovation policies in education" are as follows:

> Policy makers typically view education industries as providers of goods and services, often technology-based, to schools. They tend to dismiss the fact that innovation in education is also changing the environment in which schools are operating. Technology-based innovations tend to open up schools and learning environments in general to the outside world, both the digital world and the physical and social environment. At the same time they bring new actors and stakeholders into the educational system, not at least the education industries with their own ideas, views and dreams about what a brighter future for education could hold.
>
> Convincing schools and education systems to treat industry as a valuable partner is still in many cases a very sensitive issue. Fears about or ideological objections to a perceived 'marketisation' or privatisation of education, or outright anxieties about the displacement of teachers by computers, often endanger a potentially fruitful dialogue. The fact that the global education industry is a largely unknown entity – in contrast to the medical or paramedical industries in the health sector, for example – further adds to the difficulty. (OECD, 2016, p. 123)

Digitization and GEI mean that large cutting-edge technology corporations such as Google, Apple, Amazon, and international organizations, such as the OECD, are all united along the belief in disruptive innovation. Of course, these are not the only actors, but they are the core that propels the industry. Despite their different outlooks, charismatic personae of the digital age such as Kurzweil and Thrun have clout when it comes to education even if they are not themselves experts.

In his book *The End of College*, Kevin Carey claims that in higher education alone, disruptive innovation is a 4.6 trillion-dollar industry. Some of the most successful startups, according to an April 14th, 2015, report by the INC Magazine, are listed below. I retain the numbers of the ranking, but do not re-iterate the full list. The selection is to provide an overview of the spectrum of activities. Although many focus their activities primarily on the American market, their products can be easily adapted to fit other purposes or serve as models for similar enterprises in other contexts.

## InsideTrack

InsideTrack markets its services to universities, providing highly personalized coaching to students and assessment of whether their technology and practices accurately measure student progress. It also helps schools manage their technology and boasts testimonials from institutions including Arizona State and the University of Virginia. In addition, InsideTrack recently announced a partnership with Chegg, through which it will provide its coaching services directly to students.

## The UnCollege Movement

Thiel Fellow Dale Stephens accepted $100,000 from Peter Thiel to skip college and found The UnCollege Movement, which provides students with a 12-month Gap Year experience for $16,000. The program has four phases—residence in a Gap Year House, travel abroad, an internship, and completing a creative project. Enrollees experience some of what they would in college, such as dorm life and community, along traditional Gap Year benefits like travel and professional training.

## Udacity

Founded by Stanford computer science professor Sebastian Thrun, Udacity runs online employee training for companies such as AT&T, who were willing to pay them $3 million according to *The Wall Street Journal*. Other corporate partners include Google, Facebook, and Salesforce.

## Coursera

Coursera advertises "Free online courses from top universities," partnering with prestigious universities worldwide. With $8 to $12 million in annual revenues, according to an EdSurge estimate, it is very profitable.

All of these startups are just a fraction of what Carey describes as the larger thriving ecosystem of nonprofit and for-profit organizations for students.[8] They have to be considered not only in the context of profit and economization, but also in the more general context of schooling policies focusing on "enhanced" or "augmented" education (cf. Sheehy, Ferguson, & Clough, 2014). Along with established forms of blended learning and online formats, augmented education includes virtual reality experiences such as museum tours and lab simulations. As already mentioned, whether digitization will enhance or reduce equity in education is unclear. Access depends on investment in hardware and software, which make it easier to produce and disseminate up-to-date education materials more cheaply and easily than traditional printed publishing. Other concerns include real-time formative and skill-based assessments which allow teachers to monitor student learning as it happens, and adjust their teaching accordingly. It may also enable active participation for more students in classroom discussions. But, to take up another point raised earlier, the ethical concerns also have to be discussed. Because of the incredible headway made in storage capacity, data collection is literally insatiable, and with this information that links learning habits to all areas of personal conduct and circumstances comes the uncanny feeling that control over one's life is transferred to algorithms to make decisions which may be mistaken for sense-making.

The point is technology-supported assessment enables skill development to be monitored in a more comprehensive way than is possible without it (OECD, 2016, p. 10). These new vistas promise to monitor mistakes, but they may do much more than that. Not only are decisions delegated to non-human algorithms, but a trend is emerging that so far is rarely brought up in digitization-debates: the merging of advising and assisting systems along the lines of what Cortana, Alexa, and Siri provide in terms of digital assistance. In the next section, I will describe the successful implementation of e-advising at a large public university, then turn to an example showing how far digital technologies have penetrated the lives of individuals and the ambivalences this entails.

## e-Advising and Adaptive Learning

Digitization and algorithmization do not just result in commodification and profit when it comes to GEI. As the following example shows, they also provide services in large public institutions without the human resources to deliver these services on their own. With its current enrolment of around 72,000 students in the larger Phoenix metropolitan area, Arizona State University is one of the largest research schools in the USA. In 2016, Arizona State University (ASU) received the prestigious Phi Kappa Phi "Excellence in Innovation Award" for using two digital tools, eAdvisor and me3, to increase retention rates. eAdvisor and me3 have since become among the most widely implemented instruments in the world. How deeply they affect the learner's life depends on the regulations and laws effective in their respective countries. Generally speaking, the USA is far more deregulated in this area than countries belonging to the EU where data protection and the importance of the private sphere are emphasized. This notwithstanding, e-assistants and other forms of digital support quickly spread so that ASU's example is more a pars pro toto than an uncommon let alone "exotic" feature.

As for ASU's motivation for using technology to increase access and impact, the Phi Kappa Phi report states that, "ASU measures its success not by the number of students excluded from the university, but rather by those included and how they succeed" (Phi Kappa Phi, 2016, p. 2). As this is the report on the "Excellence in Education Award," it is laudatory and uncritical, but it does address a crucial point of public, that is, state-run universities worldwide: Although national university systems traditionally bear a variety of path-dependencies and specificities, public research universities are under similar pressures globally. Such schools must make do with stagnating or declining budgets combined with the expectation to serve an ever larger and more diverse student population. Decreasing the rate of university dropouts is expected as part of the knowledge-economy narrative promising to introduce an increasingly larger population of students to tertiary education. In order to maintain much less increase in public funding, universities must prove they successfully graduate their students, providing a market for automated tracking systems like eAdvisor.

Arizona State University's Mission Statement expresses these globalized expectations:

> Arizona State University has developed a new model for the American Research University, creating an institution that is committed to access, excellence and impact. [...] ASU takes fundamental responsibility for educating Arizonans for a better future and for the economic, social, cultural and overall health of the community it serves. As part of its charter, ASU has developed three key metrics designed to help our state succeed: a) 90% retention from freshman to sophomore year, b) 75% 6-year graduation rate and c) awarding 25,000 degrees annually by 2020. (Phi Kappa Phi, 2016, p. 2)

If an institution such as ASU commits itself to benchmarks like retention rate and number of degrees awarded, these figures will determine whether or not goals have been achieved. An algorithmic automated tracking system may be an excellent way to ensure students who may not have passed the required number of courses visit their human guidance counselors, because if they do not they are dropped from the course and not allowed to register. eAdvisor scans information pertaining to a particular student and looks for patterns such as not completing coursework on time, failing exams, or spending more hours in the gym than the library, which might signal they are at risk. If enough red flags are raised, their counselor is notified to contact the student to meet. The idea is to get students back on the right track before they stray too far. Close monitoring is justified as a money-saver for the student, who might otherwise waste money on a degree they will never complete. It also can save the student from wasting time on a major that is not engaging their interest. Indeed, eAdvisor's effectiveness seems proven by an increase in retention rates (see the appendices to the Phi Kappa Phi publication). University faculty and staff would agree that if "problem" students are recognized in time they can be helped. This may still underestimate the obstacles certain groups of students face, but it is based on decades of experience and observation. The eAdvisor narrative presents an idealized version of events legitimized by successes such as receiving the prestigious Phi Kappa Phi award for using technology to help students make better choices, as well as its proven success lowering the dropout rate.

In addition to tracking student progress, eAdvisor can also enable them to audit their success throughout the semester. Students might drop a class, transfer credit, change majors, or any number of other things that will affect their grade—all of which can be monitored with eAdvisor. eAdvisor students also receive regular updates to their student email account which has the added benefit of encouraging them to monitor it daily.

eAdvisor also provides important reminders to students on their My ASU page provided by the university. If a student falls behind, an advising hold will be placed on their record. While they may drop or withdraw from a course, they will not be able to add courses in the current semester, or register for future semesters until they have contacted their advisor to discuss strategies for improvement.[9]

Upon closer observation, various levels of rationality and legitimation may be identified associated with the implementation of digital technologies such as eAdvisor or similar systems. Clearly, they address the individual, they become part of the experience of being socialized as a student in the twenty-first century. As a consequence, habits will be formed accordingly. Chances of falling through the cracks, of slipping by without being detected when late with exams, are close to zero. The algorithm will inevitably identify students who are behind. If someone should have been selected erroneously, the face-to-face talk with the human advisor will rectify the mistake. However, the introduction of such systems also serves another purpose. It signals not only to the outside world, to stakeholders, but also to the global university community, that top of the line technology is implemented to optimize processes and tasks, that the university fulfills its teaching and qualifying role. In addition, as already brought up, the question of data collection, storage, and transfer is also crucial in this context. As tempting and promising these new technologies are both individually and institutionally, the commercial use raises significant issues especially as the growth of GEI in this sector is related to a strong interest in "big data."

This point is driven home by technology in the burgeoning field of adaptive learning. While e-advising systems keep the student on track by monitoring learning outcomes such as earned credits and exam grades, adaptive learning systems monitor progress by focusing on habits, strengths, and weaknesses to take the entire academic environment into account. The Knewton Company platforms for adaptive learning, used by ASU for their math courses, are a good example. Before detailing what the company is doing, let me emphasize that the dynamism of the field is also illustrated by the strategic moves linking Knewton with powerful corporations in the field. According to Wikipedia:

> The Knewton platform allows schools, publishers, and developers to provide adaptive learning for any student. In 2011, Knewton announced a partnership with Pearson Education to enhance the company's digital content, including the MyLab and Mastering series. Additional partners announced include Houghton Mifflin Harcourt, Macmillan Education, Triumph Learning, and over a dozen others. (Wikipedia without references)

Jörg Dräger and Ralph Müller-Eiselt published *Die Digitale Revolution* (The Digital Revolution) for a German audience in 2015. The authors mainly focus on the state of digital education in America to tell a tale of disruptive innovation. That a third edition came out in 2017, and the book was widely discussed in the media and in educational settings testifies to the attention the book received.

The Knewton business model is summarized as personalized education though data collection, a large amount of which is gathered daily. The rationale is that optimized personalized learning is possible if everything that can be known about the student is accounted for. What and how the student learns—every mouse-click, reaction, right and wrong answer—is registered (cf. Dräger & Müller-Eiselt, 2017, p. 24). The company claims the continually refined algorithm can even predict how students will perform (ibid., p. 25), rendering exams obsolete.

They acknowledge the dangers of this development in terms of access, and correctly point out that these data are more revealing and potentially detrimental than photos posted on Facebook (ibid., p. 26). Nevertheless, big data is—as a highly traded resource—the oil of the twenty-first century, and data mining is big business.

The field of automated support is extensive, and entails the consensus of professionals dealing with students in large public higher education institutions dependent on limited resources due to declining state contributions worldwide. In order to accommodate the needs of tens of thousands of students, the professional counseling staff in many higher education institutions already uses or is on the verge of introducing e-advising systems to monitor academic progression and identify students in need who are reluctant to take the initiative. As the reduced dropout rate shows, being obligated to do something by an automated system has its advantages. However, the boundaries between strictly monitoring academic progression and more extensive data collection are fluid. Though adaptive learning and advising are separate, they are linked by adaptive learning systems such as Knewton whose appetite for data is insatiable. The more that is known about the social and cultural background of the student, his routines and habits, preferences and learning style, social networks, and so on, the more precise the advice that may be given. So, while simply acknowledging academic issues such as failed courses is the first step to initiating the counseling process, more information is conducive to identifying the appropriate measures to put the student back on track. Instead of asking students numerous background questions, which they may be more or less willing to provide, from the point of view of effective counseling, it is more desirable to have a system at hand that "objectively" provides information that may prove relevant, such as the amount of hours devoted to various activities on the scale of work per week and month.

So, the next step of e-advising could easily be a direct communication with the advisee. What if an e-advising system was linked to a personalized virtual personal advising system? What if a student could directly communicate with a personalized virtual advising system that offers options for him or her what to do next? These questions raise numerous others. For example, so-called non-traditional students may find it easier to deal with a machine than with a human and his prejudices, pre-conceptions, and judgments. So, on a first glance, for some students dealing with a "machine" may be easier and less burdened by feelings of shame or inadequacy. On the other hand, what is known about the "learning" processes of algorithms is at best mixed: The result depends on which "thread" of communication and information is picked up, as machines are not value free. This danger is compounded by the fact that the development of intelligent systems is still dominated by primarily male scientists and technical personnel belonging to the privileged social classes representing dominant Western values.

Related to this is the question as to who makes the decision. This introduces the concept of algocracy or rule by algorithms (cf. Danaher, 2014). Algocracy designates a form of rulership but does not make a judgment whether the form of rule is positive or negative. Rule by algorithm takes on different forms in relation to humans. Humans can be "in-the-loop," making decisions based on information provided by the algorithm. But humans can also intervene or remain "outside" the loop, their subjective thoughts, and opinions unaccounted for. To be effective, pedagogical expert systems must penetrate deeply into the life of the individual, their relationships, and contexts in order to be effective. If the algorithm ultimately determines the student's educational success, we have entered in an area of ethical concern (for further critical discussions in this context see, for example, Hartong, 2016; Karcher, 2015; Radtke, 2009).

To sum up: With regard to GEI, e-advising and adaptive learning systems are an important sector of the industry. The OECD has already included them in their list and as the use of clouds becomes increasingly common and the technical difficulties are overcome, privacy laws and data protection will not likely prove to be obstacles. In addition, whoever develops systems that are widely used and successful in keeping young people on track will have a competitive edge and impact. Easy adaptation is among the features making these systems most attractive from an economic perspective.

## Digitization: The Human Factor

The relationship between humans and the technology we create is ever evolving and made even more complex by profit and commercialization. Both issues are important in terms of e-advising, learner interacting, and adaptive learning systems. A useful comparison is the use of technology in medicine in areas such as cancer diagnosis, where oncologists work in close collaboration with machines whose "advice" they take into account and depend on. In some areas of diagnostics, the best artificial systems are at least as accurate as humans and sometimes more precise. Developing sophisticated artificial expert systems in pedagogy remains a challenge, particularly for merging e-advising with traditional guidance counseling.

The earliest example of such a system is ELIZA,[10] a counseling program developed by Joseph Weizenbaum in the 1960s modeled on Carl Rogers' principles of human psychology. ELIZA's primitive algorithms proved inflexible and incapable of modeling the complex ethical aspects of decision making. The merger of neuroscience and computer science, along with the rise of probability models and fuzzy logic—which does a better job of approximating human concepts by allowing for partial truths—can be sensitive enough to pick up on subtleties and cues they have "learned" to look out for. Although there still remains a gap between the formal language of computer science and the natural language used by humans, the combination of progress in bio-informatics and big data processing in computer sciences promises to help bridge it for routine counseling. The danger, that is, the system reproducing stereotypes and making discriminating judgments, has already been mentioned.

The other primary man-machine relation is between the learner and the artificial assistant. Here the affective bond is decisive, because learners are encouraged to identify with the machine, which is, by definition, more distant and objective. Designers and evangelists will work closely together to create a powerful narrative around these systems which will help sell them in the GEI market. This development is based on the confluence of two powerful anthropological facts: One, humans are storytellers, and two, since Paleolithic times humans have bonded with inanimate objects (cf. Zarkadakis, 2016). In his illuminating account, *In Our Image*, George Zarkadakis traces a continuity from the appearance of the first art objects, to the awareness that others might think differently than ourselves, and therefore it is important to predict their actions (a.k.a., "theory of mind). Art serves as a common language which we use to create a symbolic universe, as evidenced by examples such as Lion Man of the Vogelherd, an ivory sculpture recognized as among the earliest examples of human artifice, as well as the famous cave paintings at Lascaux. As Zarkadakis writes:

> The realization of your inevitable death can only take place if you have a mind capable of self-awareness. In prehistoric art we discover the beginnings of religion and science, and importantly the cognitive roots of our hardwired belief that things can have minds, which also means that robots can ultimately become as intelligent as ourselves. (Zarkadakis, 2016, p. 16)

As machines become more "human," they become more able to "know" us. They help us function in our personal and professional lives, choose our partners, help with chores, and even console us when we are sad by suggesting books, films, and music. Moreover, they may actively respond and communicate with us. As they are fed with information about ourselves, our preferences, hobbies, habits, daily routines, desires, they are our "Doppelgänger."

The commercial (disruption) and relational dimensions intersect at the point of affective meaning that is not only a key trait of the corporate evangelists, but designers of technological systems as well. For example, Microsoft named its personal assistant system Cortana after a virtual heroine popular with many of its users. The disruption paradigm is facilitated, augmented, supported, and reinforced by the capacity to establish emotional bonds. Disruption does not mean everything changes; the core of the respective service or business—be it transportation, photography, health or education—remains the same. Education is learning, and learning is more than a cognitive process. It is holistic, and positive emotions and relationships play a key role. That GEI capitalizes upon this relationship is obvious. Why wouldn't it?

# Digitization, Disruption, and the Society of Singularities

In the final decades of the twentieth century, a variety of terms—the Information Society, Post-Industrial Society, Network Society, Knowledge Society—were chosen to describe how technology has transformed our world. The latest descriptor, "Society of Singularities," specifically positions us in relation to late modernity. The very idea of late modernity, addressed and elaborated by Andreas Reckwitz (2017), implies continuity, reconfiguration, re-arrangement, and the creation of new relations and hierarchies as opposed to the simple substitution of the old with the new and different. In this regard, the *"Allgemeine"*—the general—does not disappear, but rather is replaced by the singular or the extraordinary. The concepts are reconfigured.

As a general sociological theory, society of singularities claims to explain major transformations and their effects on societal relations in practice. If the analysis is correct, it is only logical that no system or essential organizations are unaffected. Politics, education, economic relations, our ways of being in the world—that is, our understanding of subjectivity—all have to be reconsidered in the light of new orientations and a re-arrangement of established relations. This may seem too mono-causal, but Reckwitz distinguishes the principle of "singularity" from the use in AI (Kurzweil, 2005). Striving for the outstanding, the unique, special, or singular, becomes the distinguishing feature of cities, regions, corporations, and the individual. It deeply affects our lifestyles, employment relations, and impacts the social structure, which Reckwitz describes in painstaking detail. The arts as well as the creative economy more generally are the model for the major shifts currently taking place. "Projects," Reckwitz insists, are the singularistic form of the social par excellence" (ibid., p. 192). Formal certificates are no longer the direct path to a profession or career, but have taken on a secondary role. No doubt they are still relevant, but the importance of individual performance and originality has superseded them.

e-Advising systems exemplify the transformation from the general to the specific, unique, particular, singular. The "norm," and the "standard" remain, but the emphasis is on individual guidance to further stimulate individual talent and potential. This is what is behind "new" paradigms such as individualized instruction and diversity. And this is why the boundaries between institutional advising and personal assistance are so easily blurred. The powerful narrative of innovation and creativity "nudges" the individual, as it were, allowing a wide variety of data to be collected and analyzed that goes far beyond being strictly course or class related.

Dave Eggers novel *The Circle* (2013) strictly speaking is not a dystopia, but an account of a present where the technological prerequisites are already almost completely in place to create full transparency. The novel tells the story of a complete synthesis of digitally available personal information, leading to the full transparency described above. At this stage, the user allows every digitally connected person to gain a full insight—total observation—into his or her life. This description lends itself to interpretation in light of the Foucauldian notion of governmentality, biopower, following Han's (2014) "psychopower," and "the society of singularities."

The GEI of new technologies adheres to the logic of disruption rather than to the traditional qualities of what we commonly associate with an industry. As I have shown, Reckwitz' diagnosis fits nicely with the key practices and ideas of many of the protagonists in the current digital transformation. Their critique of schooling resonates with what he describes at length as the importance of the performative and the strength of narrative in a "corporate evangelical" sense. This fits with his emphasis that it is the power to elicit strong emotions of identification, vision, and so on, that makes for success in the age of the singularities.

There is still much empirical work to be done; however, what I have described above shows the necessity of pursuing these questions further. It is important to view current trends in digitalization and algorithmization not as fashionable add-ons to education as we know it, but to take their disruptive potential seriously and discuss their implications. These include not only how education is embedded in notions of the public, democracy, participation, and human rights, but also how it is situated in the relationship between humans and machines. The question of the essence of the human and the meaning of a human(e) education is raised with urgency.

## Notes

1. See: World Bank (2018). *Technology & Innovation in Education*. Retrieved from: http://www.worldbank.org/en/topic/edutech [last Jul. 19, 2018].
2. See: Open Learning Exchange. Retrieved from: http://ole.org [last Jul. 19, 2018].
3. See: EC (2018). *Digital Learning & ICT in Education*. Retrieved from: https://ec.europa.eu/digital-single-market/en/ict-education [last Jul. 19, 2018].
4. See: e-Estonia (2018a). *We have built a digital society and so can you*. Retrieved from: https://e-estonia.com [last Jul. 19, 2018].
5. See: e-Estonia (2018b). *Education*. Retrieved from: https://e-estonia.com/solutions/education [last Jul. 19, 2018].
6. For example, Capterra.com lists hundreds of school-related products covering all aspects of student data administration to fund raising, including the per student costs. See: Capterra (2018). *School Administration Software*. Retrieved from: https://www.capterra.com/school-administration-software [last Jul. 19, 2018].
7. See: Christensen, C. (2018). *Disruptive Innovation*. Retrieved from: http://www.claytonchristensen.com/key-concepts/ [last Jul. 19, 2018].
8. See: Retrieved from: https://www.inc.com/ilan-mochari/16-startups-that-will-disrupt-the-education-market.html [last Jul. 19, 2018].
9. See: Retrieved from: https://eadvisor.asu.edu/students/tools [last Jul. 19, 2018].
10. ELIZA is the name of a computer program developed by Joseph Weizenbaum that simulates psychological counseling based on Carl Rogers. The name is an ironic quote of George Bernard Shaw's main character in Pygmalion.

## References

Biesta, G. (2015). What Is Education for? On Good Education, Teacher Judgement, and Educational Professionalism. *European Journal of Education, 50*(1), 75–87.

BMBF (Bundesministerium für Bildung und Forschung). (2018). *Bildung Digital*. Retrieved from: https://www.bmbf.de/de/bildung-digital-3406.html. Last 19 July 2018. Accessed 01 June 2018.
Carey, K. (2015). *The End of College. Creating the Future of Learning and the University of Everywhere*. New York: Riverhead Books.
Christensen, C., Horn, M. B., & Johnson, C. W. (2008). *Disrupting Class: How Disruptive Innovation Will Change the Way the World Learns*. New York: McGraw-Hill.
Danaher, J. (2014). *Rule by Algorithm? Big Data and the Threat of Algocracy*. Retrieved from: http://ieet.org/index.php/IEET/more/danaher20140107. Last 19 July 2018.
Dräger, J., & Müller-Eiselt, R. (2017). *Die Digitale Revolution, Der radikale Wandel des Lernens und wie wir ihn gestalten können*. München, Germany: Deutsche Verlagsanstalt.
EC (European Commission) (2017). *Digital Education Policies in Europe and Beyond. Key Design Principles for More Effective Policies* (Joint Research Center Policy Report). Luxembourg: Publications Office of the European Union.
Eggers, D. (2013). *The Circle*. New York: A. Knopf.
EPRS. (2014). *Digital Opportunities for Education in the EU*. Retrieved from: https://epthinktank.eu/2014/04/01/digital-opportunities-for-education-in-the-eu/. Last 19 July 2018.
Han, B.-C. (2014). *Psychopolitik. Neoliberalismus und die neuen Machttechniken*. Frankfurt am Main, Germany: S. Fischer Wissenschaft.
Hartong, S. (2016). Between Assessments, Digital Technologies, and Big Data: The Growing Influence of 'Hidden' Data Mediators in Education. *European Educational Research Journal, 15*(5), 523–536.
Karcher, M. (2015). Ich-Maschine – Das ‚kybernetische Selbst' im Kompetenzdiskurs. In E. Christof & E. Ribolits (Eds.), *Bildung und Macht. Eine kritische Bestandsaufnahme* (pp. 81–100). Vienna: Erhard Löcker.
Kurzweil, R. (2005). *The Singularity Is Near*. New York: Viking.
OECD. (2016). *Innovating Education and Educating for Innovation: The Power of Digital Technologies and Skills*. Paris: OECD Publishing.
Parreira do Amaral, M. (2011). *Emergenz eines Internationalen Bildungsregimes? International Education Governance und Regimetheorie*. Münster et al.: Waxmann.
Phi Kappa Phi. (2016). *2016 Phi Kappa Phi Excellence in Innovation Award*. Retrieved from: https://provost.asu.edu/sites/default/files/page/2546/asu_phi_kappa_phi_2016_final_hi_res.pdf. Last 19 July 2018.

Radtke, F.-O. (2009). Evidenzbasierte Steuerung – Der Aufmarsch der Manager im Erziehungssystem. In R. Tippelt (Ed.), *Steuerung durch Indikatoren*. Opladen, Germany: Budrich.

Reckwitz, A. (2017). *Die Gesellschaft der Singularitäten*. Berlin, Germany: Suhrkamp.

Sheehy, K., Ferguson, R., & Clough, G. (2014). *Augmented Education. Bringing Real and Virtual Learning Together*. New York: Palgrave Macmillan.

Verger, A. (2016). *The Rise of the Global Education Industry: Some Concepts, Facts and Figures*. Retrieved from: https://worldsofeducation.org/en/woe_homepage/woe_detail/4850/the-rise-of-the-global-education-industry-some-concepts-facts-and-figures. Last 19 July 2018. Accessed 01 June 2018.

Zarkadakis, G. (2016). *In Our Own Image: Savior or Destroyer? The History and Future of Artificial Intelligence*. New York/London: Pegasus.

# 12

# Writing Global Education Policy Research

Stephen Carney

## The Light

*It wasn't the heat that brought Ganesh's thoughts to a standstill, but the light. A white field that blocked the sight of the desert and mirage of the city and dulled the lessor sensations of sound and smell. Taste was a crude proxy of home and what was left of touch was always through leather gloves stiffened by dirt and sweat. The desert and city were things of hardship and separation but the light was extraordinary. It subsumed all else such that form, distance, even time, could not be trusted. Even though the working day came to an end, the sun was a malignant memory as he prepared the evening meal and it returned to fill his thoughts with foreboding as he lay down to sleep. Back in Nepal, summer could be unrelenting for sure but the sun was an ally that would flow with the seasons and the social customs built around them. The*

---

S. Carney (✉)
Department of People and Technology, Roskilde University,
Roskilde, Denmark
e-mail: carney@ruc.dk

© The Author(s) 2019
M. Parreira do Amaral et al. (eds.), *Researching the Global Education Industry*,
https://Doi.org/10.1007/978-3-030-04236-3_12

*light in the Gorkha hills brought the fields alive and gave depth to the jungles that framed his bamboo home on the outskirts of town. Here, the sun offered a light that created not only life, but a life worth living. In the Gulf, the light stole everything and life became a dozen rituals of deference and defeat. To endure its domination was a victory of sorts but one that could only be fully realized at the end of a three-year contract. Then, wages would be counted and debts squared away. The force that enabled him to carry on over there was the dream that one day, the photo of his wife and small child would be exchanged with their touch and gratitude.*

\* \* \*

New horizons and hope. Hardship and loss. Desire and seduction. Global flows of ideas and bodies. Changing relations between economies and nations. New policy problems in a world overflowing with solutions. Education and the future of schooling. Research and/or writing?

\* \* \*

This chapter confronts a glaring absence that lies at the center of global education policy studies, a genre of work that considers education policy reform in an international and comparative context. While such research provides insights into the connectedness and complexity of global reform efforts, it often misses the chance to embody that complexity through open-ended, transgressive or, even, ambivalent approaches to enquiry. Paradoxically, global education policy research *simplifies* the world. Methodologically, it appears to favor a gaze from above and across space, silencing or simplifying subaltern experiences and expressions of reform in order to trace new formations of power and their effects. Research in the service of others. Its aim is to uncover, expose and lay bare familiar and emerging political and economic interests in education, nourishing a long-running narrative of decline and loss. Such sentiment gives education policy research so much of its life force. It is an old trade, surprisingly resilient to a generation of radical critique that has left notions of reality, truth, subject, author and text in tatters.

I argue that most policy work misses its own mark, trapped in nostalgia for an earlier epoch of reason and meaning. The impulse to explanation of systems, processes, intentions and 'impact' fumbles with and, ultimately, avoids facing important aspects of our current 'situation'. The rise of multiple and 'fake' truths, digital selves, virtual realities, cloning and the code are invitations to consider how time, history, place and subject are under erasure with their disappearance into the hyperreal leaving 'room only for the orbital recurrence of models and for the simulated generation of differences' (Baudrillard, 1994, p. 3). If we can speak of 'ultimate truth' it might be the 'dematerialization of "real life" itself, its reversal into a spectral show' (Žižek, 2012, p. 16). A system built on indifference but not nihilism, for that would imply some 'imaginary of the end' (Baudrillard, 1994, p. 161). Where the moderns talked through the industrial metaphor of *production*, where things—places, histories and subjectivities—were created with value(s), we might now consider their transformation by the forces of *consumption*. Here, things are overloaded such that the system of accumulation, meaning and exchange breaks down. The world of production might focus on *subjects* (understood through a range of readings of power and its twin, desire), but a focus on consumption brings *objects* to the fore. The object is not a dormant or silent thing brought to life on demand but, rather, 'fired with passion', with 'autonomy' and, most dangerously, endowed with 'a capacity to avenge itself on a subject over-sure of controlling it' (Baudrillard, 2003, p. 4). In Baudrillard's (2008) enigmatic terms: 'it's no longer the subject which desires, it's the object which seduces' (p. 141). What might that mean for global education policy research?

\* \* \*

I began this chapter by *writing* Ganesh, a Nepali acquaintance who challenged my own preconceptions about exploitation and sorrow, schooling and hope, education reform and futures. I write the journey that Ganesh took from a village in Nepal to the world beyond his homeland and then back to himself. Ultimately, Ganesh's experiences—at least as they live in this text—are about a different sense of being, belonging and purpose. To unfold my argument, I discuss privatization efforts in public education in

Nepal and link reform processes to Nepal's fraught engagement with global labor markets and mobility (mainly to the Gulf States), distorted consumer modernity and long-term trauma of state formation. That is a rich brew but one aimed at suggesting that neoliberal tropes such as 'quality', 'effectiveness', 'commercialization', privatization and, for example, 'entrepreneurship' intersect with and invest other tropes such as freedom and self-determination, fulfillment, happiness, style, love and belonging as well as anger and disillusionment. What looks like the capture of public education by, for example, hard-nosed edu-business and entrepreneurial interests—a key concern within global education policy studies as it looks for the smoking gun of reform—is actually a much more chaotic ensemble of reason, desire, fear and *seduction*. How can we write of such things?

Stylistically, such writing could start by disrupting the 'normativities of practice' (Honan & Bright, 2016, p. 732) that dictate how one might construct the academic text. Education policy research is intensively invested in interrogating the 'real' and does so by deploying a 'conventional, reductionist and hegemonic' (p. 731) form of writing that limits the possibilities for radical or even alternative thought. That involves framing issues in terms of familiar problematics and structuring the text in ways that guide the reading experience toward certain ends. Another type of writing might challenge the exchange of meaning in educational research work (i.e. 'writing' the poor and disenfranchised within agreed universalist frames; assigning to education its rightful utopian role, etc.) thus disrupting knowledge projects that are familiar and totalizing. Instead, a 'fatal' writing might, itself, reflect the overloading of the system by undermining certainties, shaking alliances, provoking judgments (even scorn) and impeding our desire for comfort and resolution. It would avoid writing that seeks nothing more than to mirror the contours of the 'real' and which, therefore, remains stuck in the 'play of appearances' (Baudrillard, 2003, p. 21).

To challenge such conventions, the text offered here dances between three modes of presentation: the scientific, meditative and poetic. Enter this text and you will most certainly find a familiar trail of concepts, categories and 'trustworthy' academic sources aimed to win you over to the seriousness of the subject matter. You will also encounter various meditations where scientific bedrock is reinforced or questioned by subjective musings and authorial sleight of hand. These are occasionally political where cherished notions of social justice, rights or simple compassion for the desperateness of life on the global periphery serve to bind writer and reader to a shared moral project. At other times, my meditations serve to stop us in our tracks. Are things *that* desperate? *Whose* interests are at stake when reporting such desperation? Finally, disturbing these familiar genres is the *poetic*, a form of writing unhinged from any notion of objective experience, logic or rationality. Serious and frivolous at once.

Thrown together, the text contains a good deal of '(un)knowing and (un)doing' (Koro-Ljungberg & MacLure, 2013, p. 219). With the provocation that 'some truths speak only from the well of exaggeration' (Hughes, 1997, p. 609), I complicate my authority as researcher with that of writer. This aims to challenge to dominant logic of education, and of global education policy studies:

> Education is not perverted, it is perversion. Education sets down the intellectual and affective foundations for another century of rampant growth, exploitation, pollution and barbarity. The educator helps model the directionless, frantic subjectivity we too must acquire. Education sets us up so that we are already defeated by it. Education prepares our defeat by constructing frameworks of disappointment. It develops terminal subjectivities so we are forever dependent on its life-support, so we may live as if part deceased. (Allen, 2017, p. 2)

This challenge—a cynicism of sorts—is not aimed at winning you over. Instead, it seeks to induce 'personal discomfort' (p. 3), to 'confront' educational subjectivities and frameworks as 'systems of bad faith' and to resist a world that 'wants absolutely to cleanse everything, to exterminate death and negativity' (Baudrillard, 2003, p. 98). I encourage you to read the piece, twice, and dwell in its provocations. With any luck, we may 'give way to our suspicions' (Allen, 2017, p. 3).

\* \* \*

The context for my own encounter with Nepal was the 'Education for All' (EFA) movement, the 'governance' imperative that framed attempts to enhance aid effectiveness and issues as diverse as decentralization, democratization, gender equality and poverty reduction (Bista & Carney,

2002; Carney & Bista, 2009). By exploring the dynamic discourse of education reform since the introduction of EFA, it was possible to suggest that policy thinking about education had narrowed from expansive visions of democratization and nation building to one that, only ten years later, sought to distance schools from state control. Having undermined its own monopoly position as service provider, the Nepali state greedily extended the 'cultural circuit(s) of capital' (Thrift, 2005, p. 34) by explicitly encouraging the growth of private schooling. This signaled to donor agencies that the state was ideologically open to private solutions in education and pragmatic about its own capacity to reach the EFA and subsequent Millennium Development Goals (MDG) goals alone. In education, we now see huge increases in terms of private enrolments and expenditures in schooling, new actors to the sector, as well as new relations between states, teachers and communities.

Privatization efforts include the 'opening up' of the public system to new providers, especially those seeking profit, as well as a disciplining of the public sector to the assumed efficiencies and mindset of the business world (Ball & Youdell, 2008, p. 9). While contest and resistance have followed these transformations, states, service providers and consumers have largely agreed upon a new logic in/for education, one that has connected floating and diffuse terms such as quality, relevance, access, equity and social justice into one meaningful narrative of renewal and progress. With key policy entrepreneurs at the visible sharp end of this narrative, we see the 'penetration and impact of new programmatic ideas' that are packaged 'in a way that makes them appealing to a range of audiences' and which are then disseminated 'among practice communities' who 'push(ing) for them to be implemented in particular contexts' (Verger, 2012, p. 111). The processes at play here are complex, multi-dimensional and embedded. Apparently, we should be very worried by the undermining of a self-evident public good.

While much global education policy research does not intend to exclude the voices of civil society, practitioners, parents and others, it is nonetheless a concerted search for explicit interests, causality and meaning-making. What of other actors, experiences and contexts that are separate from but intersect with the educational sphere? Who (and what) disappears, or is silenced, when we restrict our gaze to the most visible and thus, presumably, most significant events and processes? When global education policy scholars talk about flows of *ideas*, how far can we push what counts as an idea?

\* \* \*

Some argue that the imagination is not only 'a constitutive feature of modern subjectivity' (Appadurai, 1996, p. 3) but *the* 'key component of the new global order (p. 31, emphasis added). However, for much of humanity and a good number of the lessor 'stakeholders' in education, the 'lines between the realistic and the fictional' are 'blurred', leading to 'imagined worlds that are chimerical, aesthetic, even fantastic' (1996, p. 35). How do disparate experiences, unfulfilled dreams and wild associations take form, for example, by investing the new and glittering object of private solutions in education with legitimacy? Is it enough to trace new formations of discourse and interests among the policy elite, assuming that they alone create the field of the possible? How do objects—having lives of their own—reach out and communicate with us? What happens when that communication is blocked or distorted by a proliferation of signs that the subject cannot hope to accumulate and exchange?

Globalization has become one popular trope with which to organize such questions. When understood as the 'spatialization of modernity' (Featherstone & Lash, 1995), it connects histories and struggles and provides new imaginary landscapes on which to play them out. In Ferguson's study of life on the Zambian Copperbelt (1999), economic boom and its attendant urbanization create new cities, connecting them and their inhabitants to the modern grid through displays of cosmopolitan identity and belonging. However, subsequent economic decline—heralded by the collapse of the copper price at a distant futures exchange—shows how promiscuous and transitory global connections can be as workers, made abject by sudden structural changes, must return to the village to renegotiate social roles and futures hemmed in by convention and envy. 'Doing modernity' becomes a precarious business. In Liechty's (2003) study of the emerging middle-class in Kathmandu, we see young people dealing with a central paradox of modernity where a 'Western' model or vision of life becomes both the 'object of intense local desire' but 'seemingly by definition an unachievable condition'. On the 'Third World periphery', 'satellite television, unemployed youth, beauty pageants, mass tourism, and countless other examples link(ing) the city to worldwide trends'(xiii), creating desire, frustration and anxiety but also innovative strategies to live life in the 'consumer present' (p. 239). What 'spaces of imitation and invention' (Thrift, 2008, p. 254) does our present phase of global cultural *disorganization* throw up?

\* \* \*

Urban Nepal is known as a place of material poverty, in part made poor by a politics of representation where a discourse of modernity and/as 'development' creates social difference (Pigg, 1992). In early post-development scholarship, a 'language of categorization' (p. 511) was viewed as connecting the cosmopolitan Nepali to global society; instigating a hierarchy of social worth that further marginalized non-urban compatriots. However, in a world of wildly proliferating signs, the promise of a connected life now seems within reach for all Nepalis. *Cosmopolitanism for All*. Even the most cursory trip around its cities will expose Nepal as a site of simulation and seduction as much as want and despair. In one short ride across any mid-size hill town, it is impossible to ignore the billboards, posters and political slogans that promise if not demand a different mode of living. In Gorkha, across from a small vegetable market, stood a clothing store with two prominent t-shirts on display. One brandished the phrase 'LA or bust', the other 'London is number 1'. Some meters away, on a telephone post next to a tea-seller was a poster of social entrepreneur Mohammad Yunus. Wrapped around this concrete artifice, accompanied by the smiling face of the global sage were the words: 'If we are not achieving something, it is because we have not put our minds to it. We create what we want!' Five minutes away, in the foyer of a low-fee private school, Bill Gates—in life size cut-out poster form—is waiting to greet parents, teachers, pupils and visitors alike, insisting that: 'If you are born poor, that is not your mistake; but if you die poor that is your mistake'. Few in Nepal will have read Kant's great call to resist the 'laziness and cowardice' of our 'self-imposed nonage', but the King of the European

Enlightenment seems very much alive on its outskirts (Kant, 1954, p. 1071). Such direct appeals to an assumed will to succeed are interspersed with messages of a more baroque kind. Back in Kathmandu, my bus stopped outside a café called 'Paris'. Here, an enormous billboard met me at eye-height, thrusting forward two well-groomed Indian male models in three-piece tweed suits offering up 'Royal Stag' scotch whiskey alongside the message: 'I have yet to become me'. Cosmopolitan sophistication? Existential fantasy? Fear of failure? The subaltern in ontological trouble or the new man of global neoliberal ideology? How do subjects embody *all* of this in semiotic terms and exchange it as part of the quest to realize a life worth living? Sapere aude!

\* \* \*

*Like some 1500 young Nepalis who gain work permits to the Gulf States each day, Ganesh saw Dubai as a city of light and hope. Soaring towers, sparkling waters and 'smart' lifestyles set free from the constraints of history and place, this gulf paradise was an obvious culmination to the jumbled imaginaries of Nepal. The recruitment agents told Ganesh that a contract in the Gulf was the ticket to freedom, and end to poverty and the only chance to change a destiny that was otherwise set. 'At home we heard stories of local boys – village boys – who made the journey to the Gulf and returned as successful men. These stories are in the newspapers and magazines and on the TV. One can go away as nothing and come home knowing Dubai style. After that, life is different. You are a big man and people respect you. This was the promise that no one can refuse'.*

\* \* \*

At the time he boarded his flight to Dubai, stories of migrant worker entrapment and exploitation were reaching Western breakfast tables. The 2022 football World Cup in Qatar provided a relevant context. In a one-month period in 2013, some 44 Nepali workers, most of whom were under 25 years of age, died while building stadiums and hotels in the emirate. More than half of these suffered heart failure, most likely the result of extreme physical hardship. Long days of grueling labor, little food or water and the threat of physical violence at the first sign of resistance or complaint led to the Nepali ambassador to Qatar calling this paradise in the sun an 'open jail' (The Guardian, 2013). In Dubai, Ganesh had to relinquish his passport and agree to defer receiving wages as an incentive not to flee. The living conditions—eight men in a metal shipping container with minimal ventilation or lighting—and restricted possibilities for freedom of movement focused his time in the Gulf on work and a new life that lay beyond the daily grind. Eventually, Ganesh was badly injured in a work-accident, being blinded in one eye and losing partial use of his left arm. In 30 months abroad, he earned a little more than 3600 US dollars but was at least glad to be returning home. Back in Kathmandu, he learnt that his wife had left him for another man, taking his young son and wages. It was a long bus ride to the village.

\* \* \*

At present, the only market for unskilled labor in Nepal lies a great distance from 'home'. The relentless flow of optimistic young men to the desert, and their return as broken bodies lumbered with the debt, represents a major social and political challenge. Some returnees question the traditional structures of social organization they attempted to flee. Others find peace with them. All must add these experiences to the whirlpool of hopes, fantasies and fears that frame their sense of 'reality'. In Berlant's (2011) terms, how does one 'live on'?

\* \* \*

*Versed in the Maoist political ideology that was the mainstay of the Gorkha region, Ganesh described the Gulf as a form of 'hard capitalism'. This was a place where men were without even the right to withdraw their labor and construction firms, in collaboration with the local authorities, were free to shape the city to the needs of total profit. 'Dubai' was an 'empty promise' but not one without meaning. Without bitterness, Ganesh suggested that it had served to expose the 'lie of Nepal' where a lingering 'feudalism' ensured that rights followed one's social status and livelihoods were always in the hands of* others: 'In the Gulf, I finally understood that in Nepal there is no state and no one to help us. We must make our way. Over there we were mistreated, but at least the foreman gave us water once per hour so that we wouldn't die. That wouldn't happen here. When there were abuses, the ambassador from the Philippines would come and help us by complaining to the management. Even though the Nepali officials stayed away because they were afraid of upsetting the construction firms, we saw that government officials could actually work on behalf of the poor. That would never happen at home. We are a poor country. Nepal has only prepared us to be slaves. In school, we learnt only how to be prisoners. From now on, we must save ourselves. Even though I have lost half my sight I now see much further'.

\* \* \*

That school was identified as a necessary element in a global circuit of hope and exploitation was a serious challenge to my own understanding of the 'development' project in Nepal. For Ganesh, more public schooling would make possible more exploitation and disappointment. Such schooling was not the answer, especially if states and donor agencies were unable or unwilling to fund it properly. Time in exile had also fostered a further iteration of hope and purpose. New objects demanding to be seen. Having experienced a more determined form of capitalism abroad and reflected on the limits of political representation in his homeland, Ganesh was receptive to the messages of heroic individualism that saturated public discourse in Nepal. Now, he planned to join with other local men and create an agricultural collective where they would pool resources to purchase land and equipment and mechanize the traditional farming processes that were etched into his body from childhood. He was also inspired to work with local community leaders to create a non-profit private college that would focus on the types of technical skills needed by Gulf State employers but that were otherwise beyond the reach of untrained villagers in the area. For Ganesh, 'the state was dead' but could be remade by 'new men and new institutions'. Sapere aude!

\* \* \*

How does global education policy research deal with objects of (mis)identification that are central to contemporary life but which are, at best, consigned to their margins? How does it respond to the types of cruel attachments (Berlant, 2011) that such (mis)identification engenders? I suggest that the phenomena I weave together here—education reform, development ideology, hard labor and consumerism—constitute an 'imaginative scape' of hope and possibility that is occasionally coherent, always intoxicating and necessarily fraught with risk. This scape invests private solutions in education with a sense of urgency and potential. Here, in one place, we find rural poverty at the heart of a still-born state project, home and its annexes in the Gulf hidden by pain and shame, images of Western consumer hedonism planted like landmines at every turn, and the glorified image of the rags-to-riches entrepreneur offering instant self-actualization. Such imaginaries create a frame for thought that is *at least as* productive as the hard-nosed business models and roll-out strategies of policy elites and educational entrepreneurs.

It might be convenient for global education policy scholars to restrict their gaze to the workings of a high-profile donor conference, foundation seminar or public-private partnership, but the unmanageable force driving change in public education may well residue in a million fractured moments, emotions and experiences of living that are impossible to gather up as 'data', let alone harness into a renewed program of high-quality public EFA. The language of education with its hope and promise of salvation and fulfillment has slipped from the policy paper, school development plan and curriculum document into the t-shirt graphic, consumer billboard, pop song lyric, political pamphlet and, even, the well-ordered slave camp but a short flight away. These are unwieldy flows and circulations that reflect the 'other' of global education policy research, by which I mean the things that can't be processed with reason or science but which speak loudly by their absence in our texts and which thus remain to haunt our analyses.

There are of course many ways to go about exploring education at a time of unheralded connectivity (Carney, 2009; Henry et al., 2001; Robertson & Dale, 2015; Schriewer, 2012; Takayama, 2015; Verger, 2012). Adhikary and Lingard (2018) note the contemporary focus mobilities—of ideas, policies and peoples—identifying how the governance of education in particular is being rescaled in ways that displace the nation state from its historically privileged position in education. Competing with—often supplementing—states are traveling policies, transnational actors, networked governance and complex circuits of social relations, all of which demand new research methodologies. How should the researcher of global education proceed? One increasingly popular strategy of enquiry, reflecting both the potential and omissions of a global gaze on education, finds form in various approaches to network analysis (e.g. Adhikary & Lingard, 2018; Ball, 2012, Larsen & Beech, 2014). Here, the 'system' or 'culture' becomes the global playing field itself and methodology a sophisticated process of tracing and uncovering the often embedded and opaque forces that shape educational decisions. The work of Stephen Ball and his colleagues (Ball, Junemann, & Santori, 2017) is but one illustrative example of an emerging focus on neoliberalization as the 'disarticulation and re-articulation of governance, the state, education policy and the delivery of educational services' (p. 1). When conceptualized as *process*, the study of neoliberal networks in education requires a different 'geographical imagination' in order to map the *space* of policy (p. 2). The research gaze here follows ideas, money, events and people as they spread thought and models across the policy network. This is one manifestation of Gupta and Ferguson's (1997) call for 'ethnography without the ethnos' where the gaze is 'up and along rather than down', 'forsaking the perspective of the subaltern' (Marcus, 1995, in Ball et al., 2017, p. 15) in order to understand the logic and function of dynamic systems.

For Ball and colleagues, network analysis invites us to interrogate new sources of data. Here, the internet becomes a key tool for 'illuminate(ing) the extent of influence of new kinds of actors, including donors, policy entrepreneurs and various brokers, on processes of policy, and the identification of new spaces of policy and conduits (both virtual and face-to-face) for policy ideas and discourses and crucially relations and interactions between actors' (Ball et al., 2017, p. 20). Unsurprisingly, such research yields enormous returns, with recent project work in India and four African countries generating over 1000 nodal points and a map that is 'partial' and 'difficult to read' visually (p. 7). And this is only a beginning. Enthused by the potential of this new gaze, they note that 'With more time and more money, we could have followed links and relationships further, through more disparate nodes, to more distant and more local points' (Ball et al., 2017, pp. 8–11).

Notwithstanding its systemic gaze, this approach identifies the personalized nature of policy networks. The Michael and Susan Dell Foundation has been of recent interest (Ball, 2017; see also Ball, in this volume). The gaze has also been directed at US philanthropist Irene Pritzker, a key supporter of microfinance strategies in low-fee private schooling. An earlier use of the methodology centered on English professor of education, James Tooley, described by Ball as a 'card-carrying Hayekian' (Ball, 2012, p. 38) and 'policy entrepreneur par excellence'; a 'policy traveler' who 'animates global circuits of policy knowledge' and 'co-construct(s)' infrastructures that advocate, frame, package and represent policy ideas'. However, such figures are more than energetic and committed individuals. For Ball (2012), such actors are 'inserted into a highly developed, long-standing, dense and effective neo-liberal advocacy network'. Studying the person 'enables us to identity key sites, connections, methods and practices of neo-liberal advocacy and policy mobility' (p. 40). Ultimately, research of this type aims to 'map and trace…before it is too late and other imaginaries are cast into the "field of memory" or excluded from rational possibility' (p. 145). This is research in the service of humanity but, equally, our 'madness' with method (Stronach, 2010). In time, such passions turn to dust:

\* \* \*

As a heuristic device, network ethnography can certainly offer us further nodal points, new associations, hunches and the possibility of dwelling in the complexities of a proliferating education project. In that sense, it resonates with my own musings. However, while it views the 'neoliberalizing' of people and bodies as occurring 'not primarily through oppressions but through anxieties and opportunities', it limits its gaze to the 'very real', mirroring the neoliberal fixation with 'measurement and comparison' that it seeks to undermine (2012, p. 145). 'Exactitude in Science' destined to consume itself:

The following Generations, who were not so fond of the Study of Cartography as their forebears had been, saw that the vast Map was Useless, and not without some Pitilessness was it, that they delivered it up to the Inclemencies of Sun and Winters. (Borges, 1998, p. 181)

The policy network is constructed and read through the language of 'science', and thus invites the reader to critique it through that same language. What other pathways to understanding and knowing are available to us? One of many lines of flight would be to re-read network research—and indeed a good deal of global education policy research—through the lens of myth that, for Levi-Strauss, represents an esthetic path to knowing 'parallel or analogous' to the more familiar objective form (Kazamias, 2009, p. 1080). Citing Bowra, Andreas Kazamias (2001, p. 1) considers myth to be 'no less useful when the dramatist is unable to see any solution to a problem and wishes to present it for its own sake, as something which troubles him and of which others should be at least aware'.

If one delves into the Greek tradition, the network becomes the labyrinth, a place of intractability and horror. If one delves into the Greek tradition, the network becomes the labyrinth. This is a place of intractability and horror: home to the monstrous half-man, half-bull Minotaur. The god Poseidon had presented a white bull to King Minos of Crete for sacrifice. Having learnt that the King had failed to carry out his will, Poseidon brought forth the Minotaur from a terrible union between man and animal. Raining terror on the people of the city, the beast was contained in a labyrinth built by Daedalus and 'so artfully contrived that whoever was enclosed in it could by no means find his way (Bulfinch, 1993, p. 188). To satisfy the beast, the King of Crete sacrificed a number of the youth of Athens each year. However, Theseus, son of the King of Athens would end this 'calamity' by slaying the monster. Arriving on the island as one of the youths to be devoured, Theseus met King Mino's daughter Ariadne who imparted the secret of the labyrinth, offering a sword with which to 'encounter' the beast and a 'clew of thread' (p. 189) with which to navigate and escape the enclosure. Completing the task, the hero fled the city with Ariadne in hand.

\* \* \*

Farfetched? The denial of myth is also a myth, indeed, 'the only true myth' (Bataille, 2006, p. 48). Myth abounds in our contemporary world as the education researcher, wrapped in modernist certainties, unknowingly fantasizes of a world of promise, fulfillment and, even, domination (Adorno & Horkheimer, 1997). Consider these parallels when we do policy work:

> *Labyrinth* = the impossible complexity of human and non-human relations in global education policy spaces?
> *Minotaur* = the 'villain' of global education reform. James Tooley? Irene Pritzker? Bill and Melinda Gates?
> *Theseus* = the hero as theory? Method? Data? The policy scholar? Myself?
> *The clew of thread* = the narrative of meaning, coherence and closure that we put in place *before* setting off on perilous journeys?

Yes, the string is our storyline: from start to finish; from good to bad and back; from reason, through chaos and back to the world of form and substance and 'reality'. Purpose. Justice. Hope. The string ties us to the world, keeps us from getting lost. Narrative has a beginning, a complication and an end. It keeps us tethered to life. Death, of all sorts, kept at bay.

\* \* \*

This line of thinking, and the association to this particular Greek myth, is used by Taylor (1984) to introduce his notion of 'erring', a way to think about science and life—including much of what counts as global education policy research—after an age of modernist certainty. Deconstruction, if by that we mean a way of thinking that is seriously troubled by Nietzsche's parable of the madman and the death of a single authoritative source of meaning, or the possibility of shared meaning-making projects, has been a central feature of education policy research for at least 30 years. This is most familiar to us through Derrida's challenge to language, Foucault's disruption of the idea of history and celebration of that temporary 'face in the sand' augmented, after a time, by Deleuze-inspired revolutionary notions of intensities and becoming. However, the 'tone' of this work in the hands of policy scholars is 'often at odds with the deliberate "production of estrangement"' (Allen, 2017, p. 160) intended by such writers.

While post-structuralist policy scholars acknowledge (although usually fail to *embrace*) the death of God and thus the impossibility of singular meaning-making projects, it appears to have been violently resisted by the modernist mainstream. Full of despair but inoculated against resignation, they fight for life through the Text which exposes a lingering attachment to History (and the myth of origins) and thus a belief in Self (as the active and conscious embodiment of God *on earth*). God, Self, History and Book: all 'bound in an intricate relationship in which each mirrors the other' (Taylor, 1984, p. 7). In the age of modern purpose, these were brought to life in UPPER CASE: authoritative, certain, confident. In our current age of post-deconstruction doubt and loss, they can be usefully embraced in the LOWER form, making possible a new mode of knowing. The call to 'err' is thus an invitation to reflect on our provisional and fragile position as transcendent Author/Creator/Master, and how we constantly invent reason through text. Ultimately, what Taylor is talking about here is the possibility and necessity of a writing without authority, books without closure and an invitation to readers to traverse personal path(s) to awareness.

Instead of the labyrinth to be penetrated and conquered, Taylor offers the image of the maze, a heuristic implying multiple possibilities to enter, explore and experience research work as journey and process. To 'maze' is to 'bewilder, perplex, confuse, daze, or stupefy'. To be 'mazed' is to be 'delirious, deluded, or to wander in mind'. A maze can thus be a 'delirium, delusion, vain amusement, dissipation, trick, or deception' (Taylor, 1984, p. 168). While a maze is still a place of paths and turns and is thus a *type* of labyrinth, *our* labyrinth is 'never-ending'; an 'abyss' with many points of entry and as many points of exit:

> There is no Ariadne to save the wandering Theseus, no thread to show the way out of the maze. Every line that seems to promise escape further entangles the drifter in a complex network of relations. Along the boundless

boundary where traces err there is neither a fixed center that orients nor an eternally present logos that directs. In the absence of center and logos, there is no special time or special place. In the eternal play of the divine milieu, die Mitte ist überall. (ibid., p. 168f.)

The radical message here is that this surface made possible by the death of God is a place where 'no-thing is truly sacred and thus nothing is simply profane'. Here, the 'extraordinary becomes ordinary and the ordinary becomes extraordinary'. Invoking Thomas Altizer (1979), we might think of the maze, and mazing, as 'a way of totally loving the world, and not only a way of loving the world but also a way of (writing) of love in a time and world in which God is dead' (Taylor, 1984, p. 169). Dionysus dancing.

\* \* \*

*The big plans that Ganesh had outlined to me on that hotel terrace in Gorkha were swept away a short time later by the devastating earthquakes of April 2015. With the epicenter in Gorkha itself, little remained. While the hotel itself still stands, much else, including the images of Mohammad Yunus on his telephone post and Bill Gates in his school of the future now rest under millions of tons of rock and top soil. Temporarily silent. Ironically, it was the farming poor, trapped in toil on the open plains, who lived through that day as their 'modern' friends and neighbors disappeared into the ancient darkness. Emergency relief work, hindered by missing roads and bridges and compounded by a formidable bureaucracy in the capital, made a return to normalcy impossible, thrusting much of central Nepal back into an earlier epoch. Funding for new projects was captured by savvy social entrepreneurs with contacts to the urban political elite and their donor partners. Same as it ever was. Ganesh now worked a few hours per week as a porter and maintenance man at the hotel. He had not reunited with his wife but she had returned their child.*

## A Different Light

*Life begins on the other side of despair.* (Sartre, in Kaufmann, 1975, p. 46)

Global education *policy* includes concerned and pragmatic policy makers, bold entrepreneurs and showmen as well as subjects drawn to the allure of irresistible objects. Global education policy *scholars* carry the DNA of each of these. Global education policy *research* is brought to distorted life in a sea of cultural and emotional flows that barely submit to the strictures of science. To place such phenomena in a maze is to acknowledge the productive potential of education discourse, the best intentions of practitioners, actually occurring hardships, dreams of fulfillment and the disappointments and false steps that follow but that are always more than just failures. It is also to acknowledge new insights and the realization that things (objects) have a life of their own. The impulse to migration gives way to return. The dream of education when disavowed is forged anew through liberal entrepreneurship which itself slips away, literally from under one's feet. And always with something unconsumed and beyond redemption. 'Somewhere there is a "remainder", which the subject cannot lay hold of, which he believes he can overcome by profusion, by accumulation, and which in the end merely puts more and more obstacles in the way of relating' (Baudrillard, 2003, p. 5). Without bitterness, open to the world but non-expectant, the subject/subject of global policy comes in and out of view. As does the writer/writing of global education policy research.

\* \* \*

*Ganesh was often drawn to the terrace, not only when foreign scholars and other-tourists held their coffee breaks between 'important' sessions of training workshops or development planning seminars, but whenever his duties made possible a moment in the warm winter sun. Mornings were indescribable with the view into the valley below encompassing multiple geographies and paradigms of living that unfolded slowly as the mist receded. Now it was dusk. The chatter from the bazar below traveled up the steep hills, as did the smoke from the wood fires of a thousand shops, cottages and tin-roofed huts. Planned power cuts would soon send the bustling valley into a darkness that was total. From that original state would come another morning, another mist folding back its protective blanket and another invitation to life.*

**Acknowledgments** As with all of my writing, it is not possible to present a text without acknowledging an ongoing dialogue with my colleague Ulla Ambrosius Madsen. The artifact presented here is mine but it builds on a shared mode of thought.

# References

Adhikary, R. W., & Lingard, B. (2018). A Critical Policy Analysis of 'Teach for Bangladesh': A Travelling Policy Touches Down. *Comparative Education, 54*(2), 181–202.
Adorno, T., & Horkheimer, M. (1997/1944). *Dialectic of Enlightenment*. London: Verso.
Allen, A. (2017). *The Cynical Educator*. Leicester, UK: Mayfly Books.
Altizer, T. (1979). Eternal Recurrence and the Kingdom of God. In D. B. Allison (Ed.), *The New Nietzsche: Contemporary Styles of Interpretation* (pp. 232–246). New York: Delta.
Appadurai, A. (1996). *Modernity at Large: Cultural Dimensions of Globalization*. Minneapolis, MN/London: University of Minnesota Press.
Ball, S. (2012). *Global Education Inc.: New Policy Networks and the Neo-liberal Imaginary*. London: Routledge.
Ball, S. (2017). Michael and Susan Go Investing. *Keynote Presentation to Symposium on Economization. Commodification. Digitalization. The Emergence of a Global Education Industry*. February 16th–17th, Goethe-University, Frankfurt am Main.
Ball, S., Junemann, C., & Santori, D. (2017). *Edu.net. Globalization and Education Policy Mobility*. London: Routledge.
Ball, S., & Youdell, D. (2008). *Hidden Privatization in Public Education*. Brussels, Belgium: Education International. Retrieved from https://www.ei-ie.org/media_gallery/2009-00034-01-E.pdf. Accessed 01 Mar 2018.
Bataille, G. (2006). *The Absence of Myth: Writings on Surrealism*. London: Verso.
Baudrillard, J. (1994). *Simulacra and Simulation*. Ann Arbor, MI: University of Michigan.
Baudrillard, J. (2003). *Passwords*. London: Verso.
Baudrillard, J. (2008). *Fatal Strategies*. Los Angeles: Semiotext(e).

Berlant, L. (2011). *Cruel Optimism*. Durham, NC: Duke University Press.
Bista, M., & Carney, S. (2002). *Human Resource Development Plan for the Education Sector of Nepal*. Kathmandu, Nepal: His Majesty's Government of Nepal.
Borges, J. L. (1998). On Exactitude in Science, *The Aleph*. London: Penguin.
Bulfinch, T. (1993). *The Golden Age of Myth and Legend: The Classical Mythology of the Ancient World*. Hertfordshire, UK: Wordsworth Editions.
Carney, S. (2009). Negotiating Policy in an Age of Globalization: Exploring Educational 'Policyscapes' in Denmark, Nepal and China. *Comparative Education Review*, 53(1), 63–88.
Carney, S., & Bista, M. B. (2009). Community Schooling in Nepal: A Genealogy of Education Reform Since 1990. *Comparative Education Review*, 53(2), 189–211.
Featherstone, M., & Lash, S. (1995). Globalization, Modernity and the Spatialization of Social Theory: An Introduction. In M. Featherstone, S. Lash, & R. Robertson (Eds.), *Global Modernities* (pp. 1–24). London: Sage.
Ferguson, J. (1999). Global Disconnect: Abjection and the Aftermath of Modernism. In *Expectations of Modernity: Myths and Meanings of Urban Life on the Zambian Copperbelt* (pp. 234–254). Berkeley, CA: University of California.
Gupta, A., & Ferguson, J. (1997). After 'People's and 'Cultures'. In A. Gupta & J. Ferguson (Eds.), *Culture, Power and Place: Explorations in Critical Anthropology* (pp. 1–29). Durham, NC: Duke University Press.
Henry, M., Lingard, B., Rizvi, F., & Taylor, S. (2001). *The OECD, Globalisation and Education Policy*. Oxford, UK: IAU Press & Elsevier Science Ltd.
Honan, E., & Bright, D. (2016). Writing a Thesis Differently. *International Journal of Qualitative Studies in Education*, 29(5), 731–743.
Hughes, R. (1997). *American Visions: The Epic History of Art in America*. London: Harvill Press.
Kant, I. (1954). What Is Enlightenment? In Columbia College & J. Buchler (Eds.), *Introduction to Contemporary Civilization in the West: A Source Book* (pp. 1071–76). New York: Columbia University Press.
Kaufman, W. (1975). *Existentialism: From Dostoevsky to Sartre*. New York: Plume.
Kazamias, A. (2001). Globalization and Educational Cultures in Late Modernity: The Agamemnon Syndrome. In J. Cairns, D. Lawton, & R. Gardner (Eds.), *Values, Culture and Education. World Yearbook of Education 2001* (pp. 1–16). London: Kogan Page.

Kazamias, A. (2009). Agamemnon Contra Prometheus: Globalisation, Knowledge/ Learning Societies and Paideia in the New Cosmopolis. In *International Handbook of Comparative Education* (pp. 1079–1111). London: Springer.

Koro-Ljungberg, M., & MacLure, M. (2013). Provocations, Re-Un-Visions, Death, and Other Possibilities of "Data". *Cultural Studies ↔ Critical Methodologies, 13*(4), 219–222.

Larsen, M., & Beech, J. (2014). Spatial Theorizing in Comparative and International Education Research. *Comparative Education Review, 58*(2), 191–214.

Liechty, M. (2003). *Suitably Modern: Making Middle-Class Culture in A New Consumer Society*. Princeton, NJ: Princeton University Press.

Pigg, S. (1992). Inventing Social Categories Through Place: Social Representations and Development in Nepal. *Comparative Studies in Society and History, 34*(3), 491–513.

Robertson, S., & Dale, D. (2015). Towards a 'Critical Cultural Political Economy' Account of the Globalising of Education. *Globalisation, Societies and Education, 13*(1), 149–170.

Schriewer, J. (2012). Editorial: Meaning Constellations in the World Society. *Comparative Education, 48*(4), 411–422.

Stronach, I. (2010). *Globalizing Education, Educating the Local: How Method Made Us Mad*. New York: Routledge.

Takayama, K. (2015). Provincialising the World Culture Theory Debate: Critical Insights from a Margin. *Globalisation, Societies and Education, 13*(1), 34–57.

Taylor, M. C. (1984). *Erring: A Postmodern A/theology*. Chicago: University of Chicago Press.

The Guardian. (2013). *Revealed: Qatar's World Cup 'Slaves'*. Retrieved from http://www.theguardian.com/world/2013/sep/25/revealed-qatars-world-cup-slaves. Accessed 01 Mar 2018.

Thrift, N. (2005). *Knowing Capitalism*. London: Sage.

Thrift, N. (2008). *Non-Representational Theory: Space, Politics, Affect*. London: Routledge.

Verger, A. (2012). Framing and Selling Global Education Policy: The Promotion of Public–Private Partnerships for Education in Low-Income Contexts. *Journal of Education Policy, 27*(1), 109–130.

Žižek, S. (2012). *Welcome to the Desert of the Real*. London: Verso.

# 13

# Conclusion: Changing Education in the GEI—Rationales, Logics, and Modes of Operation

Marcelo Parreira do Amaral and Christiane Thompson

## Introduction

Recent years saw the burgeoning of activities for which the term Global Education Industry (GEI) has been coined. Global in scope and economic in both nature and outlook, these activities literally peak annually in closed meeting GEI Summits that aim at bringing together representatives from government and business to harness the education market. Increasingly, as the discussions in the preceding chapters show, economic rationales and logics pervade educational thinking and practice; business strategies and modes of operation progressively penetrate the education sector with the active involvement of business actors and stakeholders. These developments are substantially trans-

---

M. Parreira do Amaral (✉)
Institute of Education, University of Münster, Münster, Germany
e-mail: parreira@uni-muenster.de

C. Thompson
Theory and History of Education, Goethe-University Frankfurt am Main, Frankfurt am Main, Germany

© The Author(s) 2019
M. Parreira do Amaral et al. (eds.), *Researching the Global Education Industry*,
https://doi.org/10.1007/978-3-030-04236-3_13

forming one of the remaining societal spheres where the "invisible hand" of the market did not play a primary role. The implications for education practice, policy, and research are only now beginning to be comprehensively appraised. Researching the developments examined in the previous chapters has already proved requisite in assessing how the emergence of new providers and policy actors in education reflects the fast advance of the GEI and how it is likely to transform conceptualizations of "good" and "public" education. The chapters included in this volume address various questions related to the GEI to provide cutting-edge knowledge into its several manifestations and actors, including their implications for education research, policy, and practice. They aimed at systematically discussing these actors' strategies for exerting influence and producing "evidence" to promote preferred policy ideas and business models. They also brought diverse conceptual tools to bear on the questions addressed to illuminate the work of policy advocacy networks and to elucidate the role of global infrastructures for the governance of education, both of which are imperative to examining and reflecting on the impact and consequences of the advance of the GEI for education. Questions concerning the strong intertwinement of policy and research also commanded attention as to the implications of this alignment with regard to the authorization of specific types of "expert knowledge" and the legitimation of participants as "global experts" in education policymaking.

The present volume thus represents an earnest attempt to reflect upon these developments and dynamics and offers conceptual explorations of the challenges related to education policy research, of the narratives and modes of communication in this field. A further important aspect refers to the researchers' responsibility to recognize the significance of these developments for social theory and for our aim of revealing power struggles, self-imposed dependencies, and harnessing the ability of research to cast a different light on the oftentimes distorted imageries painted in global education (policy) discourses, as skillfully argued by Stephen Carney (in this volume). In the same vein, drawing systematic attention to the rationales, processes, and impacts of current developments of the GEI has been central to this book. In this concluding chapter, we want to go beyond the particular expressions and manifestations of the GEI phenomenon by discerning different but overarching rationales, logics, and modes of operation identified from a more synthetic reading of the chapters included in this volume. The chapter is rounded out by raising questions as to the social dislocations gaped open by the GEI phenomena and interrogations of theoretical lenses that guide our analyses.

Among the myriad topics and facets of the phenomena examined in this volume, two main *rationales* transpire from the justifications of actors involved in the GEI. First, vast reference is made to the necessity and urgency of knowledge and education to create innovation and sustain economic growth; second, the involvement of the business sector is justified by the synergetic effects expected from private engagement in public education, both in terms of costs and effectiveness. Moreover, appertaining the *logics* that lie beneath the arguments, different logical chains may be distinguished that underlie the reasonings put forward by advocates of the GEI. In everyday parlance, people acknowledge arguments as logical and true when they are seen as valid, compelling, convincing, obvious, and clear. Two main related but distinct logics may be seen at work in debates around reforming education for (economic) success. We see arguments for the GEI grounded in specific ways of reasoning that privilege empiricism as a means of knowing and inferring. The veracity of these claims is bolstered by the power of quantified evidence—self-evident data, as it were—yielded from comparative large-scale assessments and more recently by (the promises of) big data. Along the same line, economism, as a theory of why and how people (inter)act following interests and incentives, appears at the tacit explanation for how education should be changed in order to yield the best results. Behavioral economics emerges here as a prominent logic behind reforming the education sector by nudging reformers in the desired direction and by creating the "right" situational conditions for educational actors to operate. Finally, in terms of *modes of operation*, those involved in advancing the GEI are also developing novel ways of exchanging and functioning that go way beyond the well-studied patterns of governance of the education sector. Alongside the customary making and shaping of any economic industry sector by state agents through policymaking, regulatory provisions, and legislation, the GEI displays modes of operation that are premised, on the one hand, on the "discursive destruction and construction" of education. Scandalizing public education produces a sense of permanent crisis, and in this constant mediatized "state of emergency," GEI activities unfold and confer upon the arguments of those proposing remedies to education's ailments the necessary authority for this change. This provides further justification as to why private and business involvement is necessary. Importantly, on the other hand, the state figures prominently in connecting new and powerful providers and policy actors, becoming more and more prone to opening education to the interest of the private sector and, indeed, itself creating business opportunities for the market. The state is indeed "a key institution in the making, maintenance and modification of" the GEI (Verger et al., 2016, p. 13); it is thus complicit in the changing of public education across the globe since the growing influence of GEI actors and stakeholders does not take place in spite of state infrastructure building, but rather their influence and activity prompt the restructuring to operate in their favor. The role of the state as a connecting agent emerges as a central facet of the GEI's new modes of operation.

To be sure, the rationales, logics, and modes of operation discussed in the following sections are not completely detached from each other. They form analytical distinctions that overlap to some extent but which prove useful in recognizing commonalities and general trends while taking into account different manifestations and activities of the diverse players and their close collaboration with governmental and non-governmental agents in fostering the education market globally. The following sections deal with each in turn.

## Insights from GEI Research

The next paragraphs introduce each of the rationales, logics, and modes of operation mentioned above and relate them to the chapters in this volume. We start with the more tangible rationales for expanding the GEI.

## Innovating, Growing, Sharing: Rationales for Expanding the GEI

Contemporary discussions about education revolve around its presumed essential role in bringing about economic prosperity through innovation. Innovation is generally understood as the process by which knowledge transforms into something new—patents, goods, services—that can be turned into value. In its newest cast, innovation is a process that starts with the *introduction* of something new, the *application* to a practical context, the adoption of new behavior or practice, culminating in the *commercialization* and the creation of value (cf. Godin, 2015). Innovation is often accompanied by attributive terms such as "major," "structural," "systemic," "paradigmatic," "disruptive," and more recently "social" or "frugal"—all of which point to the underlying assumption that innovation as planned change has become a central feature of economic, political and social realities, and that it is intrinsically good and positive. Bob Jessop has pointed out the centrality of innovation and entrepreneurship in the post-Fordist political economy, in particular the role of education in this dominant techno-economic paradigm (2002; see also Jessop, Fairclough, & Wodak, 2008). The production, diffusion, and exploitation of knowledge have become the mantra of the knowledge-based economy. The commodification and subsequent financialization of educational processes and products are only logical consequences of the economic paradigm. The involvement of business—at present first and foremost through venture philanthropies—is viewed as key to creating the most propitious conditions for entrepreneurship, economic competitiveness, and sustained growth. The latter indeed conceals an interesting ambivalence: While growth is often referred to as meaning inclusion of more people and as having a democratizing effect, in practice the actual effect is simply enlarged access to markets for those offering "solutions" to educational problems, no matter with what effect.

A second powerful rationale driving activities in the GEI may be termed shared common good. Indeed, much of the impetus behind the proponents in favor of increasing the role of private interests and profit in education is a notion of "shared value." According to the proponents of the Shared Value Initiative (cf. FSG, 2014), "[s]hared value in education is not philanthropy or corporate responsibility. Instead, [...] it is a business approach that increases profits by improving the effectiveness of education systems at scale" (Porter, 2014, p. 1). This makes the education sector not only an immense opportunity for companies to bolster their profit margins but also "an opportunity for civil society to leverage the unique capabilities of business to solve education challenges." (ibid.)

The strategic appeal here is to be seen in its merging of public and private interests by claiming to serve exactly the needs unmet by the state while at the same time raising access rates as well as quality and efficiency/efficacy standards in education. This rationale epitomizes the elision of social (moral) responsibility and economic interests, the "doing well by doing good" of "angel investors" (see Ball, in this volume), and raises important questions as to the relationship between profit and non-profit actors, as the chapter on the role of the UNESCO by Ridge and Kippels (in this volume) noted.

## Shaping Reality, Crafting Solutions: Logics of Action in the GEI

Innovation and growth, as argued above, are core pieces in the narrative of GEI proponents, and achieving these becomes then a shared value for all actors involved. The ensuing question is then related to how the solutions crafted are arrived at, and what chains of reasoning are pursued in grounding and justifying them. Two main logics of action stand out across the debates that may be termed *evidence-based reforming* and *methodological economism*.

Despite substantial differences in other respects, the education debates over the past 20 years have relied on research techniques that privilege empiricism as a preferred line of reasoning. Empiricism, as an underlying positivistic epistemology, claims that the sources of our knowledge of the world and, as a consequence, of how to act upon it must derive from experience. Much recent education research has focused on exerting greater influence on policy by expanding its impact by providing "knowledge for action," that is, "empirical evidence" that aims at neutralizing the "ideological claims" typical of the political process and at playing a greater role in shaping decisions and actions of governments and other players. Three main features are characteristic of the "empirical paradigm" of *evidence-based reforming* of education: First, a preference for knowledge generated by randomized controlled trial (RCT) studies; second, experimental designs that make claims about causal relationships; and third, the interpretation of knowledge about causal relationships as cause-effect relationships that can be put to use in social interventions (cf. Bellmann & Müller, 2011).

The shift to evidence-based research and policy has been politically induced and is premised on an economic agenda (see Parreira do Amaral, in this volume). A concerted effort of otherwise strange bedfellows operating at the national and international levels (both public and private), it has introduced dramatic changes most often led by governmental legislation in the USA, Great Britain, and Germany, to name but a few (BMBF, 2008; Feuer et al., 2002; Slavin, 2002; Tooley & Darby, 1998; see also Radtke, 2016 for a critical discussion). The changes were in line with the emphasis on large-scale assessments of educational performance testing recurrently conducted since the mid-1990s Trends in International Mathematics and Science Study (TIMSS), but especially since 2000 with the Programme for International Student Assessment (PISA).

Against this politically engendered background, many scholars have questioned the data-driven governance of education put in place through this (Bellmann, 2016; Biesta, 2007; Lingard, Creagh, & Vass, 2012; Ozga, 2009). In any case, notwithstanding whether evidence-based governance works or not, the digitalization of educational governance prompted the proliferation of data infrastructures that are deemed to provide the necessary "evidence" for effective interventions (Hartong, 2016a, 2016b, 2018; see also Hartong, in this volume). The digitalization and algorithmization of learning are further facets of the current evidence-based trend of educational reform. The assumption is that performance levels may be improved by amassing and analyzing sufficient data on student behavior (see Amos, in this volume).

*Methodological economism*—and in some instances, reductionism—refers to a second related logic of action. Some scholars argue that economics has nothing to do with money or the economy as objects. Rather, they argue, it is concerned with designing and explaining the conditions and consequences of interactions on the basis of individual calculations of advantage/disadvantage (Homann, 2006; Latour & Lépinay, 2008). Economic actors, as this line of argumentation goes, follow their projected incentives to act rationally according to respective situative conditions, that is, they rely on the—more or less approximate—calculation of individual advantages and disadvantages. From such an economic perspective, if actors are to change their behavior, it is more advisable to change their situational conditions than their preferences (Homann, 2006). Against this background, behavioral economics surfaces as a theory of action that may be seen at the basis of current attempts at changing education. Along the same line, economic agents are seen as bounded in their rationality, and behavioral economics is concerned primarily with examining how cognitive, emotive, psychological, social, and cultural factors influence decision-making, including the mechanisms that guide their choices (Heukelom, 2014; Simon, 1984). The flourishing of behavioral economics as a theory of action is directly related to the ascendance of evidence-based policymaking (Bogenschneider & Corbett, 2010), and to the popularity—in particular among international organizations (cf. OECD, 2017)—of "nudging" as a cost-neutral form of intervention (Halpern & Sanders, 2016; Thaler & Sunstein, 2008). Nudge is a cybernetic concept that entails positive and most often indirect reinforcement to influence the behavior of decision makers, as phrased by Thaler and Sunstein:

> nudge [...] is any aspect of the choice architecture that alters people's behavior in a predictable way without forbidding any options or significantly changing their economic incentives. To count as a mere nudge, the intervention must be easy and cheap to avoid. Nudges are not mandates. Putting fruit at eye level counts as a nudge. Banning junk food does not. (2008, p. 6)

The following section deals with the GEI's modes of operation.

## Constructing Crises, Industry-Making, and Connecting Interests: Modes of Operation in the GEI

The actors involved in the GEI have developed new ways of operating that go well beyond the types of interaction between governmental and non-governmental, public and private actors that are well researched in policy analysis. These modes of operation in the GEI are distinct from arrangements typical of classical economic thought, where the making and shaping of an industrial sector have been primarily influenced by (limited) governmental intervention in a self-regulating free-market environment.

A central thrust behind the activities in the GEI may be summarized under the label "*discursive destruction*" and "*discursive construction*" of education. Moreover, with special reference to the role of the state amidst these developments, a peculiar change in functions and operations becomes visible, namely that it ceased to be solely a power container regulating and controlling the activities in this industry sector and has turned into a powerful connector that initiates, facilitates, and sponsors many of the activities in the GEI.

Regarding the former, most advocates of the GEI share a deep mistrust in government and view public education as an excessively bureaucratized, inefficient, and inflexible sector that needs to be disrupted and transfigured to become fit for the future. Discursive destruction as a strategy to influence the educational debates is not new and "manufactured crises"[1] have a productive history in the field. This strategy entails semantic (mis)representations, appeals to emotions, as well as de- and re-contextualization of issues. Crisis in this context is to be viewed as productive sites that provide opportunities for those seeking to shape developments and decisions. Telling examples are the "crisis" debates in the wake of the release of the *A Nation at Risk* report in 1983 in the USA or the so-called PISA-shock in the aftermath of the publication of the first round of the OECD's large-scale assessment study in 2001, but also more generally economic crises such as that of 2007/8 (see also Peters,

Paraskeva, & Besley, 2015). As Gregory Cizek (1999, p. 739) writes, over the years almost every aspect of education—from enrollment to curriculum to efficiency—has been decried in "a baleful bonanza of epistles on emergencies" (see also Berliner & Biddle, 1995) generating a sense of permanent crisis. Scandalizing (public) education thus creates a state of emergency that proves very productive in the politics of policymaking, in particular for those advocating specific solutions and (business) models. Corresponding to this is a discursive construction of preferred educational solutions—ones that have been remarkably similar throughout the globe and recurrent across different scales (Centeno, 2017; Lingard & Rawolle, 2011). This mode of operation relies heavily on narrative practices and strategies. As developed by Thompson, authorization strategies are used to present "global expertise" as legitimate and reasonable (see Thompson, in this volume). Authorization becomes particularly productive in networked contexts where ideas are advocated and disseminated (see Lubienski, in this volume).

The recurrent summits on the GEI accurately characterize a central mode of operation in the GEI that involves networking, lobbying, consulting, and piloting "best practices." The summits correspond fairly well to what Stephen J. Ball termed "meetingness," namely:

> when network members from a range of backgrounds come together, where stories are told, visions are shared, arguments are reiterated, new relations and commitments are made, partnerships are forged, and where 'a form of 'buzz' (is) generated by the co-presence of policy makers and practitioners from a range of different contexts'. (Ball, 2017, p. 35)

In this highly connective marketplace of ideas, preferred solutions to identified (policy) problems are promoted, access to new markets negotiated, and indeed new market (needs) constituted; the latter is well illustrated by the restructuring of educational governance and the thereby resulting need for interoperability systems (Lingard, in this volume) and data infrastructures (see Hartong, in this volume). Interestingly, the nexus between reform and profit becomes clearly visible as reforming opens opportunities for making profit in the future. Very often, activities in the GEI aim at "leading the way" in tackling specific issues; by doing this, actors themselves create the so-called best practices they advocate in the sequence—for instance, through impact investment where, at first, clear and measurable effects are given priority over profit, as argued by Stephen J. Ball (in this volume).

Further, using a wide spectrum of influence strategies, networks, and resources, corporate actors have developed different ways of shaping policy by lobbying, brokering, mobilizing expertise, advocating, and/or piloting new (business) models (see Fontdevila & Verger, in this volume). At the same time, the role and function of the state as power connector have been conspicuously effective in promoting global ideas. Education has become a key "extra-economic factor" (Jessop et al., 2008) in states' attempts to enhance their competitiveness in the global economy, as illustrated by the United Arab Emirates vision of becoming an international hub in higher education. As Erfurth (in this volume) notes, the construction of a hub relies on a powerful narrative spanning various scales—relating the global education discourses to national anxieties and politico-economic projects. Indeed, as the examples in this volume show, state agents are proactive in spawning what Keller Easterling titled "infrastructure space […] a medium of what might be called *extrastatecraft*—a portmanteau describing the often undisclosed activities outside of, in addition to, and sometimes in partnership with statecraft." (2014, p. 15, emphasis in the original).

## Concluding Remarks

The GEI's expansion may be understood as a confluence of factors and developments (cf. Verger et al., 2016), and it has been driven by changing economic, political, and technological contexts that are seen to bring about and/or exacerbate social dislocations. *Technological changes* such as artificial intelligence, big data, data-mining, or digitalization bear severe implications for learning and labor, not only in terms of the competences and skills needed but also in terms of the splaying of conditions (material and otherwise), levels of access, and quality of learning and working between the winners and losers in these developments. Thus, the implications for education of the technological changes celebrated in the GEI will most probably entail important consequences for equity and equality. A further aspect pertains the implications of these changes for knowledge claims, with algorithmization developing into a key feature in decision-making processes (cf. Danaher, 2014). *Economic changes* derived from the realignment of capitalist economy and neoliberalization policies have already yielded implications. Not only have these changes prompted one of the sternest crises in welfare, health, education, and labor, these have also been "discovered" as industry sectors—as lucrative fields of investment and profit. With this, relations between capital and labor, individual and society/state, and market and consumer have been altered on a global scale, raising questions as to the contemporary meanings of concepts such as citizen, individual, employee, or market participant.

*Political changes* have also been felt, which were questioned as to how far recognized democracies are moving in the direction of a post-democratic era by losing their foundations through the lack of common goals, unbalanced debates, and being coopted by small economic elites due to the entanglement of business and politics. As Colin Crouch stated:

> A post-democratic society is one that continues to have and to use all the institutions of democracy, but in which they increasingly become a formal shell. The energy and innovative drive pass away from the democratic arena and into small circles of a politico-economic elite. (Crouch, 2013, n.p.)

Another aspect of the political transformations is related to the advent of algorithms in governance and their impact on collective decision-making. By coining the term *algocracy*—that is, the use of data-mining, predictive, and descriptive analytics to constrain and control human behavior— John Danaher has called attention to how this development affects political power, human freedom, and human rights (2014). One pertinent question concerns the relationship between the current imperative of evidence-based policymaking in education and what was termed "algorithmic hypernudging" as a hardwired form of design-based regulation (cf. Danaher, 2017). In particular, this poses questions as to the new roles and functions of the state.

The global developments dealt with in this book pose various challenges to our understanding of contemporary policymaking, of education as a right, service, and/or tradable commodity, but also of educational research and practice as these endeavors have become embedded in the economic and political calculations of a myriad players. In this way, the chapters in this volume took essential steps to explore current challenges regarding the impact of the GEI in shaping the future(s) of education, and ultimately of society.

These changes confront existing theories and narratives with significant challenges[2] and questions their ability to shed light on our understanding of the GEI as an instance of larger, structural shifts in society, culture, economy, and politics. In particular, when focusing on the implications of the developments in the GEI for education practice, research, and policy, recent developments in social theory may be instrumental in avoiding idealistic, instrumental, or moralistic conclusions and still provide conceptual subsidies for critical analysis in the sense suggested by Michel Foucault (1984).

In terms of the operative level of educational provision and the forms of subjectivation they promote, questions loom large as to whether we are witnessing a social structural change by means of which, in late modernity, the logic of the general declined in favor of a logic of the singular, as postulated by Andreas Reckwitz (2017). Reckwitz suggests that the two main motors of what he calls "singularization" are to be seen first in the economy, which has changed industrial capitalism into a cultural capitalism that values creativity and innovation (singularity), and second in technology, due to the digital revolution, which now not only standardizes but also "singularizes," for instance, through data tracking (p. 15f.). The implications for education include the psychological overload as well as social and cultural polarization of social groups and individuals, including the resulting processes of exclusion, the externalization of moral considerations ("adiaphorization," see Bauman & Lyon, 2013), the loss of common horizons of justice, value, and notions of "good" and "public."

In addition, there are challenges concerning the relationship between education and other societal sectors. These refer in particular to the internal differences in systemic logics and normativities, which raise questions as to a potential functional dedifferentiation in economy, education, and other societal subsystems. The latter has been convincingly argued by social theoretician Joseph Vogl (2015), who noted the historical economization of politics and the politization of the economy as giving shape to a current form of functional dedifferentiation. Against this background, a simple contrast of politics and economy, with the latter colonizing the former, appears as an illusion and questions as to how education as an industry in the contemporary global knowledge-based economy plays a role in securing "sovereignty reserves" (cf. ibid., p. 201ff.) come to the fore. By "sovereignty reserves" Vogl refers to the readjustment of sovereign powers formerly invested in the state, which he sees now also redistributed among private actors (ibid., p. 249).

Finally, there are challenges to our understanding of the consequences of these developments for issues of equity and equality—issues intrinsically related to education in modernity. Against the background of the dominance of the financial capitalist regime, some scholars have pointed out that we are witnessing a process of refeudalization of society. Neckel (2013, p. 49f.) argues for this and points to four related dimensions: First, with regard to social structure and social inequality, indicators are for him the polarization of social layers that no longer appear comparable and that social origin solidifies in ways reminiscent of feudal conditions. Second, and in terms of the organization of economic processes and the neo-feudal status of economic management elites prevailing in the financial markets. Third, in normative terms as the values and the justification of financial market capitalism have eroded the principle of achievement and merit as well as promoted (economic) success as inherited positions, assets, rents, and property titles. Fourth, and lastly, the refeudalization of the welfare state, which re-privatized social policy as philanthropy and charity.

Well beyond more instrumental issues of governance and policymaking as well as an understanding of the different manifestations, rationales, logics, and modes of operation of the GEI, researching the global education industry opens new vistas for critical reflections of their consequences for education practice, policy, and research. In other words, researching the GEI means developing a sensitivity for how these phenomena interact with structures of domination and hegemony, including opaque and self-imposed ones. In this way, significant areas of tension, unintended consequences, and new mechanisms of exclusion in and by education can be better scrutinized.

## Notes

1. See for instance: Berliner & Biddle (1995); Cizek (1999); Ertl (2006); Gruber (2006).
2. We would like to thank Frank-Olaf Radtke for his perceptive comments on these issues, in particular his pointing to the shortcomings of contemporary theoretical perspectives in assessing the phenomena encompassed in the GEI.

## References

Ball, S. J. (2017). Laboring to Relate: Neoliberalism, Embodied Policy, and Network Dynamics. *Peabody Journal of Education, 92*, 29–41. https://doi.org /10.1080/0161956X.2016.1264802

Bauman, Z., & Lyon, D. (2013). *Liquid Surveillance*. Cambridge, UK: Polity Press.

Bellmann, J. (2016). Datengetrieben und/oder evidenzbasiert? Wirkungsmechanismen bildungspolitischer Steuerungsansätze. *Zeitschrift für Erziehungswissenschaft, 19*(Suppl. 1), 147–161.

Bellmann, J., & Müller, T. (Eds.). (2011). *Wissen, was wirkt. Kritik evidenzbasierter Pädagogik*. Wiesbaden: VS Springer.

Berliner, D. C., & Biddle, B. J. (1995). *The Manufactured Crisis. Myths, Fraud, and the Attack on America's Public Schools*. New York: Longman.

Biesta, G. (2007). Why "What Work" Won't Work: Evidence-Based Practice and the Democratic Deficit in Educational Research. *Educational Theory, 47*(1), 1–22.

BMBF (Bundesministerium für Bildung und Forschung). (Ed.). (2008). *Wissen für Handeln – Strategien für eine evidenzbasierte Bildungspolitik*. Bonn/Berlin, Germany: BMBF.

Bogenschneider, K., & Corbett, T. J. (2010). *Evidence-Based Policymaking: Insights from Policy-Minded Researchers and Research-Minded Policymakers*. New York: Routledge.

Centeno, V. G. (2017). *The OECD's Educational Agendas. Framed from Above, Fed from Below, Determined in Interaction. A Study on the Recurrent Education Agenda*. Berlin, Germany: Peter Lang.
Cizek, G. J. (1999). Give Us This Day Our Daily Dread: Manufacturing Crises in Education. *The Phi Delta Kappan, 80*(10), 737–743. http://www.jstor.org/stable/20439557
Crouch, C. (2013). *Interview. Five Minutes with Colin Crouch*. Retrieved online: http://blogs.lse.ac.uk/politicsandpolicy/five-minutes-with-colin-crouch/. Last 19 July 2018.
Danaher, J. (2014). *Rule by Algorithm? Big Data and the Threat of Algocracy*. Retrieved from: http://ieet.org/index.php/IEET/more/danaher20140107. Last 19 July 2018.
Danaher, J. (2017). *Algocracy as Hypernudging: A New Way to Understand the Threat of Algocracy*. Retrieved online: https://ieet.org/index.php/IEET2/more/Danaher20170117. Last 19 July 2018.
Easterling, K. (2014). *Extrastatecraft: The Power of Infrastructure Space*. New York: Verso Books.
Ertl, H. (2006). Educational Standards and the Changing Discourse on Education: The Reception and Consequences of the PISA Study in Germany. *Oxford Review of Education, 32*(5), 619–634. https://doi.org/10.1080/03054980600976320
Feuer, M. J., Towne, L., & Shavelson, R. J. (2002). Scientific Culture and Educational Research. *Educational Researcher, 31*(7), 4–14.
Foucault, M. (1984). What Is Enlightenment? In P. Rabinow (Ed.), *The Foucault Reader* (pp. 32–50). New York: Pantheon Books.
FSG. (2014). *The New Role of Business in Global Education. How Companies Can Create Shared Value by Improving Education While Driving Shareholder Returns*. Retrieved online: https://www.fsg.org/publications/new-role-business-global-education. Last 19 July 2018.
Godin, B. (2015). *Innovation: A Conceptual History of an Anonymous Concept* (Working Paper No. 2). Retrieved online: http://www.csiic.ca/PDF/WorkingPaper21.pdf. Last 19 July 2018.
Gruber, K.-H. (2006). The German 'PISA-Shock': Some Aspects of the Extraordinary Impact of the OECD's PISA Study on the German Education System. In H. Ertl (Ed.), *Cross-National Attraction in Education: Accounts from England and Germany* (pp. 195–206). Oxford, UK: Symposium Books.
Halpern, D., & Sanders, M. (2016). Nudging by Government: Progress, Impact & Lessons Learned. *Behavioral Science & Policy, 2*, 53–65.

Hartong, S. (2016a). New Structures of Power and Regulation within 'Distributed' Education Policy: The Example of the US Common Core State Standards Initiative. *Journal of Education Policy, 31*(2), 213–225.

Hartong, S. (2016b). Between Assessments, Digital Technologies, and Big Data: The Growing Influence of 'Hidden' Data Mediators in Education. *European Educational Research Journal, 15*(5), 523–536.

Hartong, S. (2018). Towards a Topological Re-Assemblage of Education Policy? Observing the Implementation of Performance Data Infrastructures and 'Centers of Calculation' in Germany. *Globalisation, Societies and Education, 16*(1), 134–150.

Heukelom, F. (2014). *Behavioral Economics: A History*. New York: Cambridge University Press.

Homann, K. (2006). *Wirtschaftsethik: Ökonomischer Reduktionismus?* Diskussionspapier Nr. 2006–3. Retrieved from: https://www.wcge.org/images/wissenschaft/publikationen/DP_2006-3_Homann-Wirtschaftsethik_oekonomischer_Reduktionismus.pdf. Last 19 July 2018.

Jessop, B. (2002). *The Future of the Capitalist State*. Cambridge, UK: Polity.

Jessop, B., Fairclough, N., & Wodak, R. (Eds.). (2008). *Education and the Knowledge-Based Economy in Europe*. Rotterdam, The Netherlands: Sense Publishers.

Latour, B., & Lépinay, V. (2008). *L'économie, science des intérêts passionnés*. Paris: La Découverte.

Lingard, B., Creagh, S., & Vass, G. (2012). Education Policy as Numbers: Data Categories and Two Australian Cases of Misrecognition. *Journal of Education Policy, 27*(3), 315–333.

Lingard, B., & Rawolle, S. (2011). New Scalar Politics: Implications for Education Policy. *Comparative Education, 47*(4), 1–18.

Neckel, S. (2013). "Refeudalisierung" – Systematik und Aktualität eines Begriffs der Habermas'chen Gesellschaftanalyse. *Leviathan, 41*(1), 39–56.

OECD. (2017). *Behavioural Insights and Public Policy: Lessons from Around the World*. Paris: OECD Publishing.

Ozga, J. (2009). Governing Education Through Data in England: From Regulation to Self-Evaluation. *Journal of Education Policy, 24*(2), 149–162.

Peters, M. A., Paraskeva, J. M., & Besley, T. (Eds.). (2015). *The Global Financial Crisis and Educational Restructuring*. New York: Peter Lang.

Porter, M. E. (2014). Foreword. In FSG, *The New Role of Business in Global Education. How Companies Can Create Shared Value by Improving Education*

*While Driving Shareholder Returns*. Retrieved online: https://www.fsg.org/publications/new-role-business-global-education. Last 19 July 2018.

Radtke, F.-O. (2016). Konditionierte Strukturverbesserung. Umbau und Neuformierung der deutschen Erziehungswissenschaft flankiert von der Deutschen Forschungsgemeinschaft unter Anleitung der OECD verwirklicht von der Kultusministerkonferenz. *Zeitschrift für Pädagogik, 62*(5), 707–731.

Reckwitz, A. (2017). *Die Gesellschaft der Singularitäten*. Berlin, Germany: Suhrkamp.

Simon, H. A. (1984). On the Behavioral and Rational Foundations of Economic Dynamics. *Journal of Economic Behavior and Organization, 5*, 35–55.

Slavin, R. E. (2002). Evidence-Based Education Policies: Transforming Education Practice and Research. *Educational Researcher, 31*(7), 15–21.

Thaler, R. H., & Sunstein, C. R. (2008). *Nudge: Improving Decisions About Health, Wealth, and Happiness*. New Haven, CT: Yale University Press.

Tooley, J., & Darby, D. (1998). *Educational Research: A Critique*. London: OFSTED.

Verger, A., Lubienski, C., & Steiner-Khamsi, G. (2016). The Emergence and Structuring of the Global Education Industry. Towards an Analytical Framework. In A. Verger, C. Lubienski, & G. Steiner-Khamsi (Eds.), *The Global Education Industry* (pp. 3–24). New York: Routledge.

Vogl, J. (2015). *Der Souveränitätseffekt*. Zürich, Switzerland: Diaphanes.

# Index[1]

**A**
Adaptive learning, 227, 240–243
Advising, 16, 174n1, 228, 236, 239, 241, 246
Advisory, 51, 175n9
Advocacy Coalition Framework (ACF), 73, 75
Agenda setters, 62
Algocracy, 242, 284
Authorization, 16, 204–208, 210, 213, 216, 218, 219, 220n2, 220n5, 274, 282

**B**
Behavioral economics, 280
Belief of legitimacy, 207, 219
Blended education programs, 59
Blended learning, 39, 40, 157, 236
Boundary spanners, 24, 52, 160
Brokerage, 14, 50, 52
Business practices, 24, 41, 140

**C**
Charter schools, 40, 58–60, 72, 75, 97
Civil rights movement, 58
Commercialization, 15, 40, 135–137, 149–151, 243, 254, 277
Commodification, 4, 8, 9, 17, 38, 40, 116, 141, 157–159, 161, 166, 169, 171–173, 231, 237, 277
Connectivity, 26, 52, 205, 206, 208, 233, 262

---

[1] Note: Page numbers followed by 'n' refer to notes.

# Index

Consultancy, 7, 31, 33
Cultural Political Economy (CPE), 16, 117, 189

D

Datafication, 15, 139, 140, 142, 151, 152, 157–161, 167, 169, 171–173, 217, 218, 231
Data infrastructures, 3, 12, 15, 135–139, 141–143, 146, 147, 149, 151, 152, 279, 282
Data mining, 122, 148, 149, 241
Data-setting authority, 207, 213
Data technology, 158
De-territorialized relations of governance, 160
Digitalization, 11–13, 15–17, 35, 38, 157–161, 164, 167–169, 172, 173, 214, 225–229, 231, 232, 234, 236, 237, 239, 240, 246, 279, 283
Discursive construction, 197, 281, 282
Discursive destruction, 276, 281
Discursive relations, 25
Disintermediation, 60
Disruption, 5, 32, 226, 227, 229, 232, 233, 244, 246, 266
Disruptive innovation, 229, 232–234, 240

E

Echo-chamber effects, 55
Economism, 275, 278, 280
Ed-tech companies, 15, 135, 136, 139, 142, 144, 151, 152
EdTech Industry, 142

Edu-business, 6, 13, 15, 23, 25–27, 31, 34, 36, 37, 39, 50, 137, 139–141, 147, 149, 150, 254
Educational governance, 11, 12, 137, 140, 198, 279, 282
Educational innovation, 3, 11, 16, 204, 207, 212, 214, 218
Education privatization reforms, 48, 51
Education reform, 17, 24, 29, 54, 58, 61, 80, 96, 253, 256, 262, 266
Education space, 24, 29, 35, 40, 128
Edupreneur, 35, 53
Empiricism, 275, 278
Enlightenment, 207, 213, 218, 259
Epistemic governance, 116, 122, 123, 125, 128
Epistemology of education, 125, 127
European policy, 115, 117
Evidence-based educational research, 204, 205, 208, 213, 215, 217
Evidence-based reforming, 278, 279
Extrastatecraft, 137, 139, 140, 144–146, 151, 188, 283

F

Financialization, 4, 8, 10, 11, 26, 141, 183, 277
Formal coalitions, 53
For-profit providers, 24
Foundations, 4, 6, 23, 24, 27, 29, 33, 39, 50, 53, 54, 56–61, 92, 96–98, 100–104, 164, 184, 210
Functional dedifferentiation, 285, 286

# Index

## G

Global economy, 16, 182–183, 186, 193, 283
Global Education Industry (GEI), 1–6, 12, 13, 18n1, 23, 50, 87, 116, 128, 130, 135, 138, 140, 157, 181, 182, 185, 198, 225, 226, 229, 231, 234, 273, 274, 282, 285, 286
Global education policy (GEP), 16, 31, 198, 252–257, 262, 265, 266, 269
Global education sector, 88, 96, 97, 190
Global expert, 205
Globalized economic sector, 5, 183, 184
Government schooling system, 135, 137
Grassroots advocacy, 57

## H

Horizon 2020, 15, 115, 116, 118, 120, 126, 128, 228

## I

Imaginary, 4, 5, 8, 116, 118–120, 125, 126, 128, 129, 189, 190, 195, 196, 219, 253, 257
Impact investing, 24, 27–30, 39, 41
Individualization, 11, 210, 218
Innovation Union, 117
Intelligent Decision Support System, 122
Intermediary organizations, 14, 54, 55, 57, 74, 75, 168
International aid community, 61

International education arena, 53
International Education Hubs (IEHs), 16, 181, 184, 187, 188, 198, 199
Interoperability standards, 143, 145, 164
Intra-national policy network dynamics, 160
Investment cluster, 39

## K

Knowledge-based economy (KBE), 16, 117, 118, 127, 182, 190, 193, 195–197, 277, 286
Knowledge mobilization, 14, 50, 54
Knowledge regimes, 123, 124, 128

## L

Leading by example, 58
Learnification, 226
Lobbying, 14, 50, 51, 57, 63n1, 73, 169, 174n1, 282, 283
Low-fee private schools (LFPSs), 52, 56

## M

Market-based educational reforms, 90
Market dynamics, 24
Market-oriented interventions, 60
Millennium Development Goals (MDGs), 87, 96, 256
*Mode 1*, 124
*Mode 2*, 124, 126
Monitoring infrastructures, 167, 168
Multilateral agencies, 23
Multi-national corporations, 23

## N

Network ethnography, 25, 26, 264
Network governance, 15, 136–143, 145, 146, 151
Nodal actors, 24, 160
Non-state actors, 49, 50, 52, 70, 73, 76, 183
Nudging, 220n4, 275, 280, 284

## P

Personalization, 17, 147, 159, 227, 228
Pilot experiences, 14, 50, 53, 60
Policy actors, 3, 31, 174n3, 274, 276
Policy brokers, 77
Policy formation, 47, 138, 151
Policy learning and transfer, 121, 126
Policy-making, 3, 12, 47, 48, 54, 118, 126, 159, 160, 274, 275, 284
Policy-shapers, 47, 48
Policy solutions, 56
Policy spaces, 50, 146, 159, 172, 184, 266
Policy transfer, 40, 71
Policy transformation, 159
Political turn of corporations, 48
Power connector, 181
Private actors, 14, 47–49, 62, 74, 158, 160, 172, 281, 286
Private donors, 60
Private provision, 29, 37–38, 60
Private sector partnerships, 88, 90, 92
Privatization, 9, 10, 90, 91, 256
Prosumer, 212

Public education systems, 181
Public-private partnership, 61, 262

## R

Refeudalization, 286
Relational power dynamics, 52
Research and knowledge generation, 118
Role of the State, 181, 185

## S

School administration, 247n6
Scientifically based, 69
Scientization, 217, 218
Self-responsibility, 210, 218
Shadow education state, 24
Shared value, 41n2, 206, 277, 278
Singularization, 17, 220n8, 227, 228, 285
Social capitalism, 24, 33
Social impact bonds, 31
Social investing, 30
Social power, 205–207
Social sciences and humanities (SSH), 115
Social solutions, 38
Societal challenges, 115–119, 121, 128
Standardization of education, 209
Standardized test systems, 161
Start-ups, 23, 32, 37, 234
State monitoring systems, 158–162, 164–166, 169–171, 173
Strategic clusters, 39
Sustainable Development Goals (SDGs), 92

Systemless systems, 135, 151
Systems Interoperability Framework (SIF), 137, 145

T

Technology, 2, 3, 7, 10, 11, 13, 24, 32, 34–36, 40, 42n2, 100, 101, 104, 106, 108n3, 118, 120, 146, 150, 163, 172, 174n1, 175n9, 188, 193, 225, 229, 231–237, 239, 240, 243, 245, 285
Test-based accountability, 162

Transactional policy analysis, 82
Traveling policy ideas, 181

V

Venture philanthropy, 39, 59, 174n1
Voluntary benchmarking initiatives, 162

W

Window of opportunity, 29–30